Eugene O'Neill's New Language of Kinship

Eugene O'Neill's
New Language of Kinship

MICHAEL MANHEIM

SYRACUSE UNIVERSITY PRESS 1982

Excerpts from *Hughie* (1959), *Long Day's Journey into Night* (1956), *More Stately Mansions* (1964), and *A Touch of the Poet* (1957), by Eugene O'Neill, were published by Yale University Press and are copyrighted by Yale University Press.

Library of Congress Cataloging in Publication Data

Manheim, Michael.
   Eugene O'Neill's new language of kinship.

   Bibliography: p.
   Includes index.
   1. O'Neill, Eugene, 1888–1953 — Criticism and interpretation. 2. Autobiography in literature.
3. Kinship in literature. I. Title.
PS3529.N5Z689   812'.52   82-3190
ISBN 0-8156-2262-7   AACR2
ISBN 0-8156-2277-5 (pbk.)

Manufactured in the United States of America

Dedicated to the memory of my colleague, mentor, and friend,
CYRUS DAY

MICHAEL MANHEIM received the B.A., M.A., and Ph.D. from Columbia University. He is professor of English and chairman of the Department of English at the University of Toledo, Toledo, Ohio. Manheim is the author of *The Weak King Dilemma in the Shakespearean History Play* and articles and reviews in such journals as *Renaissance Drama, Shakespeare Studies,* and *Studies in English Literature.*

In 1924, writing program notes for an Off-Broadway production of August Strindberg's *The Dance of Death*, O'Neill made the observation that he heard in Strindberg's dialogue of spite and abuse a "new language of kinship."

Contents

Acknowledgments

THIS BOOK FIRST SUGGESTED ITSELF in the mid-1970s and was influenced in part by two powerful revivals of late O'Neill plays on stage and television: the Olivier *Long Day's Journey* and the Dewhurst-Robards *Moon for the Misbegotten*. Despite the success of these productions, what struck me most forcefully in those years was how few of my students, colleagues, and friends had any idea of what O'Neill's plays were really about. There seemed little question in anyone's mind that O'Neill was America's greatest playwright, but at the same time there seemed little desire genuinely to confront the issues he dealt with. He was gloomy, he was painful — and there was an end to it! For a *Lear* or an *Oedipus* the effort to deal unflinchingly with drama which tested the human spirit could be made, but not for an *Iceman*.

Having been deeply affected by O'Neill's last plays myself, I could not quite account for the resistance of so many people I respected, especially since audiences abroad — notably in Scandinavia (with its heritage of Ibsen, Strindberg, and Ingmar Bergman) — seemed so much more willing to confront the late plays. I began trying to counter that resistance in 1975 by offering a course on O'Neill, in which I dealt with almost his entire canon. In reading for that course, I was guided chiefly by Travis Bogard's *Contour in Time* and Louis Sheaffer's two-volume biography; and I discovered with those scholars how much one could become involved with this playwright. Almost all my research in the mid-1970s was directed toward O'Neill's life, his struggle with the ghosts of his past, and his remarkable development as a playwright *following* his great popularity of the 1920s and 1930s.

This book has resulted chiefly from a re-living on my part of some-

xi

thing of the agony which possessed the playwright through thirty years of his creative life, and the consequent development of an understanding of what this man wrote and why it can affect one so profoundly. My understanding is not the only possible understanding of O'Neill, and it may not at all times be entirely accurate. But it is, I believe, a coherent understanding; and as most of those who have dealt with O'Neill know, coherence has been almost impossible to achieve in interpreting his works.

I am grateful to a number of people in connection with this study: first, to the late Professor Cyrus Day, who shared with me his many ideas and frustrations, when we were colleagues at the University of Delaware; and to his wife, Camilla Day, for allowing me free use of Professor Day's extensive notes and papers when my work got under way in the mid-1970s. I am also grateful for the encouragement of several fellow scholars and recent graduate students for their sensitivity to the nature of my involvement with O'Neill's plays, especially the late Ernest J. Moyne of the University of Delaware, and Timo Tiusanen of the University of Helsinki (who made valuable comments on an early draft of this work). Finally, I am grateful for my heritage of interest in literature and psychology provided by my father, Leonard F. Manheim; the phenomenal support of my wife, Martha Manheim; and the incalculable assistance of our department secretary, Jean Quigley, who transcribed the several taped drafts of the work, and who saw the final drafts, with their many revisions, through to completion.

I might add that Jordan Y. Miller's annotated bibliography, *Eugene O'Neill and the American Critic* (Hamden, Conn.: The Shoe String Press, Anchor Books, 1973), has been invaluable to me, as to all O'Neill scholars of the recent past.

It should also be noted that this book was written in part during a sabbatical leave provided me by The University of Toledo in the spring of 1977.

Toledo, Ohio   MM
October 1981

Eugene O'Neill's New Language of Kinship

Introduction
Understanding the O'Neill Appeal

T HE MEANING AND UNITY of [O'Neill's] work," said Joseph Wood Krutch in 1924, lie "not in any controlling intellectual idea and certainly not in a 'message' but merely in the fact that each play is an experience of extraordinary intensity."[1] These words begin to account for the effect O'Neill has had on audiences of this century. The real impact of O'Neill is only beginning to be felt, in the process meeting the resistance that work which probes terrifying areas of man's nature inevitably meets. What has kept O'Neill alive, even during the years of his eclipse following the Second World War, has not been the attention he has received from scholars, or even journalists, but the fascination he has held and increasingly holds for the large segments of his audiences struggling to come to grips with the mysteries of human emotion — and to do so not in abstract, impersonal terms but in immediate, personal terms. It is those who can stand the glimpses of "the horror" Conrad's Mistah Kurtz found at the center of the human spirit, and feel in such glimpses a kind of vital understanding rather than pure panic, who are most openly affected by O'Neill.

Scholars and critics have approached O'Neill by a variety of means.[2] They have dealt with the intellectual and artistic influences that O'Neill most frequently acknowledges, both in the plays and in public statements. They have considered his debt to Thoreau, Nietzsche, and Freud — and to Ibsen and Strindberg. They have linked O'Neill to broad political, social, and artistic movements of the nineteenth and twentieth centuries: romanticism and Marxism, realism and symbolism. To these studies of influences, recent critics have added important studies of the aesthetics of O'Neill's drama. Approaching the plays from quite differing points of view, Timo Tiusanen's *O'Neill's Scenic Images* (Princeton, N.J.:

1

Princeton University Press, 1968) and Leonard Chabrowe's *Ritual and Pathos—the Theatre of O'Neill* (Lewisburg, Pa.: Bucknell University Press, 1976) contribute markedly to our understanding of what O'Neill achieves on stage and the ways he achieves it.[3]

Quite a few studies, both early and late in the history of O'Neill criticism, have come at O'Neill's work from a perspective which includes looking at each play in the light of O'Neill's life. Most prominent among these have been Edwin Engel's *The Haunted Heroes of Eugene O'Neill* (Cambridge, Massachusetts: Harvard University Press, 1952), and Travis Bogard's *Contour in Time: The Plays of Eugene O'Neill* (New York: Oxford University Press, 1971).[4] These works hardly ignore intellectual influences. Both seek to make as clear as possible O'Neill's debt to Nietzsche, for example, and to Freud. But both works imply that O'Neill never espoused or exploited a particular outlook for long, that he used philosophical attitudes that suited his own deeper feelings of the moment. If in the early twenties it was Emerson and Eastern mysticism that most influenced his plays, in the later twenties it was Nietzsche, in the early thirties Freud and Jung, in the mid-thirties a return to the Christianity of his youth. And with *The Iceman Cometh* in 1939, of course, it was a complete discarding of all systematized concepts of good and evil, honor and dishonor, life and death. Like many great and not-so-great playwrights before him, O'Neill not only never became the slave of any philosophical outlook, but rather used the shifting outlooks of his time as they have always worked best in popular drama — superficially. Nietzsche and Freud undoubtedly set off feelings of great intensity in O'Neill because they spoke of things he knew so well — the isolated vision of the artist, the inadequacies of the old morality, the suppression of painful memories, the overwhelming influence of "the Mother" in all human decisions. And it is with these feelings more than with intellectual concepts that O'Neill worked when he wrote his plays.

The limitations of Engel's *Haunted Heroes*, enlightening as it often is, derive from the fact that it was written before the thorough and provocative O'Neill biographies of the sixties and seventies had appeared, and even before the availability of *Long Day's Journey Into Night*. Engel had to speculate about what "haunted" O'Neill when what haunted him was to become more easily accessible with the appearance of the important work of Doris Alexander, Arthur and Barbara Gelb, and Louis Sheaffer.[5] (For me, Sheaffer's two-volume study goes beyond the purely biographical facts. It is a work of deep human understanding.) Engel's viewpoint was clearly affected by more biographical information when it became available. In his English Institute paper in 1964, he sees throughout O'Neill a "diagnosing of the playwright's own condition." Engel here calls attention to O'Neill's "fixation on Moma [sic] and Papa O'Neill, on brother Jamie, and on himself." "Obsessed," says Engel, "with the relationship between himself and his family, he repeatedly returned to the scene of whatever crimes — his family's and his own. Few playwrights have wrung so much agony and material for so many plays out of their adolescent years."[6] The important insight here, aside from the linking of O'Neill's plays so closely to his adolescence, is that Engel sees the "fixation" operating not just in the last plays, but throughout O'Neill's career. Still, even in 1964, Engel was unable to go into much detail about how the agony of O'Neill's adolescent years reflects itself in his earlier plays. And he was not yet ready to account for the "extraordinary intensity" of O'Neill's later plays, especially *A Moon for the Misbegotten*, which he considers "feeble."

The limitations of Bogard's work are different. Bogard worked extensively with the biographies, and his use of the O'Neill collection at Yale University resulted in indispensable discoveries and speculations about O'Neill's immense projected dramatic cycle "A Tale of Possessors Self-Dispossessed," of which *A Touch of the Poet* and *More Stately Mansions* are the only extant parts. (See *Contour in Time*, pp. 371–407.) The chief trouble with Bogard is that he attempts more than is manageable. He tries to add to what earlier interpreters did with O'Neill's use of historical and cultural influences; and, with the aid of the biographies, he tries to add to what Engel did with O'Neill's haunting past. He also attempts in-context interpretive statements on every play in the canon. The result is about equal parts enlightening and frustrating. His discussion of *All God's Chillun* is to my knowledge the first to make the important link between that early play and O'Neill's own family, while his discussion of *The Great God Brown* is not the first to be confusing.

While we need no convincing that O'Neill, early and late, has massive appeal, we have only scratched the surface in understanding the reasons for that appeal — what it is in the plays that makes them so fascinating, what might prompt Robert Benchley to say of the original production of *Mourning Becomes Electra* that O'Neill "gives us nothing to think about . . . but he does thrill the bejeezus out of us."[7] Is it solely, as some have claimed, that Eugene O'Neill is the true inheritor of the great tradition of nineteenth century melodrama?[8] Hardly. Audiences that have been genuinely spellbound by O'Neill have been laughing that sort of melodrama off stage and screen for years. O'Neill could use with ease the melodramatic tricks he learned from his father, but he used them strictly to achieve effects, and frequently satiric ones, not as important serious attri-

butes of his plays. If he had an instinct for making events fascinating on
stage, that instinct was the result of his ability to make audiences feel as
he felt about the subjects he was dealing with, to make them empathise
deeply with the fear and pain that were always at the center of his works.
If the Aristotelian principle of catharsis ever fit a twentieth century dramatist, it fits O'Neill.[9] Dramatic purgation has rarely been achieved in
drama as he achieves it. And the first reason is that the great pity and terror his plays evoke begins in himself — in the guilt, the frenzy over his
family, that finally became the plot of Long Day's Journey Into Night.
That guilt and that frenzy are the force that through the green fuse drives
the flower of every O'Neill play from the abortive creations of his pre-
Provincetown days to the massive Iceman.

As Engel observes, rarely did O'Neill create an important character
that was not in some way — however greatly disguised — a version of
mother, father, brother, or himself. I speak of parallels O'Neill consciously
intended in that they all become recognizable in the settings, gestures,
confessions, and exchanges of Long Day's Journey. It is with that great
autobiographical drama, and its successor A Moon for the Misbegotten,
that this study must begin and end. Most readers of this study are undoubtedly acquainted with these plays but may still not have the kind of
familiarity with them that in the chapters which follow I tend to take for
granted. The kind of familiarity I mean is that which would enable one to
quickly recall and distinguish among their plethora of autobiographical
motifs — motifs which grow out of the memories which haunted O'Neill
throughout his adult life. I speak of memories of his mother, of course, focusing first on her addiction and second on her death; but no less memories of his father, his brother, and his pre-adolescent and adolescent self.
Later in this chapter, and in this book, I shall be discussing O'Neill's last
plays from a point of view ultimately more important to understanding
the true genius of this playwright; but since so much of O'Neill's work derives from his compulsion to confess, to focus on his haunting memories
even as he was ashamed to acknowledge them, I feel a review of some of
these autobiographical motifs is needed. Such a review should help make
clear some of the disguised appearances of these motifs in O'Neill's earlier
plays and bring readers to the realization, out of which this study begins,
that O'Neill had been writing versions of Long Day's Journey throughout
his entire career.

The plot of Long Day's Journey, of course, deals in starkly direct
terms with the discovery on the part of a father and his two adult sons
that their wife and mother has slid back into a morphine addiction from
which she had seemed to recover through recent hospitalizations. The

play's sub-plot deals with the concomitantly growing evidence that the younger son (who stands for O'Neill himself) has developed tuberculosis and will shortly himself have to be hospitalized. The responses to these developments on the part of all four members of the family constitute the action of the play, and it is chiefly in these responses that the motifs emerge. It would be tedious here to include all motifs associated with the characters and situations of the play. I have attempted to delineate them more comprehensively in an appendix which readers may find useful to refer to, especially in regard to the earlier chapters. I wish here only to call attention to some of the themes repeatedly present in all the plays. Following O'Neill's own introduction of the characters in *Long Day's Journey*, I shall move from father to mother to elder son to younger son—from James Tyrone, Sr. to Mary Tyrone to James Tyrone, Jr. (Jamie) to Edmund Tyrone.

With regard to the father, the play's haunting themes are clearly James's overpowering personality, his financial insecurity, his dependency on drink and social companionship, his recollections of his poverty-stricken youth, his Irish Catholic pride, his promise as a Shakespearean actor, his famous "role," and his bitter disappointment in his wife. The motifs most importantly associated with Mary Tyrone naturally grow out of her addiction: her withdrawals into her spare room, her dilated pupils, her contempt for doctors, her denials, her ambivalence toward the fog. And following from these are the vivid memories which accompany her withdrawals: her memories of childhood and schooling, her conflicting ambitions to be nun and concert pianist, her infatuation and marriage to a matinee idol, her wedding gown, her loneliness in theatrical hotel rooms, the events surrounding the death of her second child and the painful birth of her third, her first unwitting yieldings to temptation.

The motifs associated with the Tyrone sons are as important in all O'Neill's drama as those associated with their parents. With Jamie, one thinks immediately of his charm and wit, his social conviviality, his biting cynicism, his contempt for his father, his ambivalence toward but finally great love for his brother, his uncompromising emotional honesty. And one thinks of his recollections of early disillusionment, his dismissal from college, his dissolute life, his failures — and, deriving from *A Moon for the Misbegotten*, his haunting memories of his mother's death: the death watch, the return to drink, the whore on the train. With Edmund, finally, we most frequently associate motifs commonly found in the youthful heroes of the earlier plays: the persistence of hope set against constant disillusionment, anger at his family, guilt at that anger, emulation of his brother, love of poetry and the fog, fear that he may be like his mother.

Then there are Edmund's memories: the recalled shock of learning of his mother's addiction, the sense of a lost ideal, the running away to sea and love of the sea, the prodigal return.

As motifs associated with the individual characters and their memories emerge repeatedly in varying shapes and forms throughout *Long Day's Journey*, so, too, do motifs which grow out of the encounters these characters have with one another. There are the motifs associated with the family group: mutual laughter at an anecdote concerning the humiliation of the proud, mutual recriminations between sons and father with mother in the middle, and the observation by the men of their wife-mother in the throes of complete withdrawal. Between James and Mary, there is the false hope of her rehabilitation, the mutual resentment over her addiction and his drink, the repeated themes of his land speculations and lateness for meals. James and Jamie castigate one another about similar matters: Jamie's failures and dissolute life, the father's miserliness, the question of who is responsible for Mary's downfall. The infrequent exchanges between Mary and Jamie establish motifs wherein Jamie notices his mother's dilated pupils, is viciously cynical in her presence; wherein Mary fears her son to the point that we become aware that most bona fide communication between them has broken down. Between James and Edmund we hear mutual attacks like those between father and elder son, except here we also get arguments over literary works, politics, and social causes. We also hear their mutual fears and hopes regarding Mary, and we hear the son beginning to understand what the father has been trying to tell him about the conditions of his own life.

The deepest and most painful encounters in the play are those between Edmund and Mary and between Jamie and Edmund. The chief motifs that emerge between mother and younger son are her hysterical anxiety over his health, his pleading with her to give up her drug, her refusals to acknowledge his pleas, his hurt and sense of rejection, his rage and accusation, her hurt, and the sense that communication between them is breaking down. Situations in the earlier plays which involve these motifs are especially common. Little less so are those involving the motifs of brotherly relationships: the jesting about whores, drink, and their father's eccentricities; the arguments over their mother; the elder brother's confession both of intense hatred and intense need for his younger brother.

These are some of the motifs evident in *Long Day's Journey*; and as O'Neill achieved the height of his power in this undisguisedly autobiographical play, so he is most effective in his earlier works when he employs the same motifs. His plays, early as well as late, have the greatest fascination when he deals with the motifs associated with his parental home, as he does when dealing with the timid Mrs. Keeney in *Ile* (1919), whose sudden madness resulting from her husband's proudly stubborn ambition aboard a whaling ship fog-bound in polar ice is a simply-drawn early study of Mary Tyrone's relapse amid the same ocean fog and the cold of her family's distrust. "Madness" is a code-word for addiction throughout O'Neill.[10] It suggests motifs associated with Mary's condition in character after character: Emma Crosby in *Diff'rent*, Ella Harris in *All God's Chillun*, Elsa Darling in *Days Without End*, and Deborah Harford in *More Stately Mansions*. Then there are anticipations of the father-son motifs in encounters between Ephraim and Eben Cabot in *Desire Under the Elms*, Hutchins and Reuben Light in *Dynamo*, "Father" Baird and John Darling's alter ego in *Days Without End*, and between Con and (daughter) Sara Melody in *A Touch of the Poet*. There are also powerful, often violent exchanges between siblings or sibling-like pairs, similar to the Edmund-Jamie motifs: between Robert and Andrew Mayo in *Beyond the Horizon*, Dion Anthony and Billy Brown in *The Great God Brown*, Lazarus and Caligula in *Lazarus Laughed*, John Darling and his alter ego in *Days Without End*, Orin and Lavinia Mannon in *Mourning Becomes Electra*, and finally between Hickey and Larry Slade in *The Iceman Cometh*. In all cases, the scenes and conversations I refer to are among the most powerful in the plays in which they appear.

Though I look at *Strange Interlude* later in considerable detail, that long play of the 1920s may illustrate the point I am making here in another way. Its staying power probably depends more on those elements within it which may be linked with the motifs I have been reviewing than on some of the play's more popular, and dated, soap-opera characteristics. The play deals, for example, with a series of parental deaths which offspring have trouble facing, much as James Tyrone, Jr. has great difficulty facing his mother's death in *A Moon for the Misbegotten*. It also includes a story of family insanity, of a mad old sister locked in an upstairs room (like Mary's spare room), of fears about inherited madness (like Edmund's fears) — all elements directly linked to motifs central to *Long Day's Journey*. In other words, although in *Strange Interlude* O'Neill disguised the possessing motifs of his life as carefully as he did in any other earlier play, when those motifs take hold and guide the lines and action, the play is at its most effective and durable. Similarly, other plays of the twenties and thirties make the most lasting impact, have what Chabrowe identifies as authentic "pathos," when O'Neill deals with the motifs that become the explicit subjects of his last plays.

The chapters which follow, then, will be dealing with O'Neill's earlier plays first as anticipations of the confessional aspects of *Long Day's*

Journey, as essentially tortured efforts on O'Neill's part to reveal what he was not ready openly to reveal until that later work. In each chapter I deal first with the autobiographical motifs of *Long Day's Journey* and *A Moon for the Misbegotten* as they appear in various disguises in the earlier plays and contribute markedly to the "extraordinary intensity" of those works. But there is a second element which helps give O'Neill's work even greater strength and durability — an element finally more important to what O'Neill achieved as a playwright than the first. From the beginning, even in the midst of his family troubles, O'Neill had a strong sense of the language and rhythms of human communication. He knew that people who were close to one another, or loved one another, were not necessarily good to one another. He realized, in fact, that half the time they were distinctly unpleasant to one another, and that this unpleasantness in no way took away from the fact of their closeness or love.[11] He explicitly demonstrated this insight when he said, in commenting in the early 1920s on a production of Strindberg's *The Dance of Death*, that he heard in Strindberg's harsh dialogue a "new language of kinship."[12] This insight, along with the guilt, undoubtedly grew out of O'Neill's family relationships; but it is the dramatic shape this insight took which is the primary concern of this study. That O'Neill achieved a powerful form for the dramatic confessional in *Long Day's Journey* is only half the story — and the lesser half finally. What he also brought to marvelous fruition in that play is a dramatic vision of the nature of genuine human kinship. But, as with the confession, this sense of kinship was slow in developing. In his earlier works it is evident only during O'Neill's more hopeful periods, and disappears in his prolonged periods of extreme depression and despair. A brief survey of the plays from the viewpoint of their treatment of human kinship may serve to introduce this second, all-important idea more clearly.

O'Neill's early plays, beginning with the sea plays and continuing up to the years immediately following his mother's and brother's deaths in the early twenties, are characterized by movement and dialogue which suggest a looking forward to better things, a hope, even when hope is illusory. It is hope tied to the love the central figures urgently seek, the kinship they feel will make life endurable. And that love, that kinship, is recognizable in a very specific way in these early plays — in a way most important to its revived use in O'Neill's later plays. As early as the sea plays, O'Neill gives his audiences a sense of human kinship through a rhythm of alternating hostility and affection in both monologue and dialogue. It is unreserved hostility and unreserved affection, both sincere and both temporary. It is a rhythm heard first in the monologues of

O'Neill's volatile Irishmen — Driscoll and Paddy — and comes to be the sole means by which characters like Jim and Ella Harris in *All God's Chillun* are able to communicate. This rhythm — this contrapuntal rhythm of kinship — is one in which the initial beat is made up of acid recrimination and lacerating hurt, while the following beat invariably counters the first with split-second forgiveness and total if inevitably short-lived reconciliation. It is a rhythm felt most strongly among the quarreling crew in *Moon of the Caribees,* in the tumultuous exchanges between heroine and both father and lover in *Anna Christie,* and in the violent boiler-room banter opening *The Hairy Ape.*

In the 1920s, however, the central characters in O'Neill's plays begin to lose that rhythm of kinship. They become increasingly desperate. Brutus Jones and Yank the "hairy ape" both reject the kinship each once knew (Jones on the chain gang and Yank in the boiler room), and each suffers wretched isolation as a result. Eben and Abbie in *Desire Under the Elms,* like Jim and Ella in *All God's Chillun,* having searched desperately for authentic kinship, find it only in the most desperate of circumstances. In each of these plays a rhythm of kinship is convincingly brought into being, but that rhythm is overwhelmed by forces the characters cannot control.

Then follow the plays of what I call O'Neill's "middle" period — plays written in the mid-twenties to early thirties. They include some of his best-known works: *The Great God Brown, Strange Interlude,* and *Mourning Becomes Electra.* These plays are characterized by dialogue quite different in central effect from that in the earlier plays. Here — even among characters ostensibly giving and receiving love — hypocrisy, secretiveness, deception, and manipulation are the dominant qualities. When people do try to be honest about their feelings in these plays, they are usually unsuccessful. What we get instead of the alternating but honest statements of hostile and affectionate feeling are the confused frenzy of maskings and unmaskings in *The Great God Brown,* the interior monologues in *Strange Interlude,* and the deceptions, murders, and suicides in *Mourning Becomes Electra.* The dialogue of the early plays — much of it — conveys a sense of living in spite of pain because O'Neill was seeking a way to live in spite of pain. The dialogue of the middle period, on the other hand — in which O'Neill was most frenzied, most secretive, most self-deceptive, and most violently inclined — is most accurately characterized by the terms frenzy, deception, and violence. The plays of O'Neill's middle period are his most despairing in their dramatic representation of man and life — more despairing, as we shall see, than the later *Iceman Cometh.*

O'Neill's last plays are anticipated in *A Touch of the Poet.* Written in the mid-thirties when O'Neill was probably in the most stable period of

his life, the play represents domestic relations with that rhythm heard little since the early twenties, that rhythm which keeps assuring us that the
kinship in the family represented on stage is genuine. If the moods of the
conversation in *A Touch of the Poet* are still two parts recrimination to
one part reconciliation, the bitterness is never unrelieved and the tenderness never illusory. There is also far less deception and far more direct
statement of emotion in the play. The rhythm of kinship is evident in
every exchange between father and daughter, mother and daughter, husband and wife. What we hear contains much arrogance and hostility, but
we are never in any doubt of the stability of kinship which exists.

The last plays bring to fruition the anticipated vision of human kinship that is O'Neill's great legacy. They reject the tortured struggles of
"poetic" heroes in the early plays. They also reject the retreat from life
which concludes the chief middle period plays, the escape into what is so
often called a "dope dream," the withdrawal which is the fate of many of
O'Neill's characters. The last plays label all ideals illusory and foster a
kind of stoic heroism in which the hero is the man or woman who can survive an illusionless life. But those heroes do so in the steady company of
others. As I see these plays, they most vigorously reject withdrawal. They
suggest that human beings, heroes and non-heroes alike, may endure
when they actively take part in that process which is the sole genuinely
life-sustaining process in all O'Neill's plays — the establishing and main-
taining of a thoroughly interdependent relationship with another human
being, that process most simply illustrated in the rituals by which Erie
Smith and the Night Clerk reach one another in *Hughie*. O'Neill's last
plays are most significantly a vision of the ways human beings fill the
void which all rational arguments lead to. *The Iceman Cometh*, while in
direct statement the most nihilistic of O'Neill's works, is in its representation of human kinship far less despairing than a play like *Mourning Becomes Electra*.

Finally, in the confrontations and monologues of the Tyrone family
the raw and painful qualities of human kinship are described as never before. James Tyrone and his elder son Jamie engage in an antiphony of
abuse and mutual affection that leaves us assured of the unbreakable
bond between them; and still more powerfully, James and younger son
Edmund finally recognize that their love is secure despite their devastating disagreements. Father and sons in *Long Day's Journey* establish links
which none of them can ever establish with Mary Tyrone, much as each
one tries, simply and solely because of Mary's uncontrollable withdrawals. *Withdrawal* is the great enemy of kinship and therefore of life in
O'Neill's later plays. Where there is contact, no matter how painful (and it

is usually terribly painful), there is life — and where there is withdrawal there is death. Dialogue becomes not solely a dramatic device but a life-sustaining one.

In the end, it is Jamie Tyrone who in his long confession in Act Four of *Long Day's Journey* makes explicit what has been implicit throughout so much of the dialogue in O'Neill's plays, early and late. It is Jamie, here, and again in his still longer confession in *A Moon for the Misbegotten*, who identifies directly the elements of human kinship we have been receiving undefined in earlier plays. Kinship, Jamie has learned, is made up of all-out affection alternating with all-out hostility. Neither can exist without the other, and until man can realize this he must despair. Only when both affection and hostility exist in twain, and are vigorously acknowledged, can true kinship be said to exist and hence hope be available to man. Jamie is his brother's keeper. He has been that since his disguised appearances in O'Neill's earliest produced plays, but only in the later plays does his capacity to give assume genuinely tragic proportions. He alone among O'Neill's characters is able to give *all* his love, as he is able also to pour out *all* his hate; and in the process he achieves that kind of growth and looks toward that kind of death which western man since the time of Aristotle has associated with the exultation of high tragedy.

O'Neill's career, then, begins in greatly disguised autobiography and ends in high tragedy. The explicitly autobiographical nature of his last works is but their surface. It is in his earlier works that his compulsion to act out the painful experiences of his family life is all-important. In his later works, those experiences, confronted and understood, are merely the means by which he conveys his larger vision. The nature of the appeal of O'Neill's earlier plays, therefore, is one which emanates from that which makes many works about youth coming of age popular. It resides in their dramatizing of anxieties and fantasies their audiences are intimately familiar with. The appeal of his last works, on the other hand, rather than being primarily autobiographical, is existential. Rather than enacting what we fear, they enact (and celebrate) what we are.

I

THE RHYTHM OF KINSHIP

1 The Rhythm

*T*WO RELATED OBSERVATIONS need to be developed in suggesting how O'Neill's early plays anticipate his later ones. The first is that they deal with the terrors of his adolescence and early adulthood in unexpectedly direct ways, and the second is that they are characterized by his over-riding hope, by a rhythm in monologue and dialogue which attests to his early sense of the workings of close human kinship. In the pages that follow, I shall deal first with the relationships between the plays and his life, and second with his dialogue and world view — a division which I shall roughly follow in discussing most of the plays up to and including *The Iceman Cometh*. It was, after all, O'Neill's attitude toward his suffering which prompted the kind of drama he wrote during each stage of his career. Hence, though its importance in the overall direction of this work is secondary, O'Neill's life — that is, his life chiefly as we come to know and understand it in *Long Day's Journey* — must be considered first as it relates to most of his plays.

O'Neill seems to have been ready to write a confessional play quite early in his career, had not events and new guilts turned aside the confessional force which seems to drive some of the plays of the late teens. The unproduced *Shell Shock*[1] is built around a long, melodramatic confession on the part of a guilt-ridden, shell-shocked hero which culminates in a primal scream. The result of the scream is the sudden and complete exorcising of his guilt. Although the play is not directly autobiographical, the fierceness of the hero's pent-up feelings and the all-out nature of his con-

15

fession nevertheless suggest O'Neill's psychological state at the beginning of his career and anticipate the action and the nature of monologues late in his career.[2] The early, melodramatic sea play *Ile* still more directly anticipates the Tyrone saga and indicates how strongly O'Neill wished to tell his audience about his family as early as 1917. *Ile* is the story of Captain Keeney's determination to sail ever farther northward in his pursuit of whale oil, of his fanatic belief in the importance of his quest, and of his long-suffering and weak-willed wife who is driven mad by her husband's stubborn pride. Those around the Captain complain bitterly about his ruthless treatment of them, and the crew, who appear significantly as pairs of rebellious young men, threaten mutiny because their goal has been so often pursued before and so often frustrated. These pairs also protest the Captain's relentless harassment of his wife. The ship's "family" almost precisely parallels the Tyrone family living out their hostilities "locked" together in mutual interdependence as the Captain's vessel is locked in polar ice. The Captain drives his family the way James does, and his futile pursuit of whale oil is like James's futile pursuit of financial security. The rebellious pairs of crew members suggest James Tyrone's rebellious sons, while the harassed, sensitive Mrs. Keeney parallels the harassed and sensitive Mary Tyrone.[3]

Mrs. Keeney is the most troubled character in *Ile*, as Mary is the most disturbed and disturbing character in *Long Day's Journey*. *Ile* is a catalogue of motifs paralleling those later to be associated with Mary: the wife's romanticizing of her husband's career and her insistence on making the painfully tedious trips associated with his work, the husband's attempts to please his wife with the gift of an organ (paralleling Mary's piano), the wife's desperate pleas for love and understanding, and finally the wife's withdrawal and madness (paralleling Mary's addiction). The ending of *Ile* is a precise early version of the final scene of *Long Day's Journey* as Mrs. Keeney, unable to persuade her husband to return home, loses all contact with reality and commences to play the organ, "with half-closed eyes," her fingers moving "faster and faster" while "she is playing wildly and discordantly." The image of Mrs. Keeney hysterically playing the organ, then retreating into a stupor, "a vague smile on her lips," unable to comprehend or respond, is the most obvious parallel to Mary Tyrone in any of O'Neill's earlier plays. It is almost as though O'Neill were ready to face his ghosts here with the directness and honesty which characterize his last plays.

To suggest all the ways in which O'Neill's plays of the late teens and early twenties, by reflecting his private torments of those years, directly anticipate the last plays would take far more space than this study can afford. But a few further instances devoted chiefly to the three most important figures in O'Neill's life, his mother, his brother, and himself, may suffice.

Versions of O'Neill's Mother

Versions of O'Neill's mother are in the plays from the beginning, though few so clearly as Mrs. Keeney. One is Ruth Mayo, Robert Mayo's disappointed wife in *Beyond the Horizon*, who, like Mary, thinks she realizes too late that she married the wrong man. Though Ruth must endure a poverty more grinding than anything Mary knows, their resentment of that poverty is clearly similar, as is their yearning for withdrawal. At the beginning of the third act, Ruth is described as having "aged horribly. Her pale, deeply-lined face has the stony lack of expression of one to whom nothing more can ever happen, whose capacity for emotion has been exhausted" (*The Plays of Eugene O'Neill:* III.144).[4] O'Neill continues to emphasize the "apathy in which she lives," the "slovenly" appearance of her once beautiful hair, one of Mary's most identifiable fears if not characteristics. Indifference and withdrawal characterize all Ruth says in the last act, even in her speeches to her long lost love, the hero's loyal brother Andrew. O'Neill's description of her response to Andrew's broken pleadings for reconciliation reads: "But Ruth, if she is aware of his words, gives no sign. She remains silent, gazing at him dully with the sad humility of exhaustion, her mind already sinking back into that spent calm beyond the further troubling of any hope" (III.169). The parallel with Mary both in situation and feeling is clear. One thinks, too, at this point of a later precursor of Mary's, Deborah Harford in *More Stately Mansions*, as she withdraws forever into her "little Temple of freedom."

Another character suggesting Mary Tyrone is Emma (for "Ella" O'Neill[5]) in *Diff'rent*. Emma's rejection of Caleb Williams because of a one night fling with a native girl is one outgrowth among many in the plays of O'Neill's feelings of rejection by his mother following the escapades of his early twenties. More important, Emma's withdrawal at the end of the first act is followed by a quite unconvincing portrait in the second act of her transformation into an aging nymphomaniac, a transformation which suggests the abrupt contrast between Mary's puritan Catholic rigidities and her devouring addiction. These early maternal figures are, like Mary Tyrone, all delicately attractive, extremely sensitive, and totally unable to cope with their problems. And they all escape into withdrawal which is invariably associated with madness. This withdrawal is accompanied in Emma's case by a kind of debauchery which parallels Mary's addiction.

While Mrs. Keeney, Ruth Mayo, and Emma Crosby are the most obvious representations of O'Neill's mother in his early plays, it is not only such maternal figures who anticipate Mary Tyrone. There are a few paternal figures who do so as well. Calling to mind both James and Mary is old Isaiah Bartlett in *Gold* (the revision of the earlier play *Where the Cross Is Made*).[6] Bartlett is possessed of a mad lust for his lost treasure which pulls him away from all meaningful contact with his family, and at one point in the play he is heard "pacing up and down" in his room, as Mary is heard by James and Edmund. It is, in fact, a special room the Captain has reserved for his fits of madness and unbearable remorse (as Mary reserves her spare room for her morphine and her guilt):

> The madness which has taken almost complete possession of
> him in the past year is clearly stamped on his face,
> particularly in his eyes which seem to stare through and
> beyond objects with a hunted, haunted expression. His
> movements suggest an automaton obeying invisible wires.
> They are quick, jerky, spasmodic.
>
> (II. 681)

Especially in the description of eyes and movements do motifs associated with the relapsing Mary come to mind.

Chris Christopherson in *Anna Christie* is a figure who also stands for O'Neill's father in his stubborn authoritarianism and his uncompromising rigidity. But in more important ways he too is like O'Neill's mother. O'Neill in the late teens was sufficiently obsessed by Christopherson to have written a play about him, which he later revised, of course, into *Anna Christie*. In *Anna Christie*, O'Neill lets the play's heroine, Anna, stand for his own disreputable younger self,[7] and the reunion between daughter and father early in the play anticipates the frequent powerful reunions between child and parent in later plays, which in turn anticipate the recent reunion of Edmund and Mary in *Long Day's Journey*. Old Chris is overwhelmed with joy to see his daughter, though he himself had deserted the girl years before in favor of his obsession with the sea — an obsession which frequently calls to mind Mary's with her drug. Chris cannot accept what his daughter has become, as Mary can accept neither her son's sordid life nor his resultant illness. Also significant is Chris's continuing ambivalence toward that which first made him reject Anna.

While he says he hates "dat ole Davil sea" and curses the fog which nightly seems to envelop him, he has not really separated himself from them by operating his little coal barge, and at the end is pulled back with only mild reluctance by this great lure of his life. Similarly, Mary hates her drug and curses the fog, but invariably returns to both.

Versions of O'Neill's Brother

As O'Neill's feelings about his mother account for powerful moments in his early plays, so too do feelings about his brother. It is hard to recognize in the stoic, protecting figure of Andrew Mayo in *Beyond the Horizon* the hard-drinking, volatile, and caustic figure of Jamie Tyrone of the later plays, but the parallel is there, especially in the closeness the brothers feel for each other. Andrew's level-headedness and success are not so great a disguise of Jamie when it is recalled that Andrew, like Jamie, is the success who turns failure. His achievements in the "grain" market (whiskey is made of grain, of course) are complicated when he over-speculates. That is, Andrew is associated with whiskey and with gambling, two of Jamie's prime agents of self-destruction.

But it is in the intense mutual loyalty of the brothers that the similarity chiefly resides. The sincerest embraces and statements of undying affection in *Beyond the Horizon* are those between the brothers. Robert and Andrew are also jealous and envious of each other, just as jealousy and envy are so much a part of the relationship between the Tyrone brothers. Andrew has been hurt by Ruth's rejection of him in favor of Robert, as Jamie admits his hurt in *Long Day's Journey* at what he supposes to be Mary's rejection of him in favor of Edmund. Finally, however, in the closing scenes of *Beyond the Horizon*, we are overwhelmed by outbursts of brotherly affection never again evoked so powerfully until the fourth act of *Long Day's Journey*. Despite mutual feelings of jealousy and distrust, it is brotherly love which wins out in both plays.

Another play, written shortly after *Beyond the Horizon*, presents a brotherly relationship closer still to that in *Long Day's Journey*. In the early scenes of *The Fountain*, the hero, Juan Ponce de Leon, spends a good deal of time in the company of his loyal, protecting friend Luis de Alvaredo. Like Andrew and Jamie, Luis is older than the more introspective Juan; and very much like Jamie, he is a confessed alcoholic and gambler from the start. Luis is described at his first appearance as "dissipated looking," his face having an "expression of mocking fun and raillery." This is the Jamie figure we are familiar with from the later plays. Nevertheless, written before Jamie O'Neill's death, *The Fountain* still represents the brotherly relationship in the more adolescent terms of *Beyond the Horizon*. Like Andrew, Luis shows up just in time to pull his younger friend out of scrapes, and his caustic wit is distinctly subordinate to his knightly protectiveness. There is refreshingly jocular dialogue between the "brothers" in *The Fountain* absent from *Beyond the Horizon*, but this aspect of the relationship is little developed, and Luis unfortunately disappears early from the action. The play instead concentrates on Juan, obviously the Eugene figure of the play, as the hero in search not only of eternal youth but also understanding of all life's mysteries. The characterization of Juan in fact seems almost an unwitting parody of the sophomoric yearnings an older and more self-knowing O'Neill would bring to dramatic realization in the Richard Miller of *Ah, Wilderness*.

Versions of O'Neill Himself

Which brings us to Eugene himself. As I indicated in the introduction, there is no introspective young hero in any of the earlier plays who does not anticipate Edmund Tyrone in one way or another. These figures all feel rejected or defeated, but all are easily drawn into feelings of hope and love. Like the young O'Neill, Stephen Murray (*The Straw*)[8] and Robert Mayo both have tuberculosis, and like Juan are frustrated dreamers. But the figure who embodies most precisely the characteristics of the youthful O'Neill as they are revived in the figure of Edmund Tyrone is the young Smitty of the S.S. Glencairn plays. Smitty is the outsider, educated and introspective—the uneasy, inexperienced novice in the unfamiliar surroundings of the merchant ship.[9] In the last of these plays, *Moon of the Caribees*, he confesses that he feels haunted by memories evoked in the mournful song of the natives:

> **The Donkeyman:** *(spitting placidly)* Queer things, mem'ries.
>   I ain't ever been bothered much by 'em.
> **Smitty:** *(looking at him fixedly for a moment—with quiet scorn)*
>   No, you wouldn't be.
> **The Donkeyman:** Not that I ain't had my share o' things goin'
>   wrong; but I puts 'em out o' me mind, like, an'
>   fergets 'em.

Smitty: But suppose you couldn't put them out of your mind?
Suppose they haunted you when you were awake and when you
were asleep—what then?

(I. 467)

Smitty's desolation and guilt are over his desertion by a girl and his
resultant alcoholism, though he is uncertain whether the alcoholism may
not have been the reason for her desertion in the first place. Smitty's confusion parallels O'Neill's over whether he had betrayed his mother
through his debauchery or she had betrayed him through hers. Similarly,
Smitty's sense of alienation and secretiveness are O'Neill's, that secretiveness which in O'Neill's middle period will become the chief identifying
characteristic of all his characters and all his plays.

Smitty's secretiveness, of course, fosters the melodramatic intrigue
of *In The Zone.* Smitty anticipates innumerable later O'Neill heroes in his
torment over memories too shameful and terrifying to share. In the rather
sophomoric conclusion to *In The Zone,* the crew, suspecting that Smitty
is a German spy, brutally bind and gag him, and break open his valise of
"love letters." Reminiscent of the hero's "confession" in the unproduced
Shell Shock, which was written about the same time as the *S.S. Glencairn*
plays,[10] this action may be seen as a kind of wished-for exorcism for
O'Neill. But although both the shell-shocked hero of that play and Smitty
are forced to confess their shameful secrets, the confessions themselves
are empty. O'Neill is responding only to the pressure to release what is
troubling him; he in fact releases nothing. We never hear what is in Smitty's letters. There is only shame both in Smitty and the crew at the end,
that shame which O'Neill was still entirely the slave of in thinking of what
it was "to have a dope fiend for a Mother" (Edmund: *Long Day's Journey,*
Act III). Both the shame and the secrecy were to continue as motive forces
of O'Neill's plays for many years to come.

These are but a few examples of the ways in which O'Neill reveals
his personal sufferings about himself and his family in his early plays. An
extended analysis of these plays could show other parallels with *Long
Day's Journey* both in dialogue and characterization. It is time, however,
to move on to what is more important about these early plays. Despite
their sordid themes, their deaths, and the feeling of personal rejection
which their plots exude, they are essentially plays of hope, and they are
plays of hope very probably because O'Neill, Edmund-like, still had great

hope within him. That some end happily and some sadly is beside the point. Also beside the point are the explicitly upbeat statements by leading characters—the dying Robert Mayo's positive declaration at the end of *Beyond The Horizon*, which is maudlin, or Juan's mystical realization at the conclusion of *The Fountain*, which is sophomoric.[11] What gives the plays hope primarily is the sense of human kinship to be found, especially in the earliest of these plays, the sea plays. When O'Neill works at showing characters being good or noble, he does not succeed very well; but when he allows them to deal with one another openly and directly, in mutual hostility and affection, he does succeed. In a sense, and this point carries all through the O'Neill canon, O'Neill is most hopeful when he is not trying especially to be hopeful, as he does not seem to be in the early sea plays. In the *S.S. Glencairn* plays O'Neill is simply describing, not preaching: yet in the dialogue and scenic images[12] of these short plays, he is announcing in basic, uncomplicated fashion the terms in which human existence is viable.

The sense of human kinship aboard the *S. S. Glencairn* is convincing because it is made up of human emotions that move constantly back and forth between affection and hostility, altruism and meanness, benevolence and violence. The qualities of the men are best exemplified in Driscoll, the first of a long line of O'Neill Irishmen who are uncontrollably volatile in their anger one moment and comforting to the point of being maternal the next. If Driscoll's moods are wildly disparate and unpredictable, he is nevertheless a figure of towering strength and genuine security to his shipmates. The crew know they can count on his loyalty and need never fear his rages, despite their thunder. The sense of kinship in these plays centers on Driscoll, and it is a sense never shaken by the less appealing qualities each character reveals: the pugnacity of Paddy and Yank, the sneaking malice of Cocky, the heavy stupidity of Ivan. All of these men are "thoughtless" of the feelings of others if thoughtfulness is measured by consciously (or affectedly) altruistic gestures and statements; but they have an unthinking confidence in one another far stronger than the learned formalities more educated, civilized behavior could bring them. The two characteristics which most typify their relationships are their split-second rages (mirroring Driscoll's) and their equally split-second reconciliations, which are as totally authentic as they are inevitably short-lived. The primary evidence of the kinship among these men is that their boiling points are low, their forgiveness is given freely and without reservation, and their sense of guilt is practically nil.

In *The Long Voyage Home*, what lingers rather than the cruel deceptions of the Shanghaiing intrigue is the feeling that the unfortunate Olson may not be much worse off on the moth-eaten *Amindra* than he has ever been, that his desire to return to the farm of his youth is a pipedream. As a member of his new crew, he will continue to know the kind of life-sustaining human companionship he knew aboard the *Glencairn* — in the boisterous, at times violent, but always authentic camaraderie that is ever-present there.

Then there is *Moon of the Carribees*, which is seen by some as the most successful of the group. Filled with feelings of a common lot commonly accepted, the crew in this play demonstrate their deep kinship through the explosiveness of their shared appetites and their split-second outbreaks of savage violence. The nearness of that kinship to its tribal antecedents is reinforced by the mournful song of the natives in the background, which haunts the men in spite of themselves. The crew in this play are more inter-dependent than in any of the other plays, even if their outbreaks of outrage and resentment make the men a distinct danger to one another. That feeling for the extreme counterforces rhythmically varying with one another in close human relationships, which will be the chief characteristic of O'Neill's last plays, is nowhere so forcefully anticipated as in this play. Neither primitive nor quite civilized, the crew of the *S. S. Glencairn* describe in simple, direct terms what we are.

The uniqueness of the *S. S. Glencairn* plays, and their strength, then, is not in the emphasis on the haunted Smitty, but on the kinship among the crew, which Smitty at his happier moments appears to be silently a part of. Implicit in these early plays is O'Neill's apparent realization that only by living in relation to others, as do the crew of the *S. S. Glencairn*, can humans endure. As in *The Iceman Cometh*, "pipe dreams" abound. They are the stuff of conversation, the grounds for antagonism and recrimination, the subjects of mutual reassurance. But though the men dwell chiefly on their illusions, the feelings those illusions engender are themselves quite real. The most authentic of these feelings are those shared by Driscoll and the dying Yank in *Bound East for Cardiff*, even when the two are absorbed in Yank's pipedream of settling on a farm, or in recalling past escapades which are either highly exaggerated or which never even took place. These feelings sustain these two men in a way their Captain in his self-protective aloofness can never comprehend.

Growing out of the sea plays is the sense of kinship in *Anna Christie*. Those who puzzle over the remarkable appeal of this play might consider that the rhythm of its dialogue rather than its symbols of fog and sea or its sentimental conclusion might be its real strength. The sharp reversals of emotion in the speeches of Mat Burke descend directly from those of the sturdy Driscoll and look forward to those of the indefatigable Con

Melody. Burke's authenticity as a character is entirely rooted in the fact that he regularly goes through split-second changes of mood.

Having established this trait as the essence of Burke's character, as the source of his attractiveness to the audience as well as to Anna, O'Neill conveys in his crucial last-act exchanges with the heroine his first prolonged dialogue composed, it seems consciously this time, in the alternating rhythm of kinship. Since the rhythmical variations in this kind of dialogue come across much more strongly in performance than on the printed page, illustrative quotation is all but impossible. What follows can only dimly suggest what is a strong rhythmical effect when the scene is performed by competent actors. Burke has just learned of Anna's past and is fiercely divided between his traditional male contempt and his spontaneous love for her. Anna, in similar fashion, is caught between her shame and hurt on the one hand and her great affection on the other. Burke has just announced that to get away from Anna he has signed on a steamer for Capetown:

> Burke: . . . . That I may never see another woman to
> my dying hour!
> Anna: That's what you say now, but I'll bet by the time
> you get there you'll have forgotten all about me and
> start in talking the same old bull you talked to me
> to the first one you meet.
> Burke: (offended) I'll not, then! God mend you, is it
> making me out to be the like of yourself you are, and
> you taking up with this one and that all the years
> of your life?
> Anna: (angrily assertive) Yes, that's yust what I mean!
> You been doing the same thing all your life, picking
> up a new girl in every port. How're you any better
> than I was?
> Burke: (thoroughly exasperated) Is it no shame you have
> at all? I'm a fool to be wasting talk on you and
> you hardened in badness. I'll go out of this and
> lave you alone forever. (He starts for the door —
> then stops to turn on her furiously) And I suppose
> 'tis the same lies you told them all before that
> you told to me?
> Anna: (indignantly) That's a lie! I never did!
> Burke: (miserably) You'd be saying that, anyway.
> Anna: (forcibly, with growing intensity) Are you trying
> to accuse me — of being in love — really in love —
> with them?
> Burke: I'm thinking you were, surely.

Anna: *(furiously, as if this were the last insult —*
advancing on him threateningly) You mutt, you!
I've stood enough from you. Don't you dare!
(With scornful bitterness) Love 'em! Oh, my
Gawd! You damn thick-head! Love 'em? *(Savagely)*
I hated 'em! I tell you! Hated 'em, hated 'em,
hated 'em! And may Gawd strike me dead this minute
and my mother, too, if she is alive, if I ain't
telling you the honest truth!

Burke: *(immensely pleased by her vehemence — a light beginning*
to break over his face — but still uncertain, torn
between doubt and the desire to believe — helplessly)
If I could only be believing you now!

Anna: *(distractedly)* Oh, what's the use? What's the use
of me talking? What's the use of anything?

(III. 73–4)

The subject of these lines is Anna's insistence that she hated her numerous customers, but what the lines primarily suggest is the emotional
movement in each character. Mat moves between the comically hypocritical disgust born of his stereotypes to a desire to understand born of his
love. Anna moves from the forcefulness and certainty of her protests to
the desolation that anyone can understand. And back and forth they go
in this mode through several pages of dialogue. What comes through
most in this, as in the many exchanges in the play between Anna and her
father, is not a single emotional state but the complex of contradictory
emotional states people endure during critical encounters. Mat's contempt is real, and so is his love. Anna's coarseness is real, but no less so is
her tenderness. So it is and so it will be throughout what will be the tem-
pestuous but quite probably stable marriage of Mat and Anna. The
strength of these characters lies in their capacity to give all-out utterance
to both sides of their radically conflicting emotions. The ending of the
play is, if one insists, sentimental; but the emotional pendulums in both
of these characters are as convincing as anything in the early O'Neill.
Their relationship looks forward in fact to some far from sentimental relationships to come. The chaotic rhythm of emotional self-contradiction
in the dialogue which characterizes the tragic relationships between Jim
and Ella Harris in *All God's Chillun* and Eben and Abbie in *Desire Under
the Elms* is recognizable between the lovers in *Anna Christie*. And that
chaotic rhythm is the only true foundation of affirmation in the plays of
Eugene O'Neill. Without it, there is nothing but man's animal nature in a
meaningless universe.

Biographies describe Eugene O'Neill at the beginning of his successful career as a man deeply disturbed by memories of his late adolescence and young adulthood, but charged with all kinds of hope and rebellious fervor. They also describe him as an artist bent on creating his art directly out of what was in him rather than adhering to traditions and forms. What was in him were his troubled memories, chiefly about his mother, and his determination to develop in unsentimental dramatic terms what made life worth living. These plays tell of his fear of isolation wrought by his mother's rejection, his despair wrought by the fact of her addiction, his confidence in his brother, and his longing to be reconciled with the past. They also tell of his sense that close, authentic human companionship at all levels is what gives direction and purpose to life. They tell this through their dialogue and in their scenic images of loving people reacting vigorously to one another. The truest image of the O'Neill of these years is Smitty because even though Smitty is secretive and isolated, even though he confesses that he is "haunted" by "memories," he is also seen participating in the life of the crew, happily "belonging." And what he belongs to is a segment of the human race living out its destiny of arguing and hurting, nurturing and loving. The kinship in Harry Hope's saloon, in the Tyrone living room, and on Phil Hogan's front porch grows out of the emotional counterpoint of the sea plays and *Anna Christie*.

2 Breaking the Rhythm

Noneof the plays dealt with in the last chapter ends in stoic withdrawal or violent death. A tubercular hero dies in *Beyond the Horizon* as a tubercular heroine dies in *The Straw*, but these are touching, romanticized deaths. They leave us stirred, committed to believing in people and wanting to believe in life. Other plays end with the hero encountering some kind of mystical transformation, as does *The Fountain;* or with the traditional romantic conclusion of marriage, as does *Anna Christie;* or with things continuing as they were at the start, as do three of the sea plays. And for the most part, things as they were at the start is a desirable condition in these plays. Families, brotherly friends, members of a ship's crew live in a state in which camaraderie and hostility are the two sides of a complete and ultimately satisfying human relationship. These plays, anticipating O'Neill's last plays, begin in the rhythm of kinship and tend to end with it. Memories, bad fortune, impossible dreams — the stuff which makes up their plots — break that rhythm; but once the problems are solved or the false dreams are frustrated, a kind of bearable or better than bearable status quo is re-established. While there is great sadness, there is always hope.

Plays immediately following those I have been looking at, however, show O'Neill in the grip of a growing new despair, quite possibly associated with the shocks wrought by the series of deaths of those closest to him: first his father (1920), then his mother (1922), and finally his brother (1923). The presence of these deaths begins to be evident with *Desire Under the Elms* (written in 1923) but may also be the cause of a growing sense of alienation in heroes as early as *The Emperor Jones* in 1920. Whatever the causes, there is no question that with *The Emperor Jones* and, still more, *The Hairy Ape*, O'Neill's rhythm of kinship begins to break. Central characters now begin to die in madness or self-imposed stoic withdrawal which precludes any further kinship in their lives. There are struggles in the most important plays of the early twenties to reassert kinship, but those struggles are doomed. What kinship the characters find exists under the most desperate conditions and survives only briefly. The culminating scenic images of the plays I shall now be discussing are of Eben and Abbie Cabot walking in deathly kinship to their inevitable doom and of old Ephraim Cabot withdrawing to the hard non-comfort of his "lonely God." Ephraim, in these plays, represents better than anyone O'Neill's growing sense of what heroism is coming to mean—withdrawal into a half-life where all feeling is suppressed and there are no more sounds of kinfolk. Toward kinship itself in *Desire Under the Elms* and the plays leading up to it, there is only an engulfing sense of futility.

The Emperor Jones and The Hairy Ape

The most memorable central figures of the plays of the early 1920s are panicked and ultimately suicidal. I refer of course first to *The Emperor Jones* and *The Hairy Ape*, which I see as companion pieces. In both plays, heroes break out of the relative security of kinship which fails to satisfy their ambitious egos; and in both plays, these heroes find, after a brief period of joy and release, nothing more than isolation in a totally hostile world, isolation so terrifying that they give way to panic leading to violent death. Both plays can be understood as growing out of the unspoken feelings of an author trying to shut out memories of a past which he could not separate himself from and which he feared would finally destroy him. Neither Jones nor Yank can shut out such memories, and both are indirectly destroyed by them.

Brutus Jones actually has two pasts he must escape from during his nocturnal flight. One is his past as a black American who betrayed an implied kinship with his fellow blacks of the Pullman cars[1] and escaped to his illusory mastery of a Caribbean dictatorship. This escape parallels the basic pattern of O'Neill's escape from his family (his voyage to South America) and his guilt relating to it. No offending-offended mother is explicitly referred to, but family of various sorts clearly prompts the guilt which first haunts Jones in the jungle.

Jones's second escape in the play is less obvious but more significant as an anticipation of one of O'Neill's later works. It is Jones's escape from his relationship with the treacherous cockney Smithers, who despite his unpleasant personality is Jones's sole companion on the island. Jones's relationship with Smithers, growing out of several relationships of its kind in the sea plays, is similar to one O'Neill would create years later in the two-character play *Hughie.* In both plays, a stronger, more vocal, more self-revealing character prone to nightmares is helped to survive psychologically despite terrible feelings of guilt for past offenses by a relationship with a weaker, more devious character. In both plays, a rhythm is established between the two characters whereby they feel secure as they feed each other's illusions and feel threatened as those illusions are threatened. It is a rhythm of kinship conceived in brutal terms. Although these relationships are tenuous, they do help the dominant figure in each pair to sleep peacefully at night. Erie Smith and Brutus Jones — even the choice of last names suggests a parallel between the two — both endure "eerie" torments when they are separated from their companions, nocturnal torments resulting from past memories, guilts, and panic-provoking loneliness. Erie's hotel room is very much Brutus's jungle of nightmares; and as Erie had to retire to it with all his sins upon him when the first Hughie died, so Brutus must enter his jungle having destroyed those he may have really loved and having gained short-lived rewards by outwitting simple folk with his illusory silver bullet.

Yank in *The Hairy Ape,* like Jones, runs away from a kinship which failed to satisfy his ambitions and finds only isolation and death in a cruel, indifferent world. His is the kinship of the boiler room (only a few feet removed literally as well as figuratively from the forecastle of the sea plays), and his kin are his shipmates. Unlike Jones, Yank kills no one, but he does attack the voluble, disgruntled Paddy, whose brotherly warmth is of a kind Yank longs for so desperately in his final moments that he seeks it in the arms of a gorilla. The basic rhythm of Yank's boiler room world is a loud, incessant alternation of hostility and reassurance broken suddenly by an uninvited visitor from above, the white-clad lady passenger Mildred Douglas. That Mildred is on the one hand pale, delicate, and elegant, and on the other hand deeply confused about her life suggests strongly that O'Neill is again dealing with his mother — this time in not so heavy disguise. Mildred becomes suddenly for Yank what Mary Tyrone is for her sons — both inspiration and frustration. Her spiritual beauty urges the hero on to new heights, but her cold rejection is what keeps him from ever achieving those heights. Mildred haunts Yank in a double sense: both as an image of what he could be, and, by her rejection of him, as the first and most important instigator of his terrible isolation. Everywhere Yank goes the pattern of Mildred's rejection is repeated, as O'Neill felt the pattern of his mother's rejection constantly repeated. As in the polite society of Fifth Avenue, so among his own kind in the union hall (paralleling perhaps O'Neill's theatre world), Yank is violently rebuffed. He wants to "knock all de steel in de woild up to de moon" — certainly a vigorous metaphor for O'Neill's creative surges; but everywhere he is greeted by either coldness or envious hostility. And at all times Yank keeps focusing on the rejecting Mildred, as throughout these plays O'Neill keeps focusing on his rejecting mother. All Yank does will "show her," "fix her," get even with Mildred — but all he feels is increasing isolation and increasing panic.

Both *The Emperor Jones* and *The Hairy Ape* end on a note of unqualified despair and unalloyed panic. The kinship both heroes once knew having been destroyed by the violence of their own pride and ambition, the two must face chaos, terror, and finally death. That they both possess strength and courage is part of what has made them appealing as tragic figures, but that their worlds have become empty of any kind of kinship makes them among the most despairing of O'Neill's early characters.

Two early plays still more painfully and more intricately speak O'Neill's growing despair, the "breaking" of his rhythm of kinship. They are *All God's Chillun Got Wings*, written at the time of his mother's death, and *Desire Under the Elms*, written as the effects of that death began to take hold more deeply. Unlike *The Emperor Jones* and *The Hairy Ape*, these plays are enacted love stories which contain images of tenderness, forgiveness, and reconciliation; but like them, they are plays which bespeak the ultimate futility of any kind of permanent reconciliation. Although the lovers in both cases "find" one another, they do so under conditions so terrifying or macabre as to suggest that total chaos is close at hand.

All God's Chillun Got Wings

The theme of interracial marriage is important in *All God's Chillun*, but not because O'Neill believed (in 1922) that interracial understanding was possible.[2] The hero's sister, Hattie Harris, an articulate black militant, makes clear O'Neill's own apparent conviction that black and white America were in no way ready to live in genuine kinship. Rather, the theme of interracial marriage is a displacement, important primarily in what it stands for, especially in the character of Ella Downey. Ella's identification through her name with O'Neill's mother is inescapable, and their

similarities go well beyond name alone.[3] Ella is an Irish Catholic girl of re-
spectable parents who feels debased sexually by an unfaithful white suitor
(a good-looking prize fighter)[4] and then feels further debased — much further debased — by entering into sexual union with a black man. Ella's guilt
suggests O'Neill's mother in her guilt, first her guilt at having fallen in
love with a philandering actor, then her guilt at having succumbed to her
addiction. Ella's revulsion at having sexual relations with a black parallels
Mary Tyrone's revulsion at being a "dope-fiend." This may be strong med-
icine for readers in the late twentieth century, but public attitudes regarding miscegenation at the time the play was written must be kept in mind.
Ella Downey is no society-darer or social reformer. She is a thoroughly
conventional girl who falls as the result of one bad experience into what
she considers to be another worse experience — and she suffers from her
guilt associated with the latter especially.

Having said this, I must now point out that only Ella's feelings
about having sexual relations with a black parallel Mary's feelings about
her addiction. Ella's feelings about a man named Jim Harris are another
matter entirely. The two feelings, while they contribute to Ella's madness,
are kept entirely separate throughout the play. Ella's love for Jim is as genuine as her guilt at having married him, and while that love is the love of a
woman for a man, it is also the love of a guilty mother for her condemning son. Jim's blackness prompts Ella to say some terrible things to him, as
Mary's addiction prompts her to say some terrible things to her son. But
then, in secondary guilt, Ella asks Jim's forgiveness and pledges her love
for him, as in secondary guilt Mary asks Edmund's forgiveness and
pledges him her love. In short, three factors must be considered in relation to Ella's feelings about Jim Harris. First, he is a black, and Ella's having relations with a black is like Mary's taking dope. Second, he is a kind,
loving man, and Ella quite naturally falls in love with him out of both
gratitude and genuine affection. Third, Jim Harris comes to Ella as a son,
and a share of Ella's guilt is that of a betraying mother for an innocent
son. All three of these factors are tightly interrelated in the play, of
course, but they are all readily identifiable.

For his part, Jim, even though he has O'Neill's father's name, clearly
anticipates Edmund Tyrone. Edmund will do anything to assure himself
of his mother's affection, though her persistent return to her addiction
seems constantly to deny the truth of that affection. Thus Edmund is led
to feelings of despair and morbidity. Similarly, Jim Harris will do anything
to assure himself of his wife's affections, though her persistent return to
her deep racial prejudice constantly denies for him the authenticity of that
affection, despite Ella's frequent declarations of it. Like Edmund, Jim also

becomes desperate and morbid. Edmund feels inferior to Mary for what he conceives to be her pure, superior past, as Jim feels inferior to Ella's white past. Ella's whiteness is to Jim what Mary's puritanical Catholicism is to Edmund. Hence, Jim says he is going to be Ella's "black slave" in order to win her affection. Much that Edmund says to Mary in order to assure himself of her affection is the equivalent of saying he is willing to be her slave.

Various scenes and situations in the play grow out of O'Neill's haunting past, early in the play his fantasies about that past. Anticipating later plays, O'Neill dwells on a life "before the Fall." Jim Harris and Ella Downey the "Painty Face" (rosy-cheeked) are shown as children living an idyll of love and harmony untroubled by the prejudice and guilt later life will bring. Edmund and Mary only hint at this kind of distorted reminiscence, but Simon and Deborah Harford in More Stately Mansions (a play written not long before Long Day's Journey) make it the central theme of their recurring interviews. Jim and his Painty Face are a vision of that state O'Neill longed to return to.

What gives this play its very real power, however, is not so much its reflections of the usual O'Neill haunts but the image of intense love that it communicates, love that again emerges from a rhythm of alternating hostility and tenderness. But here it is a desperate love as the hostility culminates in violent attack and the tenderness turns into a series of desperate appeals. Upon their return from Europe and their first sexual encounters, Ella begins to reveal the deep hostility which her guilt has bred. She attacks Jim's race first by attacking the many symbols of black tradition that surround her in their new home, then by attacking Jim himself. Yet the tenderness that characterized her earlier feelings for Jim regularly reasserts itself. Having spitefully hurt Jim and belittled his ambition to be a lawyer — she actually brings him to tears — she suddenly and just as spontaneously comforts him. She "kneels by Jim," "pats his shoulder," and "with kindness and love" tells him not to cry. She also pledges her love in terms as honest and compassionate as her next attack on him will be honest and pitiless. This is the rhythm of kinship in a form resembling the violent alternation of hate and love through which Anna Christie and Mat Burke pass in the recognition of their love. Only here there is no happy ending. The issues which separate the lovers are too devastating.

In the middle of the second act, Ella and Jim have their most violent encounter, one which reveals their kinship at its most intense but also its most desperate. Ella has been tormented by her fear and guilt to the point where she seems completely out of touch with reality, and Jim has been tormented by Ella to the point where he wishes he were in the same condition. He is at a table trying hopelessly to study for his exams when Ella noiselessly approaches him with a carving knife, madly determined to free herself from her shame. He turns in time to grab her wrist, and his sudden movement brings her back to reality:

Ella: Where did I — ? I was having a nightmare — Where did
they go — I mean, how did I get here? (*With sudden
terrified pleading — like a little girl*) Oh, Jim —
don't ever leave me alone! I have such terrible
dreams, Jim — promise you'll never go away!

Jim: I promise, Honey.

Ella: (*her manner becoming more and more childishly silly*)
I'll be a little girl — and you'll be old Uncle Jim
who's been with us for years and years — Will you play
that?

Jim: Yes, Honey. Now you better go back to bed.

Ella: (*like a child*) Yes, Uncle Jim. (*She turns to go. He
pretends to be occupied by his book. She looks at him
for a second — then suddenly asks in her natural
woman's voice*) Are you studying hard, Jim?

Jim: Yes, Honey. Go to bed now. You need to rest, you know.

Ella: (*stands looking at him, fighting with herself. A
startling transformation comes over her face. It
grows mean, vicious, full of jealous hatred. She cannot contain herself but breaks out harshly with a cruel
venomous grin*) You dirty nigger!

Jim: (*starting as if he'd been shot*) Ella! For the good
Lord's sake!

Ella: (*coming out of her insane mood for a moment, aware of
something terrible, frightened*) Jim! Jim! Why are you looking at me like that?

Jim: What did you say to me just then?

Ella: (*gropingly*) Why, I — I said — I remember saying, are you
studying hard, Jim? Why? You're not mad at that, are
you?

Jim: No, Honey. What made you think I was mad? Go to bed
now.

Ella: (*obediently*) Yes, Jim. (*She passes behind the portieres. Jim stares before him. Suddenly her head is
thrust out at the side of the portieres. Her face is
again that of a vindictive maniac*) Nigger!

(II. 336–37)

A mad scene? Unquestionably! And also of course filled with reso-nances of Mary Tyrone's withdrawals and recoveries. But Ella's madness is only an extreme of the chaotic reversals of feeling O'Neill finds in all close human relationships. She is murderously aggressive in her "de-mented" moments, helpless and loving in her "sane" ones; but both moods are those of the same person — one person, with two mutually exclusive sides to her nature, neither side, as it were, having any notion of the other's existence. Ella differs from others in that her aggressive side be-comes so violent that she will have to be hospitalized; yet her feelings of love and dependency exist full blown alongside the violence. Kinship in O'Neill is the hostility and the love in eternal juxtaposition. Neither com-ments on the existence of the other. There is little or no irony in his early plays. *All God's Chillun* gropes toward an understanding of human kin-ship by giving us the full impact of Ella's Jekyll-Hyde reversals and allow-ing Jim to come to sense the permanence of their relationship through per-sistent exposure to those reversals — as in the later O'Neill, the audience will grope toward understanding the nature of human kinship through exposure to similarly persistent reversals of feeling.

The sense of kinship which closes the play is again created in melo-dramatic terms. Again, the language and action create a scenic image of violent hatred countered by equally violent and mutual need. Jim has just learned that he has again failed his bar exams and bursts into a sarcastic attack on the white society which has determined to keep "Nigger Jim Harris" in his place. But Ella is overjoyed and declares wildly and trium-phantly that she has "gotten the laugh." (Ella's "laugh" is directed toward the African tribal mask in the Harris living room, which has become for Ella the focal point of her hatred and guilt.) This time it is Jim who turns actively violent, "raising his fists above her head," ready to strike her. Her cry recalls him to himself, only this time Ella does not return from her de-mented state. She follows form in suddenly turning tender and compas-sionate, but she keeps insisting that she has defeated the opprobrious mask by having gotten Jim to fail his exams. Jim realizes (like Edmund years later) that this time she has left him for good. Yet their final lines are spoken in love. Their love, their kinship, is permanent, though Ella's in-sanity now must separate them. To express that permanence, Ella, then Jim, reverts to the terms of their childhood relationship. The two ideas implicit in this reversion are first that their love can exist pure and un-damaged by the fierceness of their mutual aggression, but second that their lives have in fact been destroyed. Despite their kinship, the other re-alities of their existence have been borne in upon them to the extent that they must lose each other. In acknowledging that their kinship can no longer be of this world — he will, he says, play with Ella "right up to the gates of Heaven" — Jim directly anticipates the ending of *Desire Under the Elms*. As Eben and Abbie "find" one another as it were on the steps of the gallows, Jim and Ella "find" one another at the door of the madhouse.[5] The hope which in the early O'Neill usually resides in some sort of chaotic but close relationship between two human beings — or among a group of human beings — is clearly in decline. The relationships, the memories, have become too chaotic, too terrifying, and the only bona fide survival is the half-survival of Ephraim Cabot contemplating his hard God alone in the midst of his farm and "his stock."

Desire Under the Elms

Despite the obvious differences between *All God's Chillun* and *Desire Under the Elms* — in setting and dialect, especially — the two plays are linked. As heavily disguised re-enactments of critical family confrontations in O'Neill's adolescence and young adulthood, both plays anticipate the action of the last plays; and in their view of human kinship violently destroyed, they also anticipate the plays immediately to follow. O'Neill, beginning to reveal the longer-range effects of the deaths of his mother and brother, is beginning to find isolation to be man's natural destiny.

All four central figures of *Long Day's Journey* are represented in *Desire Under the Elms*.[6] It is easy enough to recognize in the darkly sensitive Eben one of the many anticipations of Edmund Tyrone, but it is not quite so easy to recognize Eben's rebellious and rambunctious brothers as an early variation of the Mephistophelean, alcoholic side of Jamie Tyrone in these plays. O'Neill's previous representations of his brother were in figures whose debauches are much subordinated to their protective qualities. Eben's brothers, on the other hand, are presented as ruthless competitors, hardly protective in any sense. Ten years older than Eben (Jamie is ten years older than Edmund), Simeon and Peter sell their birthright (the farm) much as the real Jamie sold his birthright (acting talent) for an illusion: "gold" for Simeon and Peter, the "good life" of the Broadway "sport" for Jamie. After years of submission, Simeon and Peter, like Jamie, finally defy a tyrant father, and in their defiance literally "whoop it up" like wild Indians, action which may stand for Jamie's irreverent, undisciplined behavior.

As Simeon and Peter anticipate Jamie Tyrone, Ephraim Cabot anticipates James Tyrone, Sr.[7] Cut from the same cloth as the stubborn tyrants in O'Neill's early plays—Captain Keeney in *Ile*, Chris Christopherson in *Anna Christie*, or Isaiah Bartlett in *Gold*—Ephraim Cabot in his dogged commitment to his farm strongly parallels James Tyrone in his commitment to his play. And as with James, that commitment has brought frustration and hardship to those around him. As James justifies himself by lengthily telling of his early struggles, Ephraim lengthily and in similar tones (if not dialect) tells of his. Such matters are of course treated with understanding and even humor in *Long Day's Journey*. *Desire Under the Elms* was written well before O'Neill had the distance and experience to treat these subjects in so detached a fashion. Nevertheless, both plays make us finally forgive and even admire their tyrannical fathers. What we admire in both the old men is their capacity to endure. James has a wife who is a seemingly incurable drug addict, Ephraim a wife who is guilty of infanticide. Both have the strength, never fully explored in either play, to survive the awesome emotional hardship each has to face. Stubborn tyrant, volatile fraud, abject confessor—these chief variations in all O'Neill's dramatic treatments of his father are linked by a consistent tone of forgiveness.

Far more complex than Ephraim, and more difficult to recognize as the representation of O'Neill's mother in *Desire Under the Elms* is the figure of Abbie Cabot. To understand what Abbie represents in this play, one needs first to consider her image at the end, where she is forgiven, as Mary is forgiven in *Long Day's Journey*. Roger Asselineau has convincingly identified the play's conclusion as an attempt to create a kind of death-transcending kinship.[8] It is an ending in which the lovers transcend the terrible event which has divided them. Abbie's murder of her baby has the same connotations as Mary's addiction. It creates in herself and others an aura of fear and disgust that go far beyond what one might associate with other "crimes." And thus the forgiveness must assume extraordinary proportions. *Desire Under the Elms*, like *Long Day's Journey*, is an attempt to dramatize that extraordinary forgiveness, and thus Abbie's links with Mary are most recognizable at the conclusion of the play.

But kinship in death is a far cry from kinship in life. The kinship of Eben and Abbie at the play's conclusion is not one of this world. Eben's responses to Abbie, like Jim's toward Ella in *All God's Chillun*, represent a determination to blot out the evil, to return to a state of innocence. In both plays, the world forces a united pair to know they must somehow leave it together if they are to remain united. This is hardly the kinship of the sea plays, or the kinship we will come to know in the later works. In fact, Abbie and Eben, like Ella and Jim, must look forward to a union that is essentially a union in withdrawal, and that is precisely the destiny figures like Simon Harford struggle against. Madness and the gallows in these plays are more an anticipation of Lavinia Mannon's or Deborah Harford's withdrawals than of the kinship in the Tyrone family or the love of Josie Hogan and Jim Tyrone. Instead of kinship, then, it might be more accurate to say that it is a morbid reconciliation that these plays yearn for.

But the figure the young hero must be reconciled with remains a figure representing O'Neill's mother.[9] I have briefly suggested that Abbie Cabot at the end of the play suggests Mary Tyrone. The problem is to recognize her early in the play in that context. If Abbie is indeed a stand-in for O'Neill's mother in this play, she does not seem so at first, during her developing relationship with Eben. Rather, she *becomes* that figure rather abruptly as the play progresses.

O'Neill's mother died shortly before this play was conceived, and Eben's reactions before he meets Abbie unquestionably have to do with that event. Eben is fiercely loyal to the memory of his recently dead mother, who he feels was the only one who loved him. But his love for her is not simple or uncomplicated. O'Neill describes the two enormous elms on each side of the house as maternal symbols, but it is "a sinister maternity." The elms "appear to protect and at the same time subdue." There is "in their aspect, a crushing jealous absorption." Clearly, Eben's sinister domination by the memory of his dead mother is O'Neill's by the memory of his.

Abbie's appearance, then, must at first conflict with everything associated with Eben's mother. With her entrance, Eben's attention is drawn away from his dead mother's memory, much as he struggles to keep that memory alive. Abbie attracts him sexually, and she attracts him maternally. As she leads him on sexually, she also refers to herself as his "new Maw." In effect, Abbie at first replaces the town whore "Min," to whom all the Cabot men have gone periodically both for sex and motherly comfort. Eben struggles against Abbie, to be sure, but it is a losing struggle. Abbie easily dominates him erotically and less easily begins to dominate him maternally. In effect, Abbie in these early scenes is an Earth Mother, the first of many in O'Neill's plays — a woman who can fulfill a man's need for both sexual satisfaction and mothering without feeling or evoking guilt in the process. She comes as a new manifestation of "Min."

But it is the sex that from the start creates the play's complications.[10] The living Abbie cannot in fact be the mythic Min. As soon as the burning, repressed sexuality bursts into open sexual encounter, guilt does set in, and the image of Abbie shifts inexorably from Earth Mother to real mother. From that point on, Abbie does more than replace Eben's "Maw."

She becomes O'Neill's Maw — a figure torn between powerful possessiveness and haunting, decimating guilt. The scene (Part Two, scene 3) in which Abbie makes her transformation most apparent warrants closer analysis. After their lust has figuratively burned down the wall between their bedrooms, Abbie, instead of making love to Eben in his room, insists that they do so in the front parlor Eben so insistently associates with his dead mother. She does this, she feels, to drive home the domination she now feels she has over Eben and the entire household, but she does not realize the strange effect this determination will have. As soon as she enters the parlor O'Neill tells us that a "change has come over the woman. She looks awed and frightened now, ready to run away." This is certainly different from her assertiveness of the previous scene and parallels once more the descriptions of the many characters who anticipate Mary Tyrone. In the parlor, at Abbie's urging, Eben begins suddenly to be reconciled to the thought of his dead mother's acceptance of what is going on. Abbie works on him through the mutual resentment both have felt for the intransigent Ephraim.

> Eben: . . . . She was soft an' easy. He [Ephraim] couldn't
> 'preciate her.
> Abbie: He can't 'preciate me!
> Eben: He murdered her with his hardness.
> Abbie: He's murderin' me!
>
> (I. 241–43)

What Abbie is doing here reflects the change O'Neill referred to. Abbie is getting Eben to identify with her in her response to her husband just as later Mary gets Edmund to feel sympathy for her treatment by the intransigent James. Mother wins son in opposition to father. But this is supposed to be a seduction scene — and so it is, in two ways. The seduction is both sexual and maternal. Abbie is possessed, says the horrified O'Neill, of a "horrible mixture of lust and mother love." Without abandoning her sexual drive, Abbie becomes in the special parlor belonging to Eben's dead mother (again recalling Mary's "spare room") a new manifestation of that mother. Abbie then commits a terrible crime in that parlor, as Mary commits a terrible crime in her spare room. She not only commits adultery, but in effect sleeps with her own son — and what follows is guilt upon guilt.

What one also comes to realize about *Desire Under the Elms* is that none of the action which follows Abbie's seduction of Eben, even the horrifying murder of a helpless infant, has the force of that seduction scene. The dramatic energy of that scene feels completely spontaneous, while that of much which follows feels contrived. Only Ephraim's feverishly grotesque solo dance at the party for the new baby seems to emanate from the kind of authentic feeling that underlies the seduction. The party itself, with its gossipy neighbors and the sulky Eben refusing to attend, lacks the ironic impact O'Neill intended for it. This is probably true because the baby and everything surrounding it is a contrivance. The baby has no identity. It functions simply as a means by which Abbie and Eben "get back" at Ephraim — that is, the means by which mother and son "get back" at father — and its murder is the terrible crime for which Eben at first violently condemns and later forgives Abbie — that is, the terrible crime for which Edmund at first violently condemns but later forgives (or tries to forgive) his mother.

Perhaps because of the sudden decline of its tone of high-pitched, extremely penetrating sexuality, perhaps because of the would-be ethereal quality assumed by the lovers facing death, the play seems wooden and artificial at the end — especially in contrast to *All God's Chillun,* which is remarkably convincing at its conclusion. Not the reunited lovers in *Desire Under the Elms* but the now totally isolated Ephraim becomes the truly heroic figure of the play,[11] and that fact brings the play to the edge of O'Neill's middle period. *Desire Under the Elms* is a play in which much space is devoted to variations on the theme of forgiveness and reconciliation, but the two successive scenic images on which the play closes deny the possibility of forgiveness and reconciliation.

The crimes that living closely with one another makes people commit against each other and against themselves are beyond any kind of practical, workable forgiveness — and thereby against any kind of practical, workable kinship. Ephraim concludes that a destiny of unbroken loneliness — the loneliness of God himself, he says — is the true "hardness" God requires of man. A God with such requirements is not a God much concerned with human kinship. He is a God who will lead many of O'Neill's forthcoming heroes and heroines to their lonely destiny, however. Ephraim finally finds in withdrawal a release from the complications of human kinship, that same withdrawal which Deborah Harford and Mary Tyrone seek and find. But that kind of release also constitutes the one totally despairing image of human existence O'Neill ever represents in his plays, and becomes one of the two terrifying alternatives between which sensitive, intelligent men and women must live suspended throughout the works of his middle period. The other, of course, is suicide.

The Emperor Jones, The Hairy Ape, All God's Chillun, and *Desire Under the Elms* reveal an O'Neill increasingly dubious that bona fide human kinship can exist — and that they were all written during the years in which he lost the three people most important to his stability and to his work supplies reason enough for the decline. What they only hint at, however, is the agony to follow — the ever-enclosing circle of guilt, frenzy and irrepressible hostility, the vortex of O'Neill's suffering between the mid-twenties and the late thirties which makes the one genuine marvel of his personal life his avoidance of suicide. Kinship might be lost in the plays just discussed, but it could be replaced by the stoic hardness of the unyielding Ephraim. What O'Neill's next plays suggest is both the loss of kinship and the utter inadequacy of that stoicism. There are no characters like Ephraim Cabot in the plays that immediately follow *Desire Under the Elms.* There was no "hardness" sufficient to cope with the nightmares to come. There was only the record of those nightmares themselves, dramatically represented in a period of extremely potent plays which won for O'Neill what for many is still the central core of his reputation.

II

THE VALLEY OF THE SHADOW

U P TO THIS POINT, I have been looking at the early plays chiefly as anticipations of *Long Day's Journey* and have sought to avoid such autobiographical motifs as do not emerge direct and undisguised in the later plays. I do this in respect to my fundamental purpose to write a study of O'Neill's plays and not his life. But O'Neill endured so many shocks in the 1920's, involving both the deaths in his family and his marital break-up, that some direct reference to them is unavoidable. They had a profound and in some cases extremely direct effect on his plays. The shocks begin with the fact that in February 1922, Ella Quinlan O'Neill died in a Los Angeles hospital, and in November 1923, James O'Neill, Jr. (Jamie) died in a sanatorium for alcoholics outside New York City. The close juxtaposition of these deaths has been noted by the biographers, the events surrounding them studied in great detail, yet the reactions in O'Neill's plays of the 1920s and 1930s has still not been fully realized. My reading of O'Neill suggests that they are the most important creative influence of his life, more important even than his feelings of rejection upon discovering his mother's addiction during his adolescence. At the very least, his reactions to his mother's death merged with his feelings about that earlier rejection. And with the addition of new feelings prompted by Jamie's death, O'Neill entered a period of depression which he was not to escape for many years.

The specific events I am most concerned with, briefly, are these. When Jamie O'Neill wired his brother early in February 1922 that his mother had suffered a stroke and urged him to come out to the coast to be with her at the end, O'Neill wired back excuses, protesting his own nervous state of mind as prohibiting such a trip. He offered the rationale that he could do little for his mother, that Jamie was there to do what could be done, and that he, Eugene, could do whatever needed doing in New York (which was very little). On the surface, O'Neill turned his full attention to the upcoming opening of *The Hairy Ape* and seemed indifferent to his mother's, and his brother's, deteriorating condition. Following the real-life episode of the "whore-on-the-train," a principal motif in *A Moon for the Misbegotten,* Jamie arrived with his mother's coffin on the very night *The Hairy Ape* opened. O'Neill, despite his seeming calm, was not only disturbed enough to be absent from the performance, but also could not face going to the train. He sent someone else in his place. Attempting to disguise his reactions, he then let it be thought that he had gone to the train but did not wish to discuss the matter. Most of the night was actually spent in an anguished walk through Central Park with his close friend Saxe Commins.

Sheaffer describes the culmination of O'Neill's conversation with Commins as follows:

> Then the floodgates opened and out poured a tide of reminisence full of old grief and bitterness about his family, matter that one day would be reworked and distilled in *Long Day's Journey Into Night.* He recalled his mother's piety and sheltered up-bringing, her falling in love with James O'Neill—a mistake, for she should never have married an actor—and her drug addiction, which had been a blight on all their lives. Thinking of his father, he recalled his despair at being chained so many years to *Monte Cristo,* his fear of poverty, and the fortune he had lost through investing in gold mines that had no gold, in oil wells without oil. And there was Jamie, who had thrown his life away, Jamie, *whom Eugene considered the more talented of the two* [emphasis added]; he was smart, he was witty, he had genuine feeling for literature, and yet it had all come to nothing, a life wasted on sex, drinking and other pleasures. Probably Jamie, his brother felt, was the most unfortunate of them all, for he had scarcely anything to sustain him, nothing except his love for his mother.[1]

This all-important conversation touches upon issues that would be central to O'Neill's plays throughout the remainder of his career, and, as Sheaffer indicates, directly anticipates many of the motifs in *Long Day's Journey.* It deals with:

1. Ella O'Neill's deeper anxieties relating to her marriage;
2. Ella O'Neill's addiction to morphine (which was known to very few people in 1922);
3. O'Neill's new capacity to sympathize with his father, and still more significant, see him objectively;
4. The pathos implicit in Jamie's debauches;
5. O'Neill's belief that his brother's creative talents were superior to his own; and
6. Jamie's total dependency on their dead mother.

These were the things on O'Neill's mind that critical night in 1922, but these were also the things O'Neill was afraid to face openly. His conversation with Commins, while highly informative, suggests no true purgation of his feelings. He had faced his father's death, but he could not face his mother's, and he was not facing his responsibilities to a desolate and deteriorating brother. He did not go to California when he was desperately needed, and he did not meet the train, although emotions associated with both were sufficient to make him miss the opening of a promising new play.

It hardly takes much clinical expertise to recognize that O'Neill's reactions the night of his brother's return reveal deep and intense fear and guilt — which it would take more than a conversation with a friend in the park to relieve. In fact, far from relieving these feelings during the 1920s, O'Neill instead developed feelings of suicidal self-hatred greater than he had ever known. These feelings are reflected first in severe eccentricities of personal behavior,[2] which are not the subject of this study, and second in his plays, which are. His growing contempt for himself for failing in his responsibilities to mother and brother in their time of death is evident in the most important plays of his middle period, beginning with *The Great God Brown* and continuing with furious intensity through *Mourning Becomes Electra.*

A lesser play which may be seen in the context of Ella O'Neill's recent death is *Marco Millions.* This play illustrates the way O'Neill's self-hatred is revealed in the better-known works to follow. It was written at about the same time as *Desire Under the Elms* though produced somewhat later. A strangely truncated, awkward work despite its scenic opulence, *Marco Millions* tells us graphically how O'Neill perceived his own reactions to his mother's death. What has puzzled many is that its hero's character seems to change so unexpectedly and improbably. In the earlier portions of the play, Marco is a callow but not insensitive youth accompanying his successful uncle on a commercial journey to the wondrous East, but in later portions he has with less than sufficient motivation become a total Babbitt: avaricious, obtuse, and insensitive. Not a trace of his earlier character remains. This change and Marco's appalling crassness late in the play have long been felt to arise from O'Neill's desire to convey a social message, an attack on the American business mentality of the 1920s. But Marco is offensive in ways which have little to do with his being a conservative midwestern businessman in medieval Florentine garb. His behavior can only be explained, it seems to me, with reference to O'Neill's severe self-hatred arising from his recent treatment of his dying mother.

Marco Millions rather closely traces some of the experiences and many of the feelings of O'Neill's young adulthood. Marco's journey to the wondrous East with his uncle parallels O'Neill's journey to the wondrous

(American) West with his father in 1913,[3] both journeys being compara-
bly commercial in purpose. The callow, confused young Marco of these
early scenes undoubtedly represents O'Neill's perception of himself as he
was before his success as a playwright. As the play progresses, however,
we see what happens to Marco after he succeeds — that is, what O'Neill
felt was happening to him in his success. First, Marco meets and falls in
love with the Chinese princess Kukachin; but with his new success, he
suddenly turns his back on the princess. Kukachin is a familiar image;
pale and sensitive, unable to come to grips with her life, she is like many
earlier characters who anticipate Mary Tyrone. But there is a difference
between Kukachin and the Mary-figures who precede her. Ruth Mayo,
Ella Downey, and Abbie Cabot all help to bring about their own downfall. In this play, all the blame belongs to Marco. We are, in other words,
now dealing with an O'Neill who has temporarily suppressed his hostility
toward his mother and is concentrating only on his guilt. Marco's rejection of Kukachin stands for O'Neill's of his mother at the time of her
death. Kukachin tries quietly and vainly to convey her love to the newly
successful Marco throughout the latter part of the play, but he ignores her
hints and finally leaves her to die alone and betrayed on foreign soil — as
O'Neill in his new success felt he left his mother to die alone and betrayed
in California. Even the death scene in the play resembles the death watch
Jamie will describe in *A Moon for the Misbegotten*.

Autobiographical elements are thus clearly evident in *Marco Millions*, but what separates the central characters and situations in this play
from the plays described in Part I is first the total saintliness of the figure
standing for O'Neill's mother, and second the Babbittry of the figure
standing for himself. This second theme becomes central in the plays that
follow and derives in part from O'Neill's altogether natural doubts about
his real abilities, doubts which frequently accompany a genuine artist's
public recognition, but which were intensified in O'Neill's case by the way
he had treated his dying mother. He felt he was betraying his art by making money, and he felt he had failed in his responsibilities as a son. It is the
combination of these feelings that results in the self-condemnation implicit in the driving, cold, and insensitive Marco.[4] That combination was
also to result in some characterizations a good deal more memorable than
Marco's, most notably the self-condemning William Brown of *The Great
God Brown* and the despicable Caligula in *Lazarus Laughed*.

What also separates *Marco Millions* from the plays previously discussed is the absence of the rhythm of kinship from its dialogue. Where

that rhythm might seem called for in the play — there is ample opportunity for Marco and Kukachin to engage in the antiphony of hostility and affection of earlier lovers — there is only blockish silence on Marco's part, and saintliness on Kukachin's. The sounds of the play are largely those of the Eastern wisdom of the Chinese Emperor, which are preachy and nondramatic sounds at best, and of Marco's insensitive Main Street bluster. There is none of the dynamic emotional movement of Mat and Anna or Jim and Ella. The central characters seem hardened into inflexible attitudes, and hence any hope of real contact between them is lost early.

Marco Millions, while among the imaginatively barest of O'Neill's plays, sets the basic pattern for the plays of O'Neill's middle period. It creates a new vision of heartless indifference (O'Neill's) set against victimization and death (his mother's), and its sounds are those of an emotional wasteland in which the rhythm of kinship is unheard. What the plays immediately to follow add to this pattern are representations of O'Neill's other "victim," his dead brother.

3 In Memory of Jamie

THE FIRST IMPORTANT PLAYS of the middle period concentrate not on
O'Neill's reaction to his mother's death but on his reaction to his
brother's more recent death, though feelings related to his late mother are
very much in evidence. After Jamie was hospitalized as an alcoholic in
1923, O'Neill, who considered him little more than an embarrassment in
the months before that hospitalization, had nothing further to do with
him. Jamie's death was certainly more unnoted than that of any member
of the family. But O'Neill was actually quite ambivalent toward his
brother, as was that brother toward him. In childhood, O'Neill had idol-
ized and imitated the seemingly heroic and much older Jamie. In young
adulthood, O'Neill came also to imitate the defiant mockery and the pro-
pensities for drink and loose women. Almost everything we know of the
young O'Neill may in fact be a manifestation of some aspect of his imitation of the immensely talented and immensely debauched Jamie. This in
spite of O'Neill's oft-stated distrust and contempt.

The Great God Brown

The Great God Brown is a play about the rivalry between two close
friends whose competition over women and professional recognition
leads to the death through alcoholism of one and the psychological disintegration of the other. It is a fantasy in which a less talented man helps
bring about the death of a more talented man and then attempts to as-

sume his identity. Its movement reveals the many complex feelings between the O'Neill brothers ranging from hysterical envy to quasi-religious adoration.

The first of the play's two heroes is Dion Anthony, the ascetic but debauched, undisciplined artist. Although usually associated with O'Neill himself, Dion seems to me primarily associated with his dead brother, while the play's other hero, the successful but fraudulent architect, William A. Brown, represents O'Neill's vision of himself in the 1920s.[1] This is not to say that these identifications hold in every instance throughout the play. Especially at the beginning, the Dion who escapes his parents to meet his girl on a pier on a festive summer evening is clearly based on O'Neill's recollections of his own youth (as it would be recalled again in *Ah, Wilderness*). And even during their exchanges in the middle of the play, Dion and Brown refer to a boyhood relationship between them in which Dion frequently stands for Eugene and Brown for Jamie. Furthermore, Dion is married, as Eugene was, whereas Brown (until he impersonates Dion) is not. But what the two characters do and say in the critical situations of the play makes their essential identities clear. Brown is the successful fraud O'Neill desperately feared he was becoming, and Dion is the brilliant but wasted Jamie who drank himself to death. Looked at this way, of course, the sarcasm of the play's title is given the emphasis it should have because it comments on what the play is essentially about: O'Neill's guilt. Brown's characterization is an extension of O'Neill's punishment exacted on himself in the characterization of Marco Polo which he would continue in the characterization of Caligula (*Lazarus Laughed*).

Until the publication of *A Moon for the Misbegotten*, the close parallels between Dion and Jamie might well not have been clear, largely because another figure, so important to both Dion and Brown in the play, seemed so inscrutable. I refer to Cybel, the prostitute who has an unusual relationship with Dion and spurns the pursuing Brown until after Dion's death. There can be no mistaking Cybel as an early sketch for Josie Hogan, and her relationship with Dion, paralleling as it clearly does Josie's with Jamie in the later play, strongly suggests the identification of Dion as an earlier portrait of the tormented brother Jamie. Cybel is the play's Earth Mother, and if by no means virginal like her later manifestation, she conducts an entirely sexless relationship with her two "lovers," both of whose desperate need for strictly motherly affection she successfully provides. Named after Cybele, ancient goddess of nature, she is described as "a strong, calm, sensual, blond girl of twenty or so, her complexion fresh and healthy, her figure full-breasted and wide-hipped, her movements slow and solidly languorous like an animal's, her large eyes dreamy with the reflected stirring of profound instincts." Cybel clearly lacks the richly human qualities of Josie, but in physical description and in their relationship to a debauched and guilt-ridden genius in the last stages of alcoholic self-annihilation, they are practically identical. Cybel is the only person alive Dion completely trusts, as Josie is the only person Jamie completely trusts; and because of that trust, these women are able to prolong for a time the lives of their dying geniuses.

That Dion must primarily be identified with Jamie is also supported by his long confession. It is essentially the same confession we are later to hear spelled out in far greater detail in *A Moon for the Misbegotten*. Reflecting on his past, Dion says the following:

> And my mother? I remember a sweet, strange girl,
> with affectionate, bewildered eyes as if God had
> locked her in a dark closet without any explanation.
> I was the sole doll our ogre, her husband, allowed her
> and she played mother and child with me for many years
> in that house until at last through two tears[2] I watched
> her die with the shy pride of one who has lengthened her
> dress and put up her hair. And I felt like a forsaken
> toy and cried to be buried with her, because her hands
> alone had caressed without clawing. She lived long and
> aged greatly in the two days before they closed her
> coffin. The last time I looked, her purity had for-
> gotten me, she was stainless and imperishable, and I
> knew my sobs were ugly and meaningless to her virginity;
> so I shrank away, back into life, with naked nerves
> jumping like fleas, . . .
>
> (III. 282)

The special relationship with the mother in young adulthood, the attitude toward the father, the reference to the dying mother as pure and virginal—these could apply to either brother. But not the image of the utterly dependent son spending two days watching his mother in her coffin. This is Jamie, especially the "shrinking back" into an existence characterized by "naked nerves jumping like fleas"—a not overly obscure reference to *delirium tremens*. Dion's speaking these lines to an indifferent Brown in this scene suggests O'Neill's obsession with guilt at his own seeming indifference to these events as they actually occurred, at his senseless jealousy of his brother. And out of that guilt there emerges in this play and its successor an image of Jamie as something of a saint, an image no more suited to him than that of the more familiar devil.

Despite touches of brotherly camaraderie between Dion and Brown which anticipate brotherly relationships in O'Neill's later plays, this play is characterized chiefly by self-recrimination — Dion's, of course (or Jamie's), but finally and most importantly Brown's (or O'Neill's). Brown begins to assume prominence in the play about the time he becomes jealous of Dion's relationship with Cybel, a jealousy which parallels O'Neill's at what he had felt was his mother's preference for his brother. Brown cannot receive Cybel's affections because he lacks Dion's vitality and true generosity. Dion (Jamie) is "alive," says Cybel, implying that Brown is thereby "dead." The active, accepted, successful Brown is really the dead one, unable to give authentic feeling as he is unable to create authentic art — while the dying failure is really the live one, the unacknowledged genius who is capable of giving in human terms as he is capable of creating. O'Neill exacts fierce punishment on himself in dramatizing the rivalry of Brown and Dion.

The focal episode of the play centers around Dion's death in Brown's library and Brown's attempt to assume Dion's identity by taking over his mask. The scene is an emblem of O'Neill's unspoken feelings regarding both his brother's death and his brother's creative gifts. Not only does the cruel Brown allow Dion to die unconsoled, he actually helps bring the death on by physically grappling with him in his final moments, in dialogue and action which again anticipates that of Edmund and Jamie late in *Long Day's Journey*. Dion accuses Brown of never having loved either Margaret or Cybel for himself but only in jealous imitation of Dion, at which point Brown makes his "frenzied" move: "You drunken bum!" he says, leaping on Dion and grabbing him "by the throat" (III. 298). Brown, like the later Edmund, strikes a helpless brother-rival at his most vulnerable, and, like Edmund, does so out of frustration. O'Neill is trying to state in dramatic terms his guilt at his coldness and hostility just before Jamie's death, a guilt which he was not in fact to come to terms with for many years — and many plays.

The play also suggests O'Neill's guilt at having "stolen" his brother's talent. Having helped to bring about Dion's death, Brown then proceeds to steal Dion's mask and replaces his own mask with it. Dion's mask has had various meanings in the play. It has made Dion preferred by women (the mask of Pan), and it has assured his identity as a genuinely creative artist — both attributes which Brown feels he lacks. Brown cannot steal Dion's basic inspiration, of course, since it was the unmasked Dion who was the real creator, but he can become a more subtle fake than ever by assuming Dion's outward characteristics. Thus, wearing Dion's mask, Brown succeeds for a time as both husband and creator. But it is only for a time. Not only does the usual pressure of the artist to be both provident and inspired tear him apart, but Brown is also terrified by the feeling that his genius is really not his own. He has stolen it. His original sense of fraud at designing buildings which were slick enough to fool the public is now compounded by his greater sense of guilt that his present work is based on someone else's abilities.

These responses are an index to the nature of O'Neill's guilt toward his dead brother and to O'Neill's psychological condition at the time he was writing the play. He had always sought to imitate Jamie, he had helped (he felt) to bring about Jamie's death through hostility and indifference, and he was now living off talents both in loving and creating which were exclusively his brother's. He could not give as husband or father (which was true enough), and his plays (he felt) were slick enough to fool the public but were not really good. Whatever genuine talents he did possess, he felt were taken from Jamie: the wit, the iconoclasm, the bursts of unrestrained emotion. All he could do was try to be like Jamie, and he could not do that for very long since his struggles in living both as man and playwright with a stolen identity were driving him to distraction. This was the state of O'Neill's mind in the mid-twenties.

The Great God Brown is powerful in part because Brown is allowed a final release from his frenzy. The conclusion approaches an exaltation more successful than that sought but never achieved in *Lazarus Laughed*, a play which in spite of radical differences in situation, setting, and tone, grows directly out of this one. The unmasked Brown at the end of the play is called *Dion* Brown both because he too is now dying (the pun intended) and because out of suffering he has earned forgiveness, as had Dion Anthony (Jamie) despite his failures. Brown has at the end earned Dion's name; it is no longer borrowed. Brown has suffered in his frantic attempts to be several different people at one time and suffered still more from the life-destroying guilt at his crimes against his dead "brother." In the final scene, Brown has stopped running; he has stopped trying to evade his guilt; he has accepted his fate. Most important, he also is capable of accepting the redemptive ministrations of Cybel as he dies — which finally make this play so anticipatory of *A Moon for the Misbegotten*. While the play reveals little of the understanding of human guilt and love revealed by O'Neill's later plays, it does show us an image of O'Neill confronting his guilt, accepting a punishment, and being forgiven — an image he would not give us again for fifteen years.

The Great God Brown is a gritty, painful play which contains no final escape or withdrawal from life's awesome accountabilities and contradictions but allows the man who confronts them the comfort and blessing of final forgiveness. In giving the play its violent conclusion, O'Neill is acknowledging his despair at ever escaping from his suffering; but he is also revealing a capacity for self-forgiveness — although in death — not to be found in any other early play. It is more genuinely a tragedy than any other play of the middle period.

But *The Great God Brown* is very much a play of this period, and not alone because of its pessimistic outlook. It rejects man's capacity to reach others. It rejects the rhythm of kinship. This may be illustrated by what has happened to the dialogue in this play. We hear the rhythm of kinship in exchanges between Dion and Brown, but these exchanges are truncated and the sense of kinship in them is extremely faint. We also hear the rhythm fleetingly in dialogue between Dion and Cybel, but it quickly gives way to something else. The alternations in feeling are present, and underline the authenticity of feeling between the two, but the spontaneity gives way to highly elliptical statements in which Dion may suddenly speak like a troubled child and Cybel may quite unnaturally sound like a nagging mother. At times Dion carries his hectic pessimism to extremes, while Cybel becomes ever more inscrutably "idol"-like. O'Neill, intentionally it seems, breaks the natural flow of the dialogue. The characters, caught between their masked and unmasked selves, become forced, stilted, and obscure in their language.

Equally illustrative of O'Neill's intent to replace the rhythm of kinship is his heavy use of monologue in the play, monologue which is full of frequently obscure metaphysical agonizing laced with quotations setting the iconoclastic Nietzsche against the ascetic Thomas a Kempis. The quotations indicate inwardly directed struggles to understand the nature of guilt and suffering, but more significantly they also indicate ever-increasing introspection and withdrawal. Few other monologues in the play are genuinely confessional in the manner of Dion's speech about his mother's death.

Above all, the play is dominated by its masks; and it is not so important I think to discover what the various masks mean — a problem which has plagued more than one critic[3] — as it is to understand that the play basically concerns maskings: deceptions, pretenses, evasions, and escapes. And it is the first of O'Neill's three important plays of this terrified middle period to have these maskings as its central concern. That it ends in a confrontation with self does not take away from the predominant attempt to escape from self — on the part of all the central characters, but especially on the part of the O'Neill-like Brown. The masks anticipate the two-level dialogue of *Strange Interlude*, and to similar effect. Through both, O'Neill asserts the individual's essential and inescapable isolation which is the basis of the despair underlying all the plays of this period and which O'Neill was later to grapple with so powerfully in *The Iceman Cometh*. We are at the opposite pole from the sea plays with their ebbs and flows of forthright human communication. The middle plays all articulate man's incapacity to reach others and render all attempts to do so as either grotesquely self-serving or so severely warped by each person's emotional deformities that they must fail utterly.

Lazarus Laughed

Cyrus Day has shown precisely how O'Neill was affected by Nietzsche in *Lazarus Laughed* and why, adhering closely to a pre-established conception while tightly restraining his natural sense of human communication, O'Neill succeeded in writing a stilted and in large measure dull play.[4] Day suggests that O'Neill's developing fascination with Nietzschean ideas begins with the characterization of Dion Anthony, who restlessly seeks a new philosophy to relieve man of his "fixation on old Mama Christianity."[5] What Dion finds, says Day, which implicitly is revealed by his own name, is a conception of the defeat of death. Dion discovers Nietzsche's version of the ancient belief in immortality through recurrence, the Dionysian "myth of the eternal return."[6] Day then goes on to demonstrate how this theme is developed in O'Neill's treatment of the biblical miracle of the risen Lazarus.

What no interpreter has yet considered, however, especially in the light of O'Neill's later drama, is the reason for O'Neill's fascination with death in the first place, a fascination which unquestionably prompted his interest in Nietzschean ideas on that subject. It is often observed that the plays of this period are all "much possessed by death" — especially *Lazarus Laughed*, which is intent on denying the very existence of death. O'Neill's fixation in this period was not so much on "old Mama Christianity" as on death itself, to him increasingly the macabre conclusion to a pointless existence, that idea which was later to terrorize Larry Slade in *Iceman*. Nietzsche's periodic suggestion that death is a phenomenon man need not fear, that lamentation for the dead is foolish, and that guilt over the death of loved ones is unnecessary spoke directly to O'Neill's greatest emotional affliction of the 1920s. It was Nietzsche's acid attack on what he considered the Christianity-conceived malady of guilt that so drew the guilt-ridden O'Neill to the rebellious German philosopher, especially in Nietzsche's guise as the eternally child-faced prophet and wanderer Zarathustra, who is, as Leonard Chabrowe has shown, the chief model for O'Neill's Lazarus.[7] I suggest that O'Neill, his guilt and fear over his mother and brother having been alleviated for a time by his reading of Nietzsche, sought to convert his new burst of conviction into a play he hoped would be as restorative as *The Great God Brown* was frenzied.

That same family group which forms the basis for so many O'Neill plays up through *Long Day's Journey* is again central to *Lazarus Laughed*[8] — in some ways more distorted than ever, but in other ways more readily identifiable. First and foremost are the parallels between Lazarus himself and Jamie, parallels undoubtedly known before the last plays only to those acquainted with the "saintly" side of Jamie's nature. There are reasons external to the play to suggest that O'Neill might link the memory of his dead brother to that biblical figure re-conceived as a Nietzschean savior. Based primarily on Zarathustra the wandering prophet, the Lazarus of O'Neill's play is also directly linked with Dionysus, the Greek god so important to Nietzsche and the great favorite of O'Neill. O'Neill might well think of Jamie as like both the Nietzschean wanderer and the joyous god. First, both Dionysus and Zarathustra are like Jamie, rebels against smug, middle-class values and attitudes—against all forms of pomposity, hypocrisy, and insensitivity. Second, Dionysus, if not Zarathustra, is always associated with the effects of alcohol, as was Jamie; and alcohol for them both is the means by which they get beyond the influence of the hypocritical attitudes of society. Third, both Dionysus and Zarathustra are conceived of as child-like and innocent, qualities which might not immediately suggest Jamie unless, linking Jamie to *Dion* Anthony, one recalls the child-like innocence of Dion's unmasked face. In both this play and its predecessor, O'Neill is seeking to suggest an unseen, sublimely benevolent side of his brother which fits well with the child-like appearance of the god and of the wanderer. Dionysus, Zarathustra, Jamie (and Lazarus): all combine severe condemnation of established society's forms and social conventions with a mien of youthful innocence.

Besides the similarities between Jamie and the mythic figures the character of Lazarus is based on, there is one direct, significant parallel between Jamie and Lazarus: their laughter, and the effects of that laughter upon others. To be sure, the laughter of Jamie was usually a cynical laughter, that of Lazarus supposedly sublime; but as it is impossible to say precisely what O'Neill had in mind for that sublime laughter, it could well be a laughter drawn from the happiest memories of his brother, as is that of another Jamie-like figure, Uncle Sid in *Ah, Wilderness*. Though certainly no hero or saint in life, Jamie through his laughter nevertheless had a Pied Piper effect on those he met in groups, and that effect may well be represented in the highly idealized scenic image of the laughing Lazarus followed by his masses of converts. O'Neill here goes as far as he ever does in blotting out his brother's debauchery and emphasizing his exceptional social magnetism. He was to dramatize the magnetism far better, of course, when he would later also give full sway to Jamie's debauchery in a figure like Hickey, but laughter in both cases is the basic ingredient of that magnetism.[9]

Then there is the theme of the play itself, the defeat of death, and its relation to Jamie. Jamie's death (like his mother's) left O'Neill with feelings of both intense guilt and intense loneliness, those twin bogeys which would later endlessly torment all the agonized residents of Harry Hope's saloon. Trying to escape his fate as the "haunted hero" slashing at "ghosts in the dark," O'Neill sought to create in Jamie a new-risen savior who could relieve man of those bogeys, both of which are rooted, O'Neill learned from Nietzsche, in the fear of death. If Lazarus bringing release from the fear of guilt and loneliness to the universal groupings which populate *Lazarus Laughed* is an exaggertion and distortion of what the real Jamie did in life, the distortion is consistent with the quite unreal quality of both language and situation throughout this play. Again, the parallels with the later Jamie-figure, Hickey, help make the point clear. Both Lazarus and Hickey bring hope of release from the fear of death which is born of guilt and loneliness. They are would-be saviors, and though in the later play O'Neill is intent on revealing the fraudulent nature of such saviors, here he is still searching for saviors and saving philosophies. Guilt-ridden and longing for his dead brother, O'Neill might naturally idealize that brother into his image of a savior.

If Lazarus is nevertheless difficult to recognize as a highly idealized image of Jamie, it should be recalled that O'Neill had given his audiences idealized images of his brother before this one — even while that brother was still alive. It is not so great a leap to the figure of Lazarus from that of Andrew Mayo in *Beyond the Horizon*, who always arrives with aid at critical moments and only once is allowed a break in his all-protecting demeanor. Andrew, like Lazarus, is hardly an image of the debauched and cynical Jamie O'Neill, but he is certainly an image of O'Neill's big brother as the playwright thought of him in adolescence and wished him to be in young adulthood. Lazarus is also like Luis in *The Fountain*, who provides strong brotherly support to the young Juan, and Joe in *All God's Chillun*, who makes his friend Jim Harris confess an inescapable fact about his being. There was certainly precedent for an idealized Jamie in plays before *Lazarus Laughed*.

Further parallels between Jamie and Lazarus are suggested by some rather familiar action in one of the play's central scenes. Lazarus's abiding concern for Miriam, his wife, and his quiet watch over her bier at the opening of Act Four precisely fits the motif of Jamie's deathwatch over his mother in California dealt with in *A Moon for the Misbegotten*. Although he is Miriam's husband, Lazarus is here described as being "like a young son who keeps watch by the body of his mother."[10] He is entirely free of the fear of remorse which possessed the real Jamie as he kept "watch over the body of his mother," but the basic elements of the tableau are there in idealized form.

Thus, the centrality of O'Neill's memory of his brother is clear in *Lazarus Laughed*. But Lazarus does not have much flesh and blood as a character. This play is a sugar-coating of memories, not an attempt to confront them. By far the more interesting character in the play is the one who directly mirrors O'Neill's own guilt and self-torment. As William Brown, the more interesting figure in *The Great God Brown*, is a representation of O'Neill's self-loathing, so in *Lazarus Laughed* is the sadistic Caligula.[11] The first description of Caligula in the play suggests his similarity to the playwright. Caligula is "bony and angular . . . with . . . hairy legs like an ape's" (I.299).[12] He wears a mask which "accentuates his bulging, prematurely wrinkled forehead" and his "hollow temples."

When the description goes on to describe a "boyish cruelty" which "has long ago become naively insensitive to any human suffering but its own," we are on more important ground. Half-consumed by a sadistic compulsion to kill and hurt others, Caligula represents in greater detail even than Brown O'Neill's horror at his treatment of his family, both in life and death. Throughout his appearances Caligula fights his compulsion to admire Lazarus as Brown fought his to admire Dion (and O'Neill his to admire Jamie). At one point, we hear from Caligula an envy the authenticity of which stands out in great relief from a play which has relatively little authentic about it:

> What is it troubles me about him? What
> makes me dream of him? Why should I—
> love him, Jewess? Tell me! You love him,
> too, I do not understand this. Why, wherever
> he goes, is there joy?
>
> (I. 330–31)

Similarly does the jealous Brown envy Dion, and similarly did O'Neill secretly envy Jamie.

Time and again, after viciously attacking the prophet, Caligula unexpectedly becomes his defender and even his spokesman. For a time Caligula feels he has been converted by Lazarus, and even seems ready to become one of his disciples. But he cannot keep this up. Just when he seems ready to become a true disciple, Caligula falls back into his old envious hostility. O'Neill describes him finally as "in a state of queer conflicting emotion, seeming to be filled with a nervous dread and terror of everything about him, while at the same time perversely excited and elated by his own morbid tension" (I. 326). Deceiver, agonizer, self-deluder, Caligula embodies those qualities which most possess O'Neill in all the plays of his middle period because they constitute the essentials of his feelings toward himself at that time. What O'Neill recognized and loathed so deeply were his great extremes of opposing feeling toward his brother and mother, and his inability to reconcile those feelings. He felt in a constant state of life-destroying ambivalence. Later, the acceptance of that ambivalence as not life-destroying but life-sustaining would be his new understanding. *Lazarus Laughed* is a representation of the ambivalence only, not yet of its mastery.

The sadistic, self-loathing Caligula gives dramatic interest to *Lazarus Laughed* because of the intensity with which he expresses the awful contradictions in his nature. But the drama of Caligula's relationship with Lazarus stresses only O'Neill's relationship with his brother. O'Neill's old guilt toward his mother appears mainly in the central speech of the fourth important figure in the play, the terrible Emperor himself. Tiberius is first presented in terms which strongly suggest James O'Neill, Sr.: "An old man of seventy-six, tall, broad, and corpulent but of great muscular strength still despite his age . . . the long nose once finely molded, now gross and thickened, forehead lowering and grim. . . . His mouth is forceful and severe. The complexion of his skin is that of a healthy old campaigner" (I. 337). But Tiberius's identification with James, Sr. is only momentary. Outward appearances notwithstanding, he shortly becomes another incarnation of O'Neill's sense of his and his brother's emotional failures toward their mother. Tiberius represents both O'Neill brothers as he describes his mother's death:

> My mother . . . I revenged myself on her. I did not
> kill her, it is true, but I deprived her of her power
> and she died, as I knew she would, that powerful
> woman who bore me as a weapon! The murder was subtle
> and cruel — how cruel only that passionate, deep-breasted
> woman unslaked by eighty years of devoured desires could
> know! Too cruel! I did not go to her funeral.
> I was afraid her closed eyes might open and look at me!

(*Then with almost a cry*) I want youth, Lazarus,
that I may play again about her feet with the love
I felt for her before I learned to read her eyes.

(I. 355)

Although the mother Tiberius refers to does not look like Mary Tyrone, her real identity is revealed by the eyes Tiberius fears might "open
and look at him," and by the love Tiberius "felt for her" before he learned
"to read her eyes." We know the motif about eyes from what the men read
in Mary's in *Long Day's Journey*, we know that it is eyes throughout the
early O'Neill which are the inevitable indicators of a woman's withdrawal
or madness. We also know about Jamie's concern about his dying
mother's eyes from *A Moon for the Misbegotten*. And we know that
Jamie "did not go to her funeral." Here Tiberius stands for O'Neill recol-
lecting the events that constitute the incurable wound underlying almost
all his plays.

Lazarus Laughed, then, is a more heavily disguised but also more
detailed statement of those agonies about his family which possessed
O'Neill in all his plays. In the mid-twenties, when father, mother, and
brother were recently deceased, he was frantically trying to escape. His
readings in Nietzsche suggested some interesting subjects for dramatic
characterization, especially in the figure of Zarathustra; but mostly they
suggested a kind of cure for his affliction: the Nietzschean conception of
the eternal return. The whole play is essentially a series of frenzied statements about guilt and the fear of death, alternating with calm prophetic
reassurances about the insignificance of guilt and death. Like Cybel, Lazarus reassures in a language intended to connote permanence, certainty,
and a kind of divinity. But throughout, language is the problem in this
play. The language by which Lazarus seeks to reassure succeeds solely in
being forced and stilted. Only in the self-lacerations of Caligula, and to a
lesser extent Tiberius, does the language come to life, and the life it comes
to must seem demented, because the characters are demented. The
O'Neill we hear in *Lazarus Laughed* is most remote from the rhythm of
kinship. The play successfully conveys only a new variation of O'Neill's
loneliness and despair. If we dismiss Lazarus, any representation of life in
this play is as empty and futile as Larry Slade later says it is — and Lazarus
is easily dismissable. He is perhaps the most artificial of all O'Neill's characters. The play lacks the power of the equally despairing *The Great God
Brown* because it attempts to anaesthetize the pain with a new dope

drawn from a superficial understanding of Nietzsche. *The Great God Brown* had demonstrated, on the contrary, a great deal of courage in facing the same pain — though no sense at all really of how to relieve it.

As it takes its lead from the play which precedes it, *Lazarus Laughed* also looks forward to plays that follow. The curative force of Lazarus's message about the defeat of death is not a lasting one in O'Neill's drama, despite all the fanfare with which it is proclaimed in the play. Lazarus's words and images convey nothing concrete, nothing recognizable; and that his creation is essentially an empty one is a realization O'Neill must have come to quickly. Rather, with the play to follow, O'Neill, exploring another fashionable philosophy of the twenties, turned away from Nietzsche and toward that kind of self-revelation he associated with the writings of Sigmund Freud. As Lazarus sought to convince us that overcoming the grip of death would relieve man of his fear and guilt, *Strange Interlude* tells us that in self-revelation lies the true relief from fear and guilt. O'Neill's first purpose in writing the later *Iceman* would be to proclaim the illusory nature of *both* these solutions.

4 *Strange Interlude* and *Dynamo*

Strange Interlude

IN *Strange Interlude*, the emphasis shifts away from Jamie, though when one recalls the very distorted Jamie of *Lazarus Laughed*, it is quite possible he may appear in guises here still more difficult to recognize than in that play. The emphasis in *Strange Interlude* seems again primarily on O'Neill himself trying to cope with all the deaths around him and, as always, with that one awful shock of his adolescence, his mother's addiction. Like so many others, the play explores his attempts to escape the pain associated with those events.

If in two previous plays O'Neill had been "much possessed by death," he was absolutely obsessed with it in *Strange Interlude*. While death, except in the early scenes, is not so explicit a subject of the play as it is in *Lazarus Laughed*, it is heavily in the background from beginning to end, tormenting all the characters in a variety of ways and directly affecting their responses and behavior. There are seven deaths referred to in this play, deaths of individuals closely related to central characters. There is the death of Professor Leeds's wife before the play opens, which the Professor finds himself unable to face. There is the earlier death of the airman Gordon Shaw, Nina's first lover, which Nina finds herself unable to face. There is the death of Professor Leeds himself, which Nina cannot "feel" anything in response to. There is the death of mad old Mr. Evans, Sam Evans's father, which his strange wife is still trying to cope with. Not long after, there is the death of Charlie Marsden's mother, whose apron strings Charlie could never cut and whose memory possesses him

60

throughout the rest of the play. There is the death of Charlie's sister referred to in Act Eight, which Charlie responds to precisely as he had to the death of his mother. And finally there is the death of Sam Evans, which no one seems to know how to respond to. In addition, these deaths are all linked by the fact that the character closest to the deceased either has trouble *feeling* the death, or *facing* it — which amounts to the same thing in the context of the play. The incapacity to feel is presented as simply an early manifestation of the incapacity to face. And so with O'Neill himself toward the deaths around him. First he could not *feel* them, then he could not *face* them.

But while death is extremely important as a force which generates people's responses and behavior, it is not the immediate or surface subject of the action. Rather, the subject is a life story, the life story of Nina Leeds, told more as a novel might present it than as a play.[1] It is also a disguised version of the life story of Eugene O'Neill, from the great disillusionment of his adolescence up to his involvement with his later wife Carlotta Monterey. Not for the first time and not for the last, O'Neill disguises an identity by changing the sex of the person intended, a simpler disguise than some because he might thereby treat certain topics more directly. The central agonies of Nina's young adulthood parallel the agonies that haunted O'Neill's existence. Although in the course of the play other characters reenact important aspects of O'Neill's attitudes and behavior, it is Nina who most comprehensively lives out the long-range fears, guilts, and frustrations which O'Neill felt were leading him to total despair.

The nine acts of this enormous play may be broken into four episodes, three relatively short, and one quite long. The first centers on Nina's relationship with her father and her response to his death; the second tells the strange tale of madness and death in the family of Sam Evans; the third traces the long, chaotic love affair of Nina Leeds and Ned Darrell; and the fourth predicts a desperate future. Although O'Neill divides the play into two major parts denoting a break of ten years, the natural story lines actually fall into the four I shall be discussing. And these four episodes follow the major preoccupations of O'Neill's adult existence: the deaths in his family, the addiction of his mother, his affair with Carlotta, and his fear of the future.

Professor Leeds, the subject of the first episode, is described in terms, and acts in ways, which suggest Mary Tyrone.[2] The change in sex from mother to father is consistent with the change that makes Nina represent O'Neill. We meet the Professor as the play opens living on the same sea-coast as Mary (New Haven substituted for New London), longing for a recently deceased (and, we infer, dominant) spouse, compulsively dedicated to the past, and unable to confront the problems of the present. He is described, like Mary, as "a fugitive from reality," "over-refined," and "temperamentally timid." He concentrates most of what he has to say in his brief appearance on his personal insecurity and on the guilt he feels toward his daughter, the recent death of whose lover both he and his daughter feel, quite irrationally, he has helped to bring about. The lover was an airman shot down during World War I, but Nina feels that had her father not prevented their marriage before the lover's departure, the lover might not, somehow, have died. Both see Gordon Shaw's death as the cause of Nina's recent nervous breakdown, and the Professor fears he may have been to blame.

Nina is described from the start in terms which suggest the young O'Neill both in appearance and in his struggle with disillusionment and guilt:

> Her face is striking, handsome rather than pretty,
> the bone structure prominent, the forehead high, the
> lips of her rather large mouth clearly modelled above
> the firm jaw . . . . Since Gordon's death [her eyes] have
> a quality of continually shuddering before some terrible
> enigma, of being wounded to their depths and made de-
> fiant and resentful by their pain. Her whole manner,
> the charged atmosphere she gives off, is totally at
> variance with her healthy outdoor physique. It is
> strained, nerve-racked, hectic, a terrible tension
> of will alone maintaining self-possession.
>
> (I. 12–13)

Like Nina, the active, athletic O'Neill was "nerve-racked," not by the idealized image of a dead airman but by the equally idealized image of a dead mother. The Gordon Shaw theme parallels that motif of a lost ideal past O'Neill represented earlier in the image of childhood to which Jim and Ella Harris long to return. With the memory of Gordon Shaw representing O'Neill's distorted recollection of his mother "before the fall," the guilt of Professor Leeds then stands for his mother's guilt after she had revealed her great crime. The nervous breakdown Nina is recovering from is symptomatically no different from the whole set of reactions O'Neill experienced following the great trauma of his adolescence. Both feel inexpressible loss and inexpressible guilt, and both try to escape into a life of unabated debauchery. To parallel his own tuberculosis sanatorium, O'Neill includes a battle-fatigue sanatorium for Nina, where she "gives herself" to patients as O'Neill "gave himself" to whores and drink. O'Neill has combined in Nina's story the debauchery of his late teens with his experience in the sanatorium. Ned Darrell makes the point about Nina that she will shortly "dive for the gutter just to get the security that comes from knowing she's touched bottom," an idea which describes O'Neill's early adult life as accurately as any.

The second act of the play, which concludes this first episode, deals with Nina's first reactions to the death of her father and grows out of O'Neill's first reactions to the death of his mother. Nina keeps repeating in a voice "flat and toneless" that she is utterly unable to "feel anything at all" about her father — as O'Neill confessed that he could feel nothing at all about his mother's death. It is in response to this inability to feel that Nina decides to accept marriage. Since there is nothing, she reasons, that can replace her mutilated ideal, she decides that she must assume the outward characteristics at least of adult behavior, a compromise O'Neill felt he had made in his marriage to Agnes Boulton and in his early career. O'Neill's understanding of his own condition is suggested by the physician Ned Darrell's diagnosis of Nina. Ned clinically announces that Nina's inability to feel (like O'Neill's) is only a result of shock, that her feelings (like his) are actually very great. O'Neill writing *Strange Interlude* had come to understand, as he had not earlier, the nature of his supposed lack of feeling; and the play's opening episode reveals the nature of the understanding. But he was far from able to find hope in that understanding.

The second of the play's four episodes is much shorter and quite different in tone from the others. It is a melodrama in one act (Act Three) presenting the same disillusionment and fear of the opening episode from a different, less reasoned perspective. Now married to Sam Evans and pregnant, Nina is briefly happy at the prospect of becoming a mother. But she soon discovers the illusory nature of her new happiness, just as she had discovered the illusory nature of her old ideal. We meet Sam Evans's mother, who is described in the old familiar terms. She is

> . . . very pale. Her big dark eyes are grim with the
> prisoner-pain of a walled-in soul. Yet a sweet loving-
> kindness, the ghost of an old faith and trust in life's
> goodness, hovers girlishly, fleetingly, about the corners
> of her mouth. . . .
>
> (I. 53)

But despite the familiar description, it is not Mrs. Evans who reminds us of Mary Tyrone in this scene so much as it is the late, withdrawn, and unstable *Mr.* Evans described by Mrs. Evans, and the insane sister she also describes locked away in an upstairs room (the spare room motif), who sits laughing to herself without a care in the world. The mood of the play suddenly becomes gothic. Nina's emotion as she learns that her late father-in-law's "madness" is an inherited one is one of horror. Her flicker of hope at the prospective child is quickly doused. The effect of the family past is haunting to her. Thus the atmosphere of the brief second episode repeats the underlying elements of the first episode but strongly counters its reasoned, clinical tone. Both the clinical and the gothic were parts of O'Neill's complex perspective of the 1920s.

The solution proposed by Mrs. Evans — that Nina have an abortion and find a substitute father for her children — leads into the play's long and best-remembered third episode, which begins with Act Four and runs through Act Seven. This is on the surface a modish 1920s love story which in its time was undoubtedly rather titillating. The relationship between Nina and Ned precisely parallels the boiling affair between O'Neill and Carlotta. "Oh, those afternoons!" the lovers murmur through much of their anguished dialogue, afternoons certainly paralleling those O'Neill spent on his increasingly long and frequent trips to New York in the mid-twenties, ostensibly to work on rehearsals, but actually to yield to the very real attractions of a quite provocative actress.[3] Here, of course, Ned Darrell is O'Neill, as his "dark, wiry" appearance suggests he sooner or later must be. But he is only O'Neill the attractive lover succumbing to a forbidden passion, not the O'Neill viewers of the plays know better, the terrified victim of an incomprehensible guilt. That O'Neill in this episode is the province of the enigmatic Charlie Marsden, a figure I shall consider in a moment.

The reason the Nina-Ned episode is so predominantly a soap opera is that, like O'Neill's earlier play on the subject of his marital and amatory problems, *Welded*, it is so engagingly superficial. It deals with that fascinating subject of people struggling with forbidden sexual attraction. It in no way deals with the conditions or causes which lead them to such activity.[4] O'Neill did something here he would never do again. He dramatized effects — which so many second-rate writers do — rather than causes, and the results were immensely successful commercially. The popularity of *Strange Interlude* was in fact very much the popularity of soap opera.[5]

These episodes are saved from utter banality, however, by Charlie Marsden, who keeps us in touch with the emotions O'Neill could not escape from, try as he might. In this episode at least, Marsden stands for O'Neill himself, more or less in the way William Brown did. Like O'Neill, Brown and Marsden are successful artists unsure of their own talents and plagued by the commercial appeal of their works. And both are, like O'Neill, overly sensitive, devastatingly self-critical, and unsure of their abilities as lovers. That last may seem strange in the light of O'Neill's active sex life, but extreme ambivalence in this area was a hallmark of all the O'Neill's. O'Neill's puritanical Roman Catholic upbringing was so full of taboos and his adolescent sexual experiences so fretted with fear and guilt that both his marriages were seriously affected by frequent periods of sexual disgust and inadequacy. The pervasive presence of that disgust in the plays is suggested by Charlie as he encounters Nina and Ned in the midst of their yearning for one another:

> lust in this room! . . . lust with a loathsome jeer taunting
> my sensitive timidities! . . . my purity! . . . purity? . . .
> purity? . . . ha! yes, if you say prurient purity! . . . lust
> ogling me for a dollar with oily shoe button Italian eyes!
>
> (I. 100)

These lines anticipate that potent atmosphere of sexual disgust particularly evident in the later plays: in the professional remarks of Cora and the Italian Pearl in *Iceman*, Edmund's recollections of his sexual initiations in *Long Day's Journey*, and Jamie's drunken sexual attitudes and behavior in *A Moon for the Misbegotten*. The Charlie Marsden we encounter in these scenes is the O'Neill who could be terribly, viscerally disturbed at the subject of sex even as he had, like his Ned Darrell, exceptional sexual appetites and, intermittently, prowess.

But more revealing still are other attitudes of Charlie Marsden's, especially in Act Six: his self-pitying lament for his dead mother and his contempt for himself as a writer, which are significantly related. He criticizes himself from the beginning of the play for being unwilling to dig deeply in his novels, afraid that he will "meet himself somewhere." In Act Six he links that fear, significantly, to the death of his mother:

> I couldn't forget Mother . . . she haunted me through
> every city of Europe. . . (Then irritatedly) I must
> get back to work! . . . not a line written in over a
> year! . . . my public will be forgetting me! . . .
> a plot came to me yesterday . . . my mind . . . is
> coming around again . . . I am beginning to forget,
> thank God! . . . (Then remorsefully) No, I don't
> want to forget you, Mother! . . . but let me remember
> . . . without pain! . . .
>
> (I. 112–13)

O'Neill's recurrent periods of inability to write are well-known, and his desire to remember his mother "without pain" is the futile effort of all these plays. Charlie tells us more a bit later:

> . . . but I might have done something big . . . I
> might still . . . if I had the courage to write the
> truth . . . but I was born afraid . . . afraid of myself . . .
>
> (I. 120)

If the audiences of 1928 were puzzled about the precise nature of that truth, those of *Long Day's Journey* some thirty years later would not be.

While Marsden and Nina represent O'Neill's anxieties about his art and about his past, Ned Darrell reflects the domestic O'Neill, revealing his guilt at having to confront his betrayed children. In Act Seven, Nina and Ned are still, in this many-years-later scene, the on-again off-again lovers, unable to part, unable to join, unable to be anything but deceptive and manipulative. Nothing new is provided about their relationship because O'Neill had nothing new to provide about his with Carlotta at that point.[6] But what he adds, quite poignantly, is his fear concerning his children. The treatment O'Neill lets young Gordon Evans give Ned Darrell, his secret father, is treatment Shane O'Neill was not too young to have awarded his father on his infrequent trips home during the courtship of Carlotta; and it feels in the play like treatment O'Neill felt he deserved. As in other instances in which guilt and hurt can be felt most intensely in O'Neill's plays, the intensity here seems the direct result of immediate experience.

But it is still essentially unexplored experience — or experience at one remove from its source. O'Neill is here dealing with behavior and responses which are *the result of* earlier unrelieved agonies, and it is only when O'Neill deals more directly with those earlier agonies that the plays probe deeply into human experience. Notwithstanding O'Neill's characterizations of Charlie Marsden and little Gordon Evans, the long third episode is maudlin. If O'Neill went further in representing the "inner" lives of his characters than he had ever gone before, he did not go much further, largely because in this play he did not have much further to go. He was mired in immediate domestic problems and in a love affair, both of which grew out of deeper problems of his past; and while he sensed the connections between past and present, he understood neither. The tedious third episode of *Strange Interlude* sheds little real light on the nature of human relationships.

The last episode of the play (Acts Eight and Nine) represents

O'Neill's attempt to achieve an idyll of withdrawal, a death in life, that condition later paralleled by Deborah Harford's in *More Stately Mansions*. It is written out of O'Neill's despair, of both past and present, and his desire to find the kind of escape the residents of Harry Hope's saloon find through their pipedreams and their nickel whiskey, but which O'Neill never could find by such methods.

There are many elements of the play present in the last episode, not all of them successfully drawn together. I shall concentrate only on those clearly enough related to O'Neill's deeper feelings to make them relevant to this study. The end of the play can best be understood through its three central characters — Sam Evans, Nina Leeds, and Charlie Marsden — in that order. For out of these characters can be seen O'Neill's two alternative routes to the eternal oblivion his despair had led him to seek in all these plays.

To begin with, Sam is O'Neill's image of what is best in life. His life and death call to mind Larry Slade's dark quotation from Nietzsche:

Lo, sleep is good; better is death; in sooth.
The best of all were never to be born.

Sam lives with his illusions intact and he dies a sudden death. Because he never knew the real conditions of his life — the madness in his family, his wife's true affections, the real paternity of his son — it could be said that he had lived a long sleep. Sam's life was a healthy pretense to O'Neill. Free from the burden of knowing reality, completely protected in his illusions, Sam has been able to achieve material success and bring security to those around him. These are qualities O'Neill envies him, and still more does he envy him his sudden death. And Sam's "son" Gordon is following directly in his supposed father's footsteps when he refuses to believe that his mother could ever be unfaithful, unable even to comprehend the news that Ned Darrell is his real father. The Evans men are of the genus that sensitive and disturbed people envy for the impenetrability of their illusions, though by the time he wrote *Iceman* O'Neill believed no one could be entirely protected from his ghosts.

More important in the episode is Nina, who represents O'Neill himself in the overall design of the play as a life story, but who from time to time suggests other important women in O'Neill's life. Her agonized exchanges with Darrell, for example, suggest Carlotta. In the last episode, through signals we are well acquainted with, she anticipates Mary Tyrone.[7] At the point in Act Eight when her selfish clinging to her son is frustrated and she is prevented by Darrell from trying to break up her son's planned marriage, she becomes increasingly remote and her thoughts become vague and confused. She imagines Charlie to be her long-dead father and confesses the great sin of her life to him in tones which suggest Mary's narcotic withdrawal.

It is quite reasonable, of course, that at this point in the play, when Nina has become the mother of a young adult, she should follow the pattern of so many troubled matrons before and after her in O'Neill's plays. What is surprising is that the character who began the play as the author's representative should end as his mother's. In fact, she represents both at the end of the play. What we see O'Neill doing in this final episode is dramatizing that aspect of his fear in which he identified with his mother's desire to withdraw. As Nina, like Mary, seeks a death in life, an insulation from all feeling, so O'Neill, nervous and guilt-ridden like both, longed for such a release so much that he was willing to betray those closest to him to find it. The Nina of the final episode is a fusion of O'Neill's anxieties concerning his mother and his anxieties concerning himself and his future — a fusion which would be central in plays to follow, especially *More Stately Mansions*.

Nina's "strange dark interlude called life," then, is O'Neill's. The play is a not-so-brief abstract of O'Neill's emotional history — "a long drawn out lie with a sniffling sigh at the end," says Nina. Now unwilling to write in the courageous if essentially suicidal terms of *The Great God Brown*, O'Neill seeks an escape in this life, and he does so through a totally new version of his Earth Mother, his Cybel, the comforting bosom on which he "might cease upon the midnight with no pain." He assigns this role to the altogether surprising figure of Charlie Marsden. The ubiquitous Charlie has represented several facets of O'Neill's experience in this play, and there are many ways to approach him, almost all of them accurate but none of them complete. We have most recently heard him uttering O'Neill's most self-pitying thoughts and thus representing O'Neill's self-condemnation in these plays. But in this final episode, he becomes something quite different from the embodiment of O'Neill's uncertainty about his talent. The first overt indication of this larger function in the last episode is when he begins thinking to himself in terms one might associate with a narcotic withdrawal:

> My life is a cool green shade wherein comes no
> scorching zenith sun of passion and possession
> to wither the heart with bitter poisons . . . my
> life gathers roses, cooly crimson, in sheltered

gardens, on late afternoons in love with evening
. . . roses heavy with after-blooming of the long,
day, desiring evening . . . my life is an evening . . .
Nina is a rose, my rose, exhausted by the long,
hot day, leaning wearily toward peace.

(I. 187)

He becomes the embodiment, in short, of escape.

In line with this function, Charlie becomes a kind of father figure to Nina. She has identified him with her father throughout the play; here she calls him father, and she yields to his love as a daughter would to a comforting father. Yet Nina has also throughout the play protested her rejection of fathers and father figures. She declares any number of times that she no longer believes in God-the-Father but has instead become a believer in God-the-Mother, the provider of nurture and comfort, a conception not far removed from O'Neill's Earth Mother, especially as she is represented in the goddess-like Cybel. So Nina's escape in the end into the embrace of a re-incarnation of her father seems contradictory — unless we recall (1) who her real father represented in the play, and (2) the androgynous terms in which Charlie earlier describes himself.

At the start of the play, when Nina could be identified simply as a young O'Neill disguised largely by a change in sex, the Professor by the same token could be identified as a version of O'Neill's mother. Nina, of course, rejects her guilty father and has difficulty facing his death, as O'Neill rejected his mother and had difficulty facing hers. In her despair late in the play, Nina seeks the forgiveness and comfort of a father — but not the still stained memory of her real father. What she seeks is that father with the stain of his guilt removed. And so O'Neill with the memory of his mother. He sought a mother with the stain of his real mother's guilt removed. Which is to say, he sought his Earth Mother, and created her in various versions in his plays. Possibly the strangest version of all is Charlie Marsden.

Several things Charlie does and says earlier in the play foreshadow this idea. He clings to Nina the way O'Neill's thoughts about the past clung to him, and he says he cannot decide whether he is a man or a woman. While the latter may suggest homosexuality,[8] there is nothing notably homosexual about the Charlie of this play. He has lost his lust, he tells us, as the result of an encounter with a whore — an experience which fits a number of O'Neill's characters, most notably Jamie Tyrone, in whom it would be difficult to identify homosexual tendencies. The point O'Neill seems to be making about Charlie is simply that he is asexual, and that is precisely what he is supposed to be at the end: an asexual, protecting comforter for Nina in her dark, despairing wait for death. Nina's final gesture in the play is to fall asleep with her head on Charlie's shoulder. Her much-misunderstood declarations earlier in the play on behalf of "God-the-Mother" are thus finally realized in the triumph of "good old Charlie Marsden."

In dividing *Strange Interlude* into what I see as its four major episodes, I have sought to cut this sprawling play down to size. Its inordinate length, like that of plays to follow, grows out of O'Neill's persistent harassment by hostility and guilt, followed by panic and withdrawal. The first two episodes re-enact his familiar set of contradictory responses to his mother's addiction and his mother's death. The third and fourth re-enact the escape, the third his escape through marital infidelity, and the fourth his desire for total oblivion. The play, like those immediately before and after it, is an extended set of variations on the theme of O'Neill's hardening despair.

Before going on to the other plays of this most desperate period in O'Neill's writing, however, I ought to say a word more about the play's interior monologues and their relation to the theme of kinship. Despite their frequent banality, they at times embody elements of the kind of dialogue O'Neill wrote earlier and would return to later. While the lines the characters speak to one another are usually deceptive or manipulative, the lines they think to themselves, when not simply self-pitying, often recall that antiphony of contradictory feelings O'Neill used so extensively in his earlier plays and would one day make basic to his language of human kinship. But although these rhythms do occur, the more important point is that they are almost always limited to the characters' thoughts. Rarely do the characters reveal their irrational reverses in feeling to others, and thus rarely are the characters in actual communication. Despite his obvious attempt to make the characters reveal their inner states, there is no true self-revelation in the play because the characters are rarely honest and direct with one another. Having told Nina that he loves her, for example, Ned Darrell thinks to himself that he is unsure that he loves her. It is quite convincing that his feelings might be so divided, but because of his fear of being hurt, Ned never makes this natural division in his feelings known to Nina. The result is the soap opera effect of pointless and ceaseless suspicion and distrust with no one the wiser or better off. There has been little real emotional confrontation, and there is little really "Freudian" about the play at all, despite the supposedly Freudian overtones of the interior monologues.

For contrast, such passages might be set beside encounters between father and son, mother and son, and brother and brother in *Long Day's Journey*. Whatever the characters in this later play feel is ultimately spoken aloud, and the result is a good deal of hurt and resentment but also a good deal of enlightenment. Only the figure of Mary, who finally must hide entirely behind her morphine screen, evokes the kind of despair that emanates from practically every scene of *Strange Interlude*. The men survive at the end of *Long Day's Journey* because they have made contact with one another — as do all three characters in *A Moon for the Misbegotten*. It is all a matter of whether the terrible extremes of human emotion are held in, breeding an aura of human separateness and despair, or whether they are released, breeding an aura of kinship. As O'Neill was far remote from any aura of kinship in his personal life of the late 1920s, so are his plays of that period.

Dynamo

Dynamo is, among all O'Neill's plays written for the professional theatre, possibly his least believable; and one reason may be that as part of its disguising veneer he attempted to create an unusual, involved plot when all he really wanted was the opportunity to reveal (while of course trying *not* to reveal) the sources of his pain. Never more than a barely adequate originator of dramatic narrative, O'Neill was best when he used ready-made stories or when he abandoned narrative almost entirely in favor of straight exploration of interacting human emotions. In *Dynamo* he gets himself tied up in an extremely clumsy tale. It is the story of a young man who in disillusionment runs away from home but returns after a brief period of dissolute living to find his mother has died as a result of his desertion. In dismay, the young man seeks reassurance and finds it, he thinks, in the worship of electricity; and in a final paroxysm of quasi-religious fervor and violence, the young man electrocutes himself by embracing a live electric dynamo. It is an unconvincing story to begin with which becomes increasingly unconvincing as it becomes more and more sensational.

True to form, O'Neill attempts to give this veneer some kind of audience-attracting modernity, and this time uses not a new fashionable philosophy, but images drawn from the avant-garde art and film of the 1920s. His descriptions of the electric plant in which the hero works seem based on Futurist paintings of the period or possibly Fritz Lang's still highly regarded Futurist film attack on twentieth-century industrial life, *Metropolis*. The play's images of brilliantly lit, idol-like "oil switches" and eternally humming dynamos suggest fascination with artistic experiments of this kind. But, again, this fascination results only in what is superficial to the play. The deeper interest is the same as it has always been. O'Neill is basically concerned with the old saga of disillusionment and guilt associated first with his mother's addiction and second with the circumstances of her death.[9] Like *Strange Interlude*, this play takes the basic form of a life story. Again O'Neill employs his interior monologues (though far less than in its predecessor), and again the play concentrates on O'Neill's feelings of entrapment by his inescapable agonies. Since it is a life story and since I wish to devote as little time to it as possible, I can perhaps most clearly approach this play by means of a brief interpretive summary, an approach which will sufficiently reveal its autobiographical elements.

Reuben Light, the central figure, except that he is the product of a working-class neighborhood (which O'Neill very definitely was not), quite resembles the adolescent O'Neill. He is a shy, sensitive, intelligent youth, who greatly enjoys reading. And his father — the rigid, ponderous, heavyset, and stubborn Reverend Hutchins Light — resembles James Tyrone, Sr. The old minister, who has a "boomingly overly-assertive" voice, melodramatically broods about earlier "wrongs done him" and is constantly "plotting revenge," calling to mind no one so much as James O'Neill in *The Count of Monte Cristo*. Similarly, Reuben's mother suggests Mary Tyrone. She opposes her son's becoming a minister in terms paralleling Mary's in response to James Tyrone's theatrical career: "I'd rather see him dead than go through the poverty and humiliation I've had to face." Like Mary, she "must have been pretty as a girl." Her face "retains its attractiveness although it has grown fleshy." She is intimidated by her husband, and seeks, like Mary, to use her son to express her bitter antagonism toward him. She also possesses quite un-Mary-like "large breasts and broad, round hips," which may be signals that O'Neill was also thinking about his Earth Mother in creating her.

But the severe disillusionment which is central to the play's narrative has less to do with Reuben's mother than with another figure. Reuben has long loved his next-door neighbor Ada Fife; but Ada's father — the iconoclastic, minister-hating Ramsay Fife — opposes their alliance and attempts to break it up by "confessing" to Reuben a terrible crime in his past. Actually, Fife has only read a newspaper account of the crime, but he convinces Reuben of his part in it.[10] Completely taken in and feeling contaminated by what he has heard, Reuben rushes home like a "frightened little boy" to tell his mother Fife's story, though he has been sworn to secrecy by the knowing trickster. The Reverend Light, with his wife's knowledge, overhears Reuben's sordid tale, however, and rushes over to the house of his old enemy Fife to threaten exposure of the crime. He is, of course, laughed at unmercifully by the Mephistophelian Fife for believing the hoax. Reuben, utterly humiliated, contemptuous of his own gullibility, enraged by his father's interference, and in particular disdainful of his mother's timidity, plays the prodigal son. He runs away to spend fifteen months in forbidden pleasures among dissolute women, thus ending the first of the play's two episodes.

These events parallel rather precisely O'Neill's own great disillusionment, although here it is the disillusionment as it had been brought on not primarily by his mother, but by his brother and his father. The Mephistophelian Fife stands for the taunting, iconoclastic Jamie as the puritanical minister stands for the condemning James; and as it was Jamie, to his father's great displeasure, who destroyed O'Neill's illusions, by first telling him of the mother's addiction, so it is Fife who destroys Reuben's, to the old minister's great displeasure. But O'Neill now felt (in 1928) that the chief cause of his disillusionment was a kind of hoax. He now felt that his mother's addiction had been blown up into larger proportions than it should have been. His mother had apparently gotten over the addiction, and O'Neill now felt that his severe reaction to it was the result of his immaturity. This play puts its stress on O'Neill's later reactions to his adolescent shock rather than upon the shock itself.

The play's second episode is about Reuben's prodigal return, which parallels Edmund's return in *Long Day's Journey*, except that this return takes place after the mother's death. By this means O'Neill signals that the second episode concerns more his adult state of mind than that at the time he returned from his travels. Not having been told of his mother's death until his return — O'Neill had all but *ignored* his mother's death — Reuben, like O'Neill, is consumed with a guilt which builds to increasingly hysterical proportions. He goes to work for Ramsay Fife, who is superintendent at the local electrical power station, thus defying his old-fashioned father and allying himself with his father's unbelieving adversary — as O'Neill rejected his father's orthodoxies and emulated his brother's cynical iconoclasm. But as O'Neill could never adhere faithfully to his brother's cynicism, or so effectively exhibit his biting wit, so Reuben cannot perform Fife's work properly. Moreover, Reuben must be a believer in something. Described several times in the play as being "like his father," as O'Neill often was, Reuben begins to make a religion of his new work and in his father's same booming, inflexible terms describes this new religion to all who will listen. That his new religion parallels while it opposes his father's old one suggests that Reuben's dedication to electricity may parallel O'Neill's to the theatre.

Finally, Reuben's relationship with one character in the play seems to parallel heroes' relationships with Earth Mothers in O'Neill's other plays, though it is not long before this relationship becomes a parody of those earlier ones. The rotund Mrs. Fife certainly has the dimensions of an Earth Mother. In terms directly anticipating those used to describe Josie Hogan, Mrs. Fife is "well over 200 pounds" though her figure "is not formless or flabby" but "suggests . . . an inert strength." And as she is directly related to the play's Jamie figure, Ramsay Fife, she also recalls the Cybel before her and anticipates the Josie to follow. Reuben is at first quite taken with Mrs. Fife, but as she is basically a shallow, stupid woman, his feeling for her quickly disappears. Though she follows him about in the last part of the play with all the devotion of a religious disciple, she has increasingly become a grotesque figure whom Reuben turns away from once his hopes in her prove futile.

Unable to find the comfort he is seeking in Mrs. Fife, Reuben finally turns to that which he considers the basis of all Earth Mothers — nature itself. But it is a strange vision of nature O'Neill now provides. In a long, strained, and convoluted speech late in the play, Reuben explains to the uncomprehending Mrs. Fife how nature, which he believes will provide him peace and solace, is no longer to be associated with the earth, or even with the sea (which for O'Neill was usually the essence of existence), but is now to be associated only with electricity, the mystical qualities of which were first suggested to him during an electrical storm in the play's first act. It is electricity, Reuben concludes, which is the true abstract of all that nature has to offer. He therefore makes electricity a god to be worshipped, and the main dynamo[11] in the electric plant, which resembles a "massive female idol," will for him replace all living Earth Mothers. In this spirit, which O'Neill makes no attempt to show as anything other than crazed, he actually gets the foolish Mrs. Fife to kneel and pray with him before the monstrous, purring machine. And not only Mrs. Fife, but also Ada, whose bloody fate becomes the incontrovertible evidence of Reuben's insanity — in case we needed any. Having denied himself all amorous activity in the puritanical zeal of his new religion, Reuben (recalling Eben Cabot) succumbs to Ada's charms and makes love to her in the very chamber presided over by his whirring goddess. Then, in hysterical guilt over breaking his vow, he seizes a revolver and kills the surprisingly docile Ada, who earlier in the play appeared anything but docile. This is followed by his embrace of the dynamo and, in a flash of "bluish light" his immediate electrocution. Reuben finally finds his Earth Mother — in a manner reminiscent of Yank and his affectionate gorilla.[12]

It does not seem difficult to recognize what O'Neill was telling us about himself in this play, which was written, not surprisingly, shortly following his running off with Carlotta. His unending guilt about his mother's death — the resentment over her addiction here temporarily transferred to the informers Jamie and James, Sr. — was, he felt, driving him mad, and his mood was distinctly suicidal. For the first time, he here suggests the absurdity of his search for an Earth Mother,[13] identifying that longing as one of those pipe dreams he would later deal with far more convincingly in *The Iceman Cometh*. He begins by making Mrs. Fife a relatively appealing symbol, but by the end his own Slade-like hold on reality must render her into an immense buffoon. There are in fact no Earth Mothers in this play. There are only a dead mother, a large, fat woman who disappoints the hero's expectations, and a half-baked theory about nature and electricity. There is also terrible panic, which is what this play is really about, a panic which must grow out of most immediate experience. Like Reuben, who kills Ada because she is attractive to him, O'Neill had recently abandoned a wife and family he genuinely loved. Then assuming he had found the Earth Mother he had been seeking, he was dismayed to discover that prolonged exposure to his new wife was rapidly proving the folly of that assumption. (O'Neill's travels with Carlotta in the period before his divorce went through, as described in Sheaffer, were a series of altercations, escapes, and troubled reunions — the pursuing lady not to be put off by what she considered O'Neill's lack of fortitude.[14]) Thus, the grim, frenzied, wretched-without-respite Reuben Light is probably the clearest image we have of how the seriously disturbed playwright felt about himself in his frantic movements about the world in 1928–29. Clearly the kind of obliteration Reuben inflicts upon himself was contemplated by O'Neill in these hectic months.

The play warrants little more discussion. Its dialogue, far from manifesting any rhythms suggesting kinship, seems totally taken up with introspective, irrational verbal meanderings countered by several varieties of emotional over-reaction. All the characters in it seem socially and psychologically warped; and even its long paean to nature and the sea, which parallels two of O'Neill's most successful lyric passages in *The Hairy Ape* and *Long Day's Journey* has, intentionally, it seems, been made to seem at the edge of lunacy as Reuben builds upon it his strange, fanatic deification of electricity. Like O'Neill's other recent plays, this one was written out of a spirit of severe self-contempt. All we see is a steady build-up of panic and hysteria.[15] Whatever else can be said of the play to follow this one, *Mourning Becomes Electra* reveals that O'Neill was more in control of himself.

5 Mourning Becomes Electra

P ERHAPS THE BEST REMARKS made on *Mourning Becomes Electra*, certainly O'Neill's most ambitious play of his middle period and for many still the most successful of all his works, were those of Robert Benchley, who in reviewing the play said he had no idea what the play was all about but that it "sure did scare the bejeezus out of you."[1] Few would deny that as dramatic treatment of an old aristocratic family decayed by years of rigidity, frustration, and distrust this play is as powerful as any family play O'Neill wrote. The dialogue can be genuinely penetrating at times and the pathos convincing when handled by very competent actors. But at the same time, as Benchley sensed from the start, the air never seems to clear. Just as one feels he is beginning to understand the motives of a particular character, something is said or done which makes earlier conclusions seem unlikely. Perhaps, despite its clearly Freudian overtones,[2] the play is only a more polished nineteenth century melodrama—a tale of the irrational, of a monstrous old family living in a "haunted house"? This possibility, which evokes responses like Benchley's, at times seems the most plausible. Taking the play as simply a skillful melodrama recalling the kind of fare popular when O'Neill's father was in his prime may be the fairest way to describe it.[3] That is, unless one considers details of the play as versions, once more, of the great personal crisis from which O'Neill could not free himself.

Much has been made of the play's connections with the *Oresteia* of Aeschylus, from which the plot and structure clearly derive. All O'Neill's plays from the sea plays to *Long Day's Journey* suggest that he cared little about originating dramatic intrigue but preferred to probe ready-made emotional situations. He was at his best working on the nearly plotless

Bound East for Cardiff and at his worst trying to develop plot complications for the hapless *Dynamo*. His best plots were usually the ones already provided him by others, and the plots of *Desire Under the Elms* and *Mourning Becomes Electra*, both provided by ancient Greek sources, are probably the best plots of all. These ancient stories were excellent for O'Neill because both provided opportunity for the development of emotional situations precisely suited to his obsessions. The *Oresteia* is a story of betrayal, guilt, and punishment; and it shows noble, attractive young people unable to throw off the sins of their ancestors. It was a ready-made vessel for O'Neill to fill with the various and contradictory facets of his personal agony, but at the same time its precise events were such that it is difficult to recognize O'Neill's own story in them.

O'Neill focuses on the two family strains in this play—Mannon and Brantome (later Brant)—because these two strains parallel the two rival strains in O'Neill's own background. The Mannons—proper, rigid, secretive, and remote—are to O'Neill like his mother's "lace-curtain Irish" family. That they are also exceedingly guilt-ridden identifies them with both his mother and himself. The Brantome side—poor, hard-headed, emotional, and loving—is to O'Neill like his father's "shanty-Irish" family. The only Brantome to appear, of course, is Adam Brant, who is half Mannon; but the story he tells of his mother lets us know plainly whom we are dealing with. The mother, we are told, was the vigorous Canuck family nurse Marie Brantome, who after her Mannon husband hanged himself, slaved through a miserable existence and finally died of malnutrition. This almost precisely parallels the story told late in *Long Day's Journey* by James Tyrone, Sr. about his mother and her sufferings on his behalf. Tyrone even alludes to a long-departed father who was rumored to have hanged himself, as did David Mannon. And it is the same story Con Melody, who also stands for O'Neill's father, tells of his background in *A Touch of the Poet*. Through the story of the Mannons and Marie Brantome, then, O'Neill presents us with the two forces he felt made up his nature as it derived from both mother and father: the sensitive, nervous, withdrawing side and the outgoing, boisterous, emotional side. He also suggests through the action of this play the losing battle he feels the outgoing side of him was waging at the time he wrote it.

Before going into the play's three parts, I must emphasize two points, one of which was made earlier in relation to *Strange Interlude*. The first is that increasingly in his drama, O'Neill's thoughts and feelings about his past flow from character to character. Attitudes suggesting his mother, for example, may at one moment be apparent in Christine Mannon, at another in Ezra Mannon, and at a third again in Christine. So, too, do his feelings about his own state at the time he was writing the play move back and forth between characters — for the most part between Lavinia and Orin Mannon. The second, and closely related, point, is that a character's sex has little to do with the figure he or she represents in O'Neill's mind. The daughter Lavinia is the chief figure to stand for O'Neill himself in Parts One and Two, the father Ezra one of the two figures to stand for O'Neill's mother in Part One.

As for the play itself, Part One seems most heavily dependent on Aeschylus and therefore most remote from O'Neill's experience. In other words, O'Neill's experience is most heavily disguised in Part One. Part One also, however, directly reenacts some experience very recent to him. Christine Mannon's periodic escapes to New York City to be with her lover are too close to O'Neill's visits to Carlotta to go unnoticed. Even the geography is the same, and the lovers' attitudes are strongly reminiscent of the Nina-Ned sequences in *Strange Interlude*, which also mirror those visits. Happily, O'Neill does not dwell long on this episode, nor does Christine in any other respect suggest O'Neill as philandering husband. Rather, what is stressed in these scenes is the cold rage of Lavinia Mannon, Christine's resentful daughter, who has discovered her mother's infidelity and views it as a terrible crime which she, Lavinia, must somehow avenge. It is Lavinia's relationship with her mother in Part One which I shall consider first.

The major confrontation between Lavinia and Christine before Ezra returns in Part One suggests several parent-child exchanges in *Long Day's Journey* — even including one between James Tyrone Sr. and Jr. But it anticipates none so prominently as that exchange which precipitates Edmund's explosion at his mother's addiction. In the earlier play, Christine's adultery, which Lavinia has been observing with the same barely controlled rage with which the Tyrone men observe Mary, finally provokes Lavinia's most direct attack upon her mother:

> Stop lying, I tell you! I went upstairs! I
> heard you telling him — "I love you, Adam" — and
> kissing him! (*With a cold bitter fury*) You vile — !
> You're shameless and evil! Even if you are my
> mother, I say it!
>
> (II. 30)

"Upstairs" suggests a familiar enough motif, and Edmund's calling his mother a "dope-fiend" is not too far removed from the spirit of these insults. Nor are the attributes of Mary's addiction far removed from those of Christine's desire for Adam. Christine longs to be taken off to the "enchanted isles" Adam keeps referring to, a retreat of eternal peace and happiness which closely parallels Mary's morphine in its described effects. Lavinia's attitudes toward Christine in Part One thus represent O'Neill's recurrent hostility toward his mother for her addiction.

Lavinia's attitudes toward Ezra Mannon, on the other hand, suggest O'Neill's equally recurrent guilt. Ezra's murder is saturated with feeling and intensity which call to mind O'Neill's whole complex of responses to his mother's death, but since the details of the myth itself greatly disguise the parallels, clarity here must derive from Ezra's personality and from his daughter's uncompromising devotion to him. When we consider Ezra, we must think of all those characteristics of the Mannon family referred to earlier and of their proximity in O'Neill's mind to his mother and his mother's family: the sensitivity, the nervousness, and the over-developed puritan sense of guilt. Following her confession of her love for Adam, Christine ceases for a time to be like Mary. It is rather Ezra who takes on the characteristics of O'Neill's mother, and now not the betraying mother suggested by Christine but the betrayed mother, the dead mother of O'Neill's imagination, the prompter of his enormous guilt.

The murder scene and Lavinia's part in it are presented in the play chiefly from Lavinia's point of view and take place in the ambience of *her* helplessness and *her* rage, which are of course O'Neill's — his feeling of helplessness in responding to his mother's death and his rage at himself following it. O'Neill's own set of feelings not only results in the fierce representation of Lavinia's responses at the end of Part One, but helps account for the very different quality of those events in O'Neill's play and that of its ancient source. O'Neill was dealing with his own feelings, Aeschylus with ritual and justice.

Even before the end of Part One, however, Christine once more becomes the betraying mother, and we are back where we started (which accords with the increasingly circular nature of the plays we are looking at). Ezra's last words identify Christine as his murderess, and Christine once again becomes the perpetrator of a terrible crime against her family. Murder has now replaced illicit love as the substitute for Mary's addiction. And for her crime Christine must be driven to suicide by her offspring. O'Neill must punish his mother again, and he must dramatize the guilt again — and again and again. The repeated punishment and the repeated guilt grow into an inescapable circle from which O'Neill and his characters seem unable to escape.

Parts Two and Three, as in Aeschylus, are devoted to the revenge of Lavinia and Orin against their mother and her lover, and to their own ensuing punishment. In these events, O'Neill's process of self-revelation becomes more precise. With the appearance of Orin, O'Neill divides his own personality in two.[4] Lavinia and Orin represent the opposing aspects of O'Neill's personality defined by his contradictory responses to his mother. Lavinia clearly becomes O'Neill's vindictive side in Parts Two and Three. She operates out of cold, controlled rage and is quite unforgiving. She demands an eye for an eye, and she seems free of guilt at her own crimes because she feels they are justified. Most significantly, once her revenge has been exacted, she is ready to live a normal life, with no pangs of conscience, with no remorse, as she would were it not for Orin. She is O'Neill's rational, some would say his "adult," nature which wants its revenge clean and precise and which could then live at peace, were it not for the demands of the other side of his nature.

Orin Mannon is the other Eugene O'Neill — that is, the O'Neill whose pain shaped his plays. Far more than even Charlie Marsden, he is spokesman for O'Neill's deeper, irrational responses; and while these might be viewed as immature responses, Orin is until Part Three, in some ways more mature than Lavinia. Explosive, vacillating, dependent, and forgiving, he is all the things Lavinia is not. Ezra Mannon's first reference to him in Part One makes the parallel with O'Neill and his sufferings practically explicit. Having been wounded in the head, Orin "got brain fever from the shock" — the "shock," of course, being O'Neill's first learning of his mother's condition, and the "brain fever" all that followed.[5] He is obviously the O'Neill who tries to confront his ghosts, who acknowledges his pain — but the effort proves more than Orin can bear.

Warned by his rational counterpart, Lavinia, not to believe the lies their mother will tell him in Part Two, Orin does believe — as Edmund always accepts his mother's assurances — only to be shocked, and shocked again, into tortured acceptance of the incontrovertible evidence of his senses. The scene in which Orin confronts his guilty mother is a more frenzied version of the dialogue in Part One between Lavinia and Christine, and more directly than ever anticipates the Edmund-Mary dialogues of *Long Day's Journey*. Christine tells Orin of the "lies" Lavinia has been spreading precisely as Mary tells Edmund of Jamie's "lies," and Orin's responses might at times substitute for Edmund's without an audience being much aware of the difference:

> Christine: Oh, Orin! You pretend to love me! And
>   yet you question me as if you suspected me, too!
>   And you haven't Vinnie's excuse! You aren't out
>   of your mind! . . . .

Orin: No! I swear to you! . . . Mother! Please!
    Don't cry! I do love you! I do!

        . . . .

Orin: . . . . Did you really want me to come back, Mother?
Christine: (. . . *her eyes are terrified and her voice trembles)*
    What a foolish question, dear!
Orin: But your letters got farther and farther between—
    and they seemed so cold! It drove me crazy! . . . .
    I longed to be here with you—like this!

                                (II. 88 and 89)

Orin's fear that his mother has forsaken him for her lover is expressed in phrases very much like Edmund's regarding his mother's addiction. And the knowledge that she has a lover is followed, of course, by the other, still more terrible knowledge that his mother is a husband-murderess. Both crimes stand for the monumental single crime of the later play.

The revenging murders seem to follow closely those in Aeschylus, but there are some striking differences in detail that can best be accounted for by O'Neill's attitudes toward his dead parents. Adam Brant, whom I have already identified on his Brantome side with O'Neill's father, is dedicated to his ship the way James Tyrone, Sr. is dedicated to his play. And his swift, "clean" murder, which once accomplished does not prey upon the mind of either avenger, is in effect like the death of O'Neill's father. Orin feels some guilt for his murder of Adam, but nothing like the guilt he feels over the death of his mother, although he only helps bring the latter about. That O'Neill had largely made peace with the memory of his father is suggested by the compassion and even admiration O'Neill makes us feel for Adam Brant, especially at his death, admiration which is hardly consistent with Aeschylus.

The death of Christine, and especially Orin's responses to it, are far more complex, and they reflect the persistent, devastating conflict in O'Neill toward the memory of his mother. It is significant that O'Neill does not have either Orin or Lavinia actually kill Christine but lets her suicide be the result of Orin's brutal accusations. This makes Orin's way of "killing" his mother precisely like O'Neill's. Neither did it directly. Furthermore, Christine's suicide is surprisingly noble, in the Roman stoic sense. (It resembles more that of Sophocles's Jocasta than Aeschylus's Clytemnestra.) Having faced in full the evil of her life and having utterly dismissed all her pipe dreams, she swiftly ends her life. This nobility in death despite the seriousness of her crimes grows once more out of the intense guilt which alternates and vies with the equally intense resentment in all O'Neill's relentless memories of his mother. The dead Christine thus is quickly forgiven her crimes by Orin, but he must now deal with his guilt at having brought her death about. Orin's long-range response to his mother's death, and finally Lavinia's, constitutes the chief subject of Part Three, which is thus more than ever a play about O'Neill's state of mind when he wrote it.

The gothic flavor of Part Three is O'Neill's attempt to suggest the state of Orin's guilt-ridden mind (and his own). It is full of references to the macabre: to spirits, eerie sounds, unlit chambers, sickly pale visages, and other paraphernalia of the tale of terror. The Mannon mansion itself, now considered "haunted" by the neighbors, is like its chief male inhabitant (i.e., like O'Neill) — still recognizably dignified on the outside but consumed by nameless fears on the inside. As the emphasis in Part One and still largely in Part Two is on Lavinia, the supposedly rational and certainly vindictive part of O'Neill's nature, that in Part Three is on Orin and his swarming, bat-like fears. This contrast is a far more successful extension of the opposition between the rational, clinical effect of the opening episode of *Strange Interlude* and its sinister, terrifying second episode, with its demented sister quietly laughing her life away in an upstairs room. Here Lavinia contributes to the clinical effect, Orin to the gothic.

Not the first of O'Neill's "haunted heroes" and certainly not the last, Orin in Part Three is the most recognizably O'Neill-like figure of all his characters, more even than Edmund Tyrone because Edmund represents O'Neill at a considerably earlier stage. The main reason Orin is so like O'Neill is that he is setting down his great agony in the form of a long book — a book which tells *the whole truth* about his family, like the play O'Neill would write within ten years of this one. Nevertheless, Orin is not prepared to tell that truth straight, as O'Neill was not yet prepared to tell his truth straight. Orin must make it a tale of recurrent crime, guilt, and retribution in the entire Mannon family (following Aeschylus and the House of Atreus), a pattern which, while it fits O'Neill's family as he saw them, also fits the relentless chain of responses in O'Neill himself. Orin's book is also important because it forecasts O'Neill's projected dramatic "cycle," which was intended, in a historical family framework, to tell the same tale over and over again *ad infinitum* — as O'Neill was living his tale over and over again *ad infinitum*. (It was not without reason that O'Neill's planned cycle went from seven to nine, to eleven, to thirteen projected plays — all of them nine or more hours in length. The cycle in O'Neill's mind literally would not end.)

The narrative of Part Three, anticipating several plays to follow in the thirties, concerns a struggle between the rational and the irrational, between vindictiveness and guilt, between adult self-control and childhood terror. It enacts the struggle between Lavinia and Orin Mannon over whose outlook will prevail following their flight from the scene of their crimes and their brief respite—at any rate, Lavinia's brief respite, since Orin can find no respite anywhere. And Orin in the end is the clear victor in that he escapes into death, while Lavinia finally becomes the haunted one. The damage done by the past is finally too much even for the seemingly clear-headed Lavinia. Orin blackmails Lavinia with his book, the contents of which would result in criminal prosecution, then withdraws to the world of the past and commits suicide. It is not the stoic suicide of Christine either, but rather the "beautiful" suicide of Ibsen's Hedda Gabler, who dies amid visions of vine leaves in a hero's hair. Orin's suicide is his retreat into the never-never land of his fantasy childhood— before his disillusionment, before "the Fall" —and thus also anticipates the fate O'Neill's later Simon Harford (*More Stately Mansions*) barely avoids. It also suggests the kind of suicide O'Neill must have been toying with, though restrained persistently by his Lavinia, his highly developed reason, his basic sanity, his inescapable grasp on reality. (Lavinia's leading successor Larry Slade, it will be remembered, could not commit suicide although he had fully convinced himself of its desirability.) Orin could take his own life (like the later Don Parritt), but Orin is only one side of O'Neill. The Lavinia side must live on—no matter how total the despair.

Lavinia's story, like Larry Slade's to follow, is one of total withdrawal without illusion, that most painful but heroic of human destinies for O'Neill. Having evened the score with her wicked mother, having achieved her "justice," she is free to give sway to her natural human instincts. She could enjoy her native lover, as O'Neill could his native lovers, during the period of her escape; and she could come, as the Orin half of O'Neill could not, to love and be loved. Lavinia is about to accept the long-suffering Peter Niles as her husband when she is blackmailed by Orin and his book. The haunting past could not let the otherwise self-sufficient present alone. She could not let the world know what was in that book, as O'Neill could not let the world know what was really in his plays. So Lavinia withdraws, with no hopes and no illusions. Fully possessed of all she knows, unflinching before her understanding of what she has done, she will live out her life with the awesome legacy of matricidal guilt Orin has left her, totally uncommunicating and unsolaced. The rational Lavinia cannot escape "the truth," as her earlier decision to marry, she decides, was an attempt to do. What she considers her sense of justice is finally too developed for her to do anything other than accept her punishment. Her reason has led her, as it was leading O'Neill, from the simple idea that "the past can be ignored" to the equally simple idea that "the past can*not* be ignored"; and that latter idea is to be the sum and substance of her personal Hell. She will live out her life only with the past and with no illusions about the past. "With Lavinia," says Frederic Carpenter, O'Neill "symbolically returned to his own land, renounced his dreams, and locked himself in with the ghosts of his family past."[6]

The one ameliorating factor in all this is that Lavinia does not enter her mansion entirely alone at the end of the play. She has her old retainer Seth to serve her in her life-long penance; and just who Seth is, what he represents, and how he functions are extremely important in this play. A discussion of Seth will lead me to some concluding observations about the essence of O'Neill's view of existence in the middle of his career.

Seth is a perfectly suitable puritan New England name, of course, but there is every reason to believe O'Neill had the biblical Seth in mind when he selected it. Seth in the Old Testament was either the third son of Adam or the first, depending on which biblical interpretation one accepts — and either interpretation fits O'Neill's use of the name in *Mourning Becomes Electra*. As the third son, referred to in Genesis 4, he was given by God to Eve as recompense for her loss of Abel. And as the first son (Genesis 5), he is simply the second in that long line of biblical patriarchs beginning with Adam (the "begats"). In neither case is he directly related to the Fall or to Cain's murder of Abel. Either he must be considered an instrument of God's forgiveness of man for his transgressions *or* he is simply a transmitter of that seed of successive offspring which is evidence in itself, in biblical terms, of God's continuing endorsement of human existence. In the play, then, he might stand for forgiveness of the Man*n*ons, or he might be a sign of the fact that since man endures, existence has value — two ideas which are, in fact, not mutually exclusive.

In the play, Seth, although a life-long associate of the Mannons, has been in no way affected by their crimes, either as perpetrator or victim. Nor is he particularly shocked at their activities. In his own narration of the past, he says he watched as Abe Mannon and his brother David competed for the affections of Marie Brantome, and had watched as the favored David was driven from the house by his revengeful brother. He then watches as the news of Ezra Mannon's murder is made public, knowing instinctively what has happened; and he watches as Lavinia and Orin take revenge upon their mother and her lover. In Part One, Seth recognizes that Adam Brant is a long-lost Mannon, but that information is of benefit only to Lavinia. It in no way affects Seth. His typical response to Lavinia's deceptions is that he will accept anything she tells him. He is a constant, unvarying presence of whose existence no one except Lavinia seems even cognizant. He does show the prying public the family homestead and restrains their excessive curiosity, but this action is not directly related to the events of the play.

Seth opens the play by singing an old sea chanty, "Shenandoah," that warrants some consideration. In Part One, the chanty sets a mood which is shattered the moment the Mannons take the stage, a mood of nostalgic yearning and a mood of peace, that quality the Mannon household seems so remote from at all times:

> Oh, Shenandoah, I long to hear you
> A-way, my rolling river
> Oh, Shenandoah, I can't get near you
> Way-ay, I'm bound away
> Across the wide Missouri.[7]
>
> (II. 6)

Again like his biblical namesake, Seth by his nearly anonymous existence in the play and by his song testifies to the ongoing assurance that nature, of which man is but one, prodigal offspring, is constant, although man has lost his ability to reach her. And he also testifies, if one wishes, to God's perpetual readiness to forgive man the atrocities the play so vividly reveals him committing. As both interpretations of the biblical Seth are possible, so are both interpretations of what Seth means in the play possible.

Seth has a stand-in in Part Two, an old drunken chantyman reminiscent of the old black spiritual-singer in *All God's Chillun*. The chantyman, in addition to singing the oft-repeated "Shenandoah," follows it with a chanty quite opposite to it in mood and pointedly related to what is going on in the play's action. This other chanty is called, appropriately, "Hanging Johnny":

> They say I hanged my mother
> Away-ay-i-oh!
> They say I hanged my mother
> Oh, hang, boys, hang!
>
> (II. 107)

Evoking the figurative "hanging" of their mother Orin and Lavinia will shortly be guilty of, and the still more figurative "hanging" of his mother O'Neill felt guilty of, the "Hanging Johnny" chanty is O'Neill's musical emblem of the play's chief mood and action, against which "Shenandoah" and Seth stand as testaments to the universal harmony of nature which man in his jealousies, intrigues, and domestic violence has irrevocably lost touch with.[8] Like the chantyman in Part Two, Seth in Part Three adds two brief lines to his "Shenandoah" rendition which suggest that part of what man has lost touch with is the ability to love well in ways akin to the singer's love for the river:

> Oh, Shenandoah, I love your daughter
> A-way, you rolling river.
>
> (II. 103)

The Mannons have lost the ability to love women deeply — as though they were the daughters of rivers — though Adam Brant (from the Brantome line) retains a trace of that ability.

Recalling, then, that Lavinia is one part of O'Neill, and the part that O'Neill feels must go on living no matter what, it is possible to see Seth as a kind of Earth Mother in this play. He has always been most closely associated with Lavinia, the figure for her of an old protector who could always be trusted and occasionally even confided in (a rare event in these plays). And his song has clearly stood for what O'Neill's Earth Mothers stand for: a manifestation of the eternal presence of constant, consoling nature. But Seth must remain Earth Mother only *in a sense*, because that all-important gesture in the relationship between William Brown and Cybel, between Nina and Charlie Marsden (even insanely between Reuben and his dynamo), is missing here: the embrace. It is the night-long succoring, life-giving embrace of Jamie Tyrone by Josie Hogan which is the culminating image in O'Neill of man finding peace, and here it is missing. Despite the peace that Seth represents, the absence of his touch, perhaps Lavinia's (O'Neill's) rejection of it, leaves the darkness of despair at the end of this play almost total. Though Seth's Shenandoah will flow on forever, man in fact can*not* get near her in this play. Lavinia retires to live in the permanent company of an Earth Mother from whom she will receive no nurturing comfort. O'Neill could at this point envision no solace to his pain, and the end of the play is bleaker than anything in O'Neill, including *The Iceman Cometh*.

There is also a contradiction, quite basic to this play, in what nature and peace stand for. It is focused chiefly in the image of the "blessed isles" Adam Brant talks of and the morbid Orin is taken on a journey to by the shrewd Lavinia. The two deeply contradictory strains suggested by this image are these. On the one hand, the isles, like Seth and the "Shenandoah" chanty, suggest the positive, natural force man has lost touch with.

One strong indication of Christine's relatively healthy passion for Adam Brant, whose background as a Brantome makes him vigorous and purposeful, is her desire to run away with him to the "blessed isles." And Lavinia, who actually does go there and just possibly has a liaison with an island prince, finally confesses her own love for Adam Brant in the light of her island experience. Everything associated with Adam Brant, right down to his name, seems intended to suggest the virile and unstained — despite his complicity in cold-blooded murder. But here the contradiction becomes apparent. Adam's isles, and Adam himself, also stand for withdrawal — withdrawal which, given its narcotic characteristics, seems intended to parallel Mary Tyrone's withdrawal. That which most symbolizes the free and healthy in the play also symbolizes the most decadent and demented.

This contradiction suggests thoughts that could only be at the Slade-like nadir of O'Neill's consciousness. If the "Shenandoah" vision of a harmony with nature man has lost be but a pipedream, a desire for withdrawal no different from that produced by Mary's morphine, then the absurdity of existence is absolute. And Mary's retreat in her dope dream is, after all, into a distant, untroubled past, as Seth's chanty deals with a distant, untroubled past. The virile Adam (whose name is that of the first man himself) would then be but one part of a pipe dream because he is certainly to be equated with his blessed isles. But he is also equated with the vigorous, physical Marie Brantome, who was certainly no pipe dream. We are caught on the very large horns of a dilemma — or O'Neill is — and there is no release from it in the play. It is also O'Neill's persistent dilemma, never resolved in philosophic terms in any of his plays, though it is implicitly resolved in other terms. The return to nature in the plays we are dealing with and shall be dealing with is O'Neill's last bastion, his sole barrier against total despair. Yet the longing for such a return, as it is evoked in the image of the blessed isles,[9] is so like Mary Tyrone's longing for her dope that even O'Neill's last bastion begins to erode, as have all bastions for the nihilistic Larry. But then there is also the image of Marie Brantome — the Earth Mother — who derives for O'Neill from the story of his own family told him by his vital and alert father; and the two yearnings once more seem quite distinct.

Mourning Becomes Electra is the culminating work of O'Neill's terrible middle years. The Aeschylean pattern gives the play a sense of formal organization so often lacking in O'Neill's plays, and within its controlling framework O'Neill works and reworks the old cycle of fear and guilt more penetratingly than in any earlier play other than *The Great God Brown*. But the play is entirely devoted to crime, violence, and guilt. It is as distant in spirit from the sea plays, with their untrammeled ebbs and flows of human love and hostility, as it is possible to get in O'Neill. And thus, it is certainly O'Neill's most despairing play of all. Those who would find it less despairing than the bleak *Iceman* miss a very essential difference between these plays, a difference which grows out of the texture of life represented in them rather than their relative degrees of nihilistic statement. The dialogue in *Mourning Becomes Electra*, like that in the plays most recently preceding it, is enveloped by deception, scheming, and back-biting, and taken together with the other plays we have been looking at constitutes a kind of "No Exit" period for O'Neill, his true dark night of the soul, his vision of Hell. Though the characters are bound together, there is no kinship here. And while it is impossible to say what was in those cycle plays destroyed by O'Neill in the 1940s, it is possible to suggest that they are plays in which the essential elements of *Mourning Becomes Electra* are repeated over and over again without relief. O'Neill's published plays to follow, on the other hand, suggest his desire to break out of his unending circle of guilt and fear, fear and guilt — and they will suggest an O'Neill unwilling to be like either his Lavinia or his Orin. But none of the plays until the mighty *Iceman* itself approaches the terrible fascination of *Mourning Becomes Electra*.

III

THE TRANSITION

6 *Days Without End* and *Ah, Wilderness*

W HY O'NEILL ABANDONED his "cycle" and destroyed its two longest completed works no one knows, of course, but it is possible to assume that the predictions of Orin Mannon were coming all too true. The cycle—that massive investigation of an American family looking back into the eighteenth century and forward into the twentieth—would always find the same pattern of deception and hurt, conspiracy and betrayal, disillusionment and withdrawal, guilts and ghosts all dogging the sensitive younger members into despair or death.[1] Despite his conviction by the early 1930s that his agony was permanent, however, that there was no escape from the eternal return of his nightmares, O'Neill instinctively could not go on with the apparent endless repetition of these plays—as he was also instinctively not a man who could accept stasis in his life, even if he could see no escape from it. In short, he had to "break out of" the pattern, even if he had no idea where the breaking out would lead him.

The four plays which survive from the period between *Mourning Becomes Electra* and *The Iceman Cometh* all were written during his, on the surface at least, more peaceful existence of the 1930s. Two of them do not come from the cycle—possibly pre-dating it, though he had the cycle in mind throughout that period—and two of them are from the cycle itself. All four represent characters in one way or another breaking out of their personal circles of discontent. John Loving's rediscovery of his Roman Catholic faith in *Days Without End*, Richard Miller's happy maturation in *Ah, Wilderness*, Con Melody's destruction of his aristocratic illusions in *A Touch of the Poet*, and Simon Harford's last-ditch escape from paranoid withdrawal in *More Stately Mansions* all counter in spirit and direction the plays I have been looking at from O'Neill's desperate middle period. The four plays are quite different from one another in plot, tone, and even the relative sentimentality of their endings; but they have in common the struggle of their central figures to break away from what seems to them inescapable despair. And what is equally important is that in the dialogue of all these plays we begin to hear and sense the rhythm of human kinship reawakening. The secretiveness, the deception, and the conspiratorial tones which characterize so much of the dialogue in the plays of the middle period begin to give way to the kind of dialogue which more truly attests to the genius of this playwright.

Days Without End

Though he dislikes the play, Louis Sheaffer finds that in *Days Without End* a "decisive impulse" was driving O'Neill "to write more plainly, more nakedly."[2] There is no question of the accuracy of this statement. In its relative directness of autobiographical statement, the play is far ahead of any play so far, rivalled only by *A Touch of the Poet* in this period as a play demonstrating O'Neill's deepening understanding of himself and of human beings in general. For some, the hero's final return to the Roman Catholicism of his youth damns the play; but for others deeply affected by O'Neill, that would not be damning in the least.[3] Rather, it is that the ending is an escape, a new retreat to O'Neill's childhood never-neverland that makes one dubious. The ending is in no way the "facing of ghosts" the characters early in the play discuss with so much animus. If there is a real conversion in this play — secular or religious — it takes place not before the Cross at the conclusion of Act Four, but in the first scene of Act Three, one of the most lucid debates among conflicting viewpoints in O'Neill's plays.

In subtitling this play "Plot for a Novel," an autobiographical novel, O'Neill is as explicit about what he is doing with his own life in a play as he ever gets until *Long Day's Journey*. In the play, John Loving's novel tells the story of a psychologically disturbed hero's confused adolescence and young adulthood. The novel's hero falls in love and marries, but soon has an affair with his wife's best friend which so shocks his wife when she discovers it that she grows ill and dies. At the opening of the play, John Loving is undecided how to end his novel, whether to have his hero commit suicide out of guilt for betraying his wife, or whether to have him survive by means of a newly-discovered religious faith. The events of the novel are a straightforward representation of John Loving's life, except that John's wife Elsa has not yet discovered that he has had an affair with her best friend Lucy. That John Loving's novel is autobiographical is a simple signal of the fact that the author's play is also autobiographical[4]; and in having John at one point in the play *deny* the autobiographical nature of his novel, when everyone knows the contrary, O'Neill is telling us not just about this play but about all his previous plays — which kept being more and more revealing even as he kept straining to distort and disguise his insistent "truth."

In this play, O'Neill reveals his truth by dividing the two facets of his personality into separate speakers — John and Loving — who represent the opposing sides of the hero John Loving. The division is somewhat like that in *Mourning Becomes Electra,* with the sensitive, believing, easily-swayed John paralleling Orin, and the vindictive, ultra-rational Loving paralleling Lavinia. But while John is clearly enough the Orin-like O'Neill, Loving is something more than simply the rational, vindictive side of his nature.[5] Unlike Lavinia, Loving has a biting cynical wit, the tone of which can only be that of O'Neill as he assumes, as he so often did, his brother Jamie's mask of brilliantly ironic nihilism. It is Loving who urges accepting realities for what they are and putting aside all escapes into illusion. In dialogue typical of much in modern drama where the reader feels he has "missed something" but has only missed what the playwright has intended him to miss, Loving tries to get John to stop evading the truth about his past in his novel, as O'Neill was evading the truth about his past in his plays:

> **Loving:** And I was thinking, too, that it would be
>   interesting to work out your hero's answer to
>   his problem, if his wife died, and imagine
>   what he would do with his life then.
> **John:** No! Damn you, stop making me think — !
> **Loving:** Afraid to face your ghosts — even by proxy?
>   Surely, even you can have that much courage!
> **John:** It is dangerous — to call things.

"To call things" what? is the inevitable question. To call things what they are seems the probable answer.[6] The obscurity here is an evasion on O'Neill's part, but it is not much of an evasion. Loving continues:

> **Loving:** . . . . I'm only trying to encourage you to make
>   something of this plot of yours more significant —
>   for your soul, shall I say? — than a cowardly
>   trick!

> John: You know it's more than that. You know I'm
> doing it to try and explain to myself, as well
> as to her.

Who precisely is the "her" in question, one wonders: the wife "Elsa," or possibly the memory of a mother named "Ella":

> Loving: (*sneeringly*) To excuse yourself to yourself,
> you mean! To lie and escape admitting the ob-
> vious natural reason for—
> John: You lie! I want to get at the real truth and
> understand what was behind—what evil spirit of
> hate possessed me to make me—
> Loving: (*contemptuously—but as he goes on a strange
> defiant note of exultance comes into his voice*)
> So it's come back again, eh? Your old familiar
> nightmare!
>
> (III. 495)

In spite of the halting quality of this dialogue, O'Neill has brought us to the very edge of hearing what he will later tell us in *Long Day's Journey*, the ultimate revelation of his "old familiar nightmare."

The solution for Loving, however, can only be suicide. Anticipating Larry Slade, Loving feels that the abandonment of illusion is the test of a man's strength, but having abandoned illusion, one's natural next step must be self-annihilation. One's "honor" demands it, says Loving. He considers all of John's proposed endings except suicide illusory—and he reserves a special contempt for John's claims to a renewed religious faith, which Loving finds the greatest illusion of all. He calls it a "cowardly yearning to go back," identifying religious faith not only with John's (O'Neill's) earlier Catholicism, but with everything associated with the fraudulent idealism of the hero's life before his adolescent disillusionment—before the Fall.

At this point in the play, as though sent from Heaven, Father Baird—John Loving's priest, uncle, and former guardian—makes his appearance. The biographers identify the Father with O'Neill's father, and some of his phrases do suggest James Tyrone, Sr. But he is in no way the "boomingly assertive" stubborn old campaigner, and his religious outlook accords more nearly with the precepts of modern psychotherapy than with the rigidly conservative Roman Catholicism of the O'Neills. I find Father

Baird a variant of the wish-fulfillment father O'Neill will shortly create in Nat Miller of *Ah, Wilderness*. The later Con Melody is the real anticipator of James Tyrone, Sr. and Con is everything Father Baird is not. But whomever he suggests, Baird certainly describes John Loving's past as one practically identical to O'Neill's. The Father reviews John's successive flirtations with all the "isms" of the day, from those associated with Nietzsche, Marx, and Zen Buddhism to his present commitment to "evolutionary scientific truth." (These of course parallel O'Neill's own successive flirtations.) He also refers to John's "middle hide-and-go-seek period," which rather aptly describes the plays of O'Neill's middle period. Then O'Neill establishes the relationship among the play's three male figures which will be so important in their crucial encounter in Act Three. There commences an antiphony of countering attitudes between Father Baird and Loving, with John in the middle, like the figure representing mankind in the medieval morality play listening to his good and evil counselors. Baird cannot know of Loving's separate existence, of course, but as a good priest-therapist he understands man's Janus-like nature and "answers" Loving as though he were in fact separate from John. Strangely enough, however, the priest does not tell John anything that Loving has not already been telling him. Like Loving, Father Baird insists that any effort on John's part to find the "truth" must "finally turn back to home." Both John's "good" and "evil" advisors tell him he must reveal, confess, release his terrible guilt — the only difference being that the Father contends such a purgation will lead John to the Cross, while Loving holds out for what he considers the more authentic "peace" of the grave. O'Neill reveals the intense pressure from both sides of his nature to tell all.

At Baird's urging, John Loving begins to relate the plot of his novel, which tells the story of O'Neill's upbringing and adolescence with only the fact of his mother's addiction omitted. As in other plays, parental death — O'Neill's second great shock — is moved up to the place of the first. John's hero's downfall begins with the death of his father and mother when he was fifteen, the very age of O'Neill's first big blow, and it drives him, in Loving's words, "into a panic of superstitious remorse." O'Neill precisely describes his own reactions further as John and Loving continue:

> **Loving:** . . . He saw his God as deaf and blind and
> merciless — a Deity Who returned hate for love and
> revenged Himself upon those who trusted Him!
> **John:** His mother died. And, in a frenzy of insane
> grief —

Loving: No! In his awakened pride he cursed his God and
denied Him, and, in revenge, promised his soul
to the Devil — on his knees, when everyone
thought he was praying!

(III. 511)

The situations referred to, of course, cover both O'Neill's first wave
of disillusioned God-cursing, and his second, following his mother's
death. The actual image of the hero whose mother has just died vengefully
denying his Maker while on his knees ostensibly praying may actually be
Jamie's experience as described in *A Moon for the Misbegotten*, but in any
case we are certainly again dealing with O'Neill's vortex of despairing
emotion since his mother's death. In the opening act of *Days Without
End*, O'Neill has thus told us almost all the elements of his life's abiding
agony. He is still disguising, but only the central facts.

Act Two deals largely with the play's romantic intrigue — John's illicit liaison with Lucy Hillman — and except that it portrays Elsa Loving's
impenetrable certainty of her husband's fidelity has few autobiographical
resonances. Elsa is full of the proud, stubborn idealism we have seen in
the Mannons and which is central to Mary Tyrone's inability to accept the
real world. As it is implicit in *Long Day's Journey* that O'Neill felt he had
trouble living up to his mother's expectations, so it is part of John's trouble that he cannot live up to his wife's. That much of O'Neill's life is represented in the second act. But the more effective aspect of this act has less
to do with plot than with dialogue, which definitely seems more open and
natural than does the dialogue in any play of the middle group. Here, Elsa
and Lucy speak to one another as friends who have had their differences.
Their exchanges contain envy and resentment which are explicitly acknowledged and quickly countered by sincere loyalty and uncomplicated
good will. Sudden, openly stated shifts in emotion reminiscent of the early
O'Neill suggest a renewed desire to convey the ups and downs of sincere
human communication. Lucy is not entirely open, of course. In confessing her adulterous escapade to Elsa, she neglects to mention that it is John
who was her lover. Nevertheless, there is in what she says a compulsion
to confess plus the emotional release associated with confession. Elsa's response is a credible mixture of shock and understanding. The dialogue in
this scene has the quality of people trying to withhold information but
hardly succeeding. Revelation tends to burst the bonds of secretiveness.

Lucy's confession suggests in still other terms an awareness on
O'Neill's part of the counterpoints in human relationships which lead
back to feelings underlying the earlier plays. In Act One, he divided his

hero in a schematic manner and made thereby a strictly cerebral point. By creating John and Loving, he gets at man's divided nature as might an abstract artist of the period — by intentionally and systematically distorting reality. But in Act Two, Lucy reveals that same division in John Loving without the distortion. First, she refers to her own divided nature. Her affair, she says, was inconsistent with what she is "really" like. She thereby parallels in naturalistic terms John's earlier protests that "Loving's" statements are not "really" those of John Loving. Then Lucy tells of the man she seduced:

> I got him in my bedroom on some excuse. But he pushed
> me away, as if he were disgusted with himself and me.
> But I wouldn't let him go. And then came the strange part
> of it. Suddenly, I don't know how to explain it, you'll
> think I'm crazy, or being funny, but it was as if he were
> no longer there. It was another man, a stranger whose eyes
> were hateful and frightening. He seemed to look through
> me at some one else, and I seemed for a moment to be watch-
> ing some hidden place in his mind where there was something
> as evil and revengeful as I was. It frightened and fas-
> cinated me — and called to me, too; that's the hell of it!
>
> (III. 522)

Described here is the John Loving we never see in this play — the complete human being with his opposing natures fiercely alternating in a situation of sexual enticement. We see in Lucy's description the kind of lover Jamie suddenly becomes with Josie Hogan in *A Moon for the Misbegotten*, and just as suddenly stops being. O'Neill is here describing quite explicitly the Jekyll-Hyde duality he finds absolutely basic to human nature and which he will use as the basis for his dialogue in his plays to follow. There is no dialogue here, of course, because Lucy is simply describing a situation she has experienced, but O'Neill seems, through her description, to be laying the groundwork for the form of later situation and dialogue. Act Two of *Days Without End* is a more prophetic scene in the development of O'Neill's art than its importance to the plot of the play might suggest.

The opening scene of Act Three constitutes the old reenactment of a mother's death and John Loving's alternating hate and guilt in it follows the pattern of Lavinia's and Orin's conflicting responses in *Mourning Becomes Electra*. That Elsa does not actually die is unimportant. In at least two of O'Neill's eight drafts of the play she in fact does die,[7] and in the published version she goes through all the motions of dying but is miraculously saved by John's sudden religious conversion. In this scene, John continues relating the plot of his novel to Father Baird, this time, however, with Elsa present. When he gets to the part about the hero's adultery, Elsa slowly recognizes what has been going on from Lucy's earlier confession. Elsa is struck by each successive piece of information in the novel as though it were a death blow. It is Elsa's responses that create the central effect of this scene. Dream-like death blows are what she seems to be receiving as John's novel gets closer and closer to home. In other words, O'Neill kills his mother over and over in this scene and play. He kills her first in Elsa's reaction to hearing the novel's hero confess his adultery, second by reacting to the death of the fictional hero's wife in the novel, third by feeling Loving's cold stare at her after her series of shocks. As if to link the situation more specifically with his mother, O'Neill also has the distraught Elsa rush off into the cold, rainy night to catch her death — as Mary is described in *Long Day's Journey* as having rushed out into the fog in the midst of an earlier drug-frenzy. Finally, in Act Four, O'Neill again reenacts the death of his mother by placing Elsa in the familiar deathwatch posture under the loving-hating eyes of her divided husband.

The overall effect of all the killing and all the hysterical guilt in John which ensues is to bring John, John's hero, and perhaps O'Neill himself closer to Loving's prescribed suicide. One version of the play does in fact end with John's suicide. So we are back where we started in *Mourning Becomes Electra* — the circle of ever-recurrent hostility and ever-recurrent guilt seemingly never to end.

But in marked contrast in tone to what precedes it and what follows, we get Act Three, Scene Two — a scene full of relative calm and intellectual clarity. Thinking Elsa has simply gone to bed, John, Loving, and Father Baird settle down to discuss the implications of what has just happened. They begin by discussing the great economic depression the country is then in the throes of, which John sees as an explicit metaphor for the depression he is in the throes of, and O'Neill is thus making a metaphor for the depression *he* is in the throes of. John says that the only way for people to achieve "freedom" from their "terror" is to have the "courage" to face it, but that for most people, himself included, courage itself means terror. They are more afraid of the unknown results of their courage than of the terror they already know. Like the denizens of Harry Hope's saloon, they accept the "slavery" of the status quo. Loving, trying to deflate John's call for courage, labels "freedom" a "romantic delusion." "We are all," he says, "the slave to meaningless chance — electricity or something, which whirls us — on to Hercules!" Loving intends this phrase to indicate that life is mechanistic, philosophically meaningless; but John picks up the phrase:

> **John:** (*with a proud assertiveness*) . . . Very well!
> On to Hercules! Let us face that! Once we
> have accepted it *without evasion,* we can begin to
> create new goals for ourselves, ends for our
> days! A new discipline for life will spring into
> being, a new will and power to live, a new ideal
> to measure the value of our lives by!
>
> (III. 542. Emphasis added)

John believes that real change can come about only by the abandonment of evasion. The discussion is thus being forged into three mutually exclusive options, options which logically lead into the various alternative endings of the play, each version suiting one of the tentative intellectual resting-points of the rapidly shifting O'Neill. One resolution is Loving's terrifying nihilism, which can only lead to suicide; another is Father Baird's message of total confession and the acceptance of Christ (as in the published version); and the third is all that might be included under the banner "On to Hercules!" — the sheer physical and emotional strength to accept life as it is, without illusion.

In this scene, the Slade-like Loving seems to get the upper hand. John, he points out, is still being messianic. Evoking the rejected Lazarus, Loving calls John's new tone and message "the pseudo-Nietzschean savior I just evoked out of my past" and refers to that image as "an equally futile ghost." Loving throws everything into his barrel of illusions. Man's Herculean strength to endure without myths is but one more myth, he says. It is not John the realist he is attacking, of course, but still John the dreamer, who must always collapse before the hard-bitten realism of his iconoclastic side. There can be no saviors of any kind, says the O'Neill who will in a few years write so elaborately on this point in *The Iceman Cometh.* John is left to choose between blind suicide and blind faith.

The scene's strength, its intellectual clarity, also reveals O'Neill's weakness. O'Neill was still fighting his battle privately and intellectually. The certainty of John's reasoned hope is precisely countered by the certainty of Loving's reasoned lack of hope; and if the "leap of faith" required by Father Baird is possible for some, it was not possible for O'Neill, despite the version of the ending selected for presentation. What is missing in this discussion, as it is still missing in the unending ironies of Larry

Slade's rhetoric, is any sense of unreasoned human contact, of kinship like that evoked between Elsa and Lucy in the quite uncerebral second act. No real hostility flows among the characters in this third act scene. Loving states his position with irony but without genuine feeling; and the Father, so human early in the play, seems here reduced to a principle. Their attacks on one another are persuasive, but they never bite deep emotionally, and true human communication in O'Neill involves deep-biting emotional conflict. Nor do the characters seem to have much genuine affection for one another — unlike Elsa and Lucy. Father Baird, earlier genuinely fatherly, is now all Priest, as Loving is all Mephisto. And the abstract debate, that interminable debate in O'Neill's mind, cannot resolve the ancient and crucial problem to be or not to be.

The play's published ending is an escape. Involving none of the confession which has been promised, it is full instead of adolescent messianic outburst. The all-important "death" of Loving is, especially in the light of Lucy's earlier description of her self-contradictory lover, inconsistent and disappointing. By this action, O'Neill intends John to be "exorcising" the nihilistic part of his nature, but people do not throw off the evil halves of their natures in great mystical flashes — as though those halves could in fact be separated as Loving is from John. Both halves are inextricably intertwined in a single personality. All they can do is learn to recognize and accept — in short, to know themselves, and in knowing themselves to begin to know others. There are not two individuals, like John and Loving, in the personalities of Sid Davis, Con Melody, Theodore Hickman, Larry Slade, or Jamie Tyrone. In each case, there is just a single individual fiercely at war with himself. And true conversion, when it does occur in an O'Neill play, will not resemble John's sudden seeing of the light. It will rather be the acceptance of the ongoing shifts in everyone's feelings about reality. There is true conversion in O'Neill's drama, I believe, but certainly not the one which closes *Days Without End.*

Nevertheless, the ending of the play does suggest O'Neill refusing suicide and refusing to accept the permanence of desolation. It implies, really, not that a solution was at hand but that constant change in philosophical outlook was inevitable. O'Neill was here beginning to explore the nature of happy outcomes. Here it was religious conversion; in another play it would be the implicit acceptance of illusion; in a third it would be the rejection of illusion. Nothing worked, of course, but all the plays of this period in O'Neill's writing were leading him to the absolute confrontation with his "truth" of his last plays. *Days Without End* was the most significant step yet made toward that confrontation, a good deal more significant a step than the play which follows it.

Ah, Wilderness

Because of its great similarity to *Long Day's Journey* in setting and characters, *Ah, Wilderness* has been a more tempting subject for autobiographical probing than any other play except that later work.[8] Its parallels to the later play are obvious enough — I hope to point out some that have perhaps not been noticed — but it is important to note that in spite of its seeming autobiographical directness, this play is a good deal less "plainly" and "nakedly" revealing than *Days Without End* before it and the two cycle plays to follow in this discussion. The play is about ninety percent wish-fulfillment and ten percent the real thing. If anything, it is O'Neill's attempt to dramatize not his early life so much as his idealized recall of life before the Fall. The play is distinctly a yielding to illusion, and it may well be more than incidental that plays to follow it dwell so heavily on how desperate illusory memories of the past can make one when the day of "truth" arrives.

The parallels with *Long Day's Journey*, and with O'Neill's early life in general, are many; but the distortions far outnumber them. Nat Miller, the hero's father, is at times like James Tyrone, Sr., but far more often is his opposite. Nat tends to be pompous, he likes to drink, he is compulsively devoted to his profession, and he is the prisoner of certain illusions — all characteristics of the aging actor-father — but the pomposity is short-lived, the drinking controlled, the compulsion healthy, and the illusions — which concern a distaste for bluefish — the subject for a good deal of harmless family mirth. Nat, unlike James, is truly generous with his money, and as a result of his openness and good nature sees his financial condition improve at the play's end. Further, at the urging of his son, he actually reads and enjoys some of the modern authors he and his wife have earlier been so apprehensive about, whereas the elder Tyrone sticks stubbornly to his Bible and Shakespeare. Nat also treats his son's adolescent interest in sex with great understanding, which hardly accords with what we know of the senior O'Neills.

Similarly, Essie Miller is represented as a trifle snobbish, a little guilt-ridden, and a touch hysterical — but hardly in ways to approach the excesses of Mary Tyrone. Her snobbery is short-lived, her guilt concerns her being over-weight, and her hysteria relates chiefly to her son's keeping late hours. She communicates openly with everyone, her little deception about the bluefish is largely a family joke, and she is attentive to the feelings of others. Her emotions are balanced throughout — just uncontrolled enough to enable her to release all her hostility and all her affection. In her great emotional stability, Essie is an even more romanticized mother-figure in the play than her husband is a romanticized father-figure. We get nothing here of a troubled past; she seems miraculously free of deeper anxieties.

The characters who come much closer to anticipating central figures in *Long Day's Journey* are the withdrawn spinster Lily Miller and the alcoholic gambler Sid Davis, Essie's brother who cannot keep a job. Lily is far more like Mary Tyrone than is Essie, and Sid directly parallels brother Jamie. Lily is caught up in a past she never discusses explicitly but which haunts her persistently. She is also puritanical about drink, Sid's greatest failing, but she is inseparably tied to Sid, as O'Neill's mother was to Jamie. She is alternately rigid and sympathetic toward Sid, who has been wooing her unsuccessfully for close to twenty years. When troubled, Lily retires to rest in a parlor which, like so many alcoves and upstairs rooms in O'Neill's plays, suggests the spare room which is Mary's addictive retreat. But in several all-important respects, Lily is unlike Mary. She has been spared the pain of childbirth so devastating to Mary, and she has been spared the immediate anxieties of marriage, which Mary cannot contend with. Lily is also capable of being Sid's Earth Mother. Their strangely satisfactory relationship in fact constitutes one of the most important statements of the play. Such relationships are the best that troubled people achieve on this planet, O'Neill seems to be saying — and for O'Neill, troubled people means most people, the contented Millers being merely a fantasy. Sid the sinner will forever sin, and Lily the forgiver will forever forgive. They can never marry, though, because Lily can "never marry a man who drinks" and Sid can never triumph over that "good man's failing." The relationship of Lily and Sid is almost precisely what Hickey tells us about his relationship with his wife Evelyn in *The Iceman Cometh*, but without the murderous guilt, and without marriage. Unlike Evelyn and Hickey, Lily and Sid are totally protected from one another, even though like them they are totally inter-dependent. A mock stability has been created out of instability, and O'Neill seems to be pleading that it be left at that. Of course it can only be left at that because of the storybook generosity, financial and emotional, of the Millers.

Modelled on Jamie,[9] whose alcohol rendered him the uproarious buffoon and whose sobriety found him submissive and crestfallen, Sid is here freed from the mask of savage cynicism which the far more insecure Jamie could never escape. Sid dominates the stage when he is on it, as does Jamie in all his dramatic variants. In some ways, Sid is the most Jamie-like character of all. The texture of his revelry at the dinner table in Act Two — exploding Nat's bluefish illusion and too-often told tales, decimating Lily especially with laughter — is a vision of Jamie often referred to in other plays but never so vividly dramatized, except perhaps in the Jim-Phil Hogan exchanges in *A Moon for the Misbegotten*. Sid is Hickey the dispenser of joy as recalled from earlier days by the misbegotten band in *The Iceman Cometh*. He is not Hickey the false savior. Sid's antics at the dinner table leave us physically weak with laughter, beyond the reach of despair — until the next morning. And as the dispenser of joy, the Jamie-figure in this play is probably no romanticizing of the past. Sid at the Miller's festive board is the true lord of misrule that the real Jamie could be at those marvelous moments so treasured by O'Neill.

Not altogether romanticized either are Sid's more sober relations with the hero Richard, relations which constitute a fairly precise replay of the O'Neill brothers' relations at the time of O'Neill's earliest escapades with wine and women. To be sure, the tempting Wint of the play who comes to lure Richard into "evil ways" is also Jamie in his mask of cor-rupter of younger brothers. But the understanding Sid who holds Rich-ard's head following his night out and who talks with him in morning-after wisdom about the effects of his roadhouse adventure reflects Jamie in the way O'Neill would eulogize him in the remainder of his plays. Miss-ing in the Sid-Richard relationship are the less friendly exchanges which culminate in Edmund's attack on Jamie late in *Long Day's Journey*, but the warmth of mutual love and trust so movingly captured in the later play are also persuasively rendered at moments in *Ah, Wilderness*.

But the moments are too few. Dialogues between Sid and Nat, Nat and Essie, Nat and Richard, and Richard and Essie all are dominated by O'Neill's determination to trowel honey over bitterness. While there are traces in each exchange of attitudes and situations in *Long Day's Journey*, all encounters are forced to turn positive. The hostility in them is quickly suppressed and broad affection easily dominates. Sid and Nat do not compete; they converse in man-to-man respect and understanding. Nat more than tolerates his wife's nagging concerns and she his surface petu-lance. Richard and Nat at one point directly prefigure Edmund and James Tyrone, Sr. as Richard proclaims radical doctrine and lauds the new icon-oclastic literature, but Nat responds with the patience of a good bourgeois father and later reads Shavian wit in chuckling delight. Though the rhythm of the dialogue occasionally has the effect of true kinship, the un-happiness seems so trivial and the happiness so emphasized that the effect too often verges on rank sentimentality. Nat's grumpy stubbornness, Sid's alcoholic aggressiveness, and Essie's mental fogginess are all played so as to achieve the effect of harmless crotchets. There is little authentic swing-ing of the pendulum between the hostile and the loving in this play.

Of Richard Miller himself, who by rights should be central to this discussion, there is little really to say. O'Neill has in fact done what he said he did: written a play indicating what "he would have liked [his] boyhood to have been"[10] — and such plays by their nature do not go very deep. The great shock of O'Neill's adolescence is here made into the common disillusionment associated with adolescent love, and the result has all the conviction of situation comedy today. Paralleling O'Neill's rebellious escape following his terrible discovery, Richard, on learning of his beloved Muriel's defection, goes off to the roadhouse for his encounter with a "tart." This episode, which certainly contributed to the play's notoriety, is a trivializing of O'Neill's late adolescent adventures. The gum-chewing Belle herself is a creditable first sketch for the tarts in *Iceman;* but Richard's gawkish reactions, his fight with the bartender, and even his drunken poetry are appropriate fare for Tuesday night television. The hurt in the play being inconsequential, the reactions are essentially trumped up. And so are they even more in Richard's reunion with his beloved Muriel on the pier, a sort of counterpoint to the roadhouse scene. In both scenes, O'Neill wants to capture the alternating rhythms of emotional conversation. Muriel, like Belle, goes from attraction to repulsion and back to attraction in split-second reversals — with the malleable Richard responding in kind. But as the effect of the bar scene is merely adolescent embarrassment, the effect of the later scene is merely adolescent sentimentality. Though O'Neill wants to get back to authentic human relationships in these scenes, he has not created true human beings to work with. Richard's Adam's apple works very hard in this play, but he never convinces us that he feels any kind of real pain or joy. O'Neill, trying to write about his adolescence as though there were no Fall, ends with a central figure the least successfully conceived of any among his later plays.

Nevertheless, despite the determination to evade in *Ah, Wilderness,* there is also the determination to forgive. The forgiveness is perhaps most apparent in his characterization of Jamie in Sid Davis. Jamie had of course long been forgiven by O'Neill. In *Lazarus Laughed* O'Neill had grossly distorted his brother's personality in attempting to forgive him. Sid's characterization suggests a truer forgiveness, one which refuses to whitewash, to bend his brother's better qualities into saintliness. Appealing as he is, Sid will remain the rest of his days a drunk and ne'er-do-well. And O'Neill's next play will continue the trend toward forgiveness without whitewash, this time dealing with his father. O'Neill was in the process of forgiving his family well before *Long Day's Journey,* but he was still a long way from forgiving himself—and the creation of Richard Miller did little to advance him in that direction.

Both *Days Without End* and *Ah, Wilderness* are plays in which O'Neill reveals himself unwilling to accept the stasis implicit in the ending of *Mourning Becomes Electra* and very possibly in the discarded plays of his long cycle. Both have endings which can only be described as wish-fulfilling, but both contain dialogue in which the old rhythm of kinship is heard anew—perhaps without O'Neill's having been quite aware of it. Stated in other words, when O'Neill tried to think through his problems, he could only come up with unsatisfactory solutions which he quickly rejected; but as he let his natural instinct for human communication flow again, he communicated a sense of the ambience of deep human relationships of the sort we encountered first in *Bound East for Cardiff*. To be sure, Lucy and Elsa have only one scene in *Days Without End* before O'Neill returns to his mental diagramming; and *Ah, Wilderness*, despite the sporadic efforts of Sid Davis, keeps falling back into its never-never land atmosphere. But the instinct once again set loose in these plays was to gather force. It is not the attempt at a happy ending in *A Touch of the Poet* which is best remembered but the personality of its central figure and the closely related texture of its dialogue. For the first time since the sea plays, in fact, the rhythm of kinship was once more to be a play's dominant quality.

7 Remnants of a Cycle

A Touch of the Poet

DECEPTIVELY SIMPLE on the surface, *A Touch of the Poet* is actually among O'Neill's more complex plays and must be approached from a variety of directions. I shall therefore divide this discussion into three conventional categories—characters, plot, and dialogue—though these categories will be treated always in terms dictated by the theme of this study as a whole. My discussion of characters will focus on the "characters" of O'Neill's family, my discussion of plots will suggest that O'Neill was here departing from the past in the way he constructed a play, and my discussion of dialogue will deal with the re-emerging rhythm of kinship.

Character

There should be little doubt that *A Touch of the Poet* is primarily a play about James O'Neill, Sr.: actor, father, and proud Irishman. Con Melody is a proud man who, having known success in earlier days, is now forced to live in what he considers undeserved obscurity. He is also like the old actor in that the past he recalls seems linked to the role O'Neill's father played throughout so much of his career. Con thinks of himself as having once been a kind of young Edmond Dantes in his brilliant Napoleonic uniform,[1] and like that character Con feels wronged by ill-meaning adversaries, against whom he must seek revenge. Con, like James Tyrone, uses his illusions about his glorious past to obscure his humble, shanty-Irish origins. Both behave like lords of a manor that exists more in their imaginations than in fact; and for both, the money needed to perpetuate their illusions is in short supply. It is their insistence upon living out their fantasies without the wherewithal to do so that irritates their outspoken offspring. Sara Melody, like the Tyrone brothers in regard to their father, views her voluble father as a figure who ought to "know better."

But Con's illusions go farther than do James's and take us into the realm of O'Neill's own problems rather than strictly his father's. Con's recall of the "Melody Castle" of his childhood — the very name suggesting its illusory nature[2] — stands squarely for O'Neill's illusory recall of existence before the Fall, his earthly paradise with mother yet unstained. Similarly does the end of illusion as represented in this play have more to do with O'Neill himself than with his father. Con in the end must murder the little *mare* who symbolizes his aristocratic pipe dreams, as O'Neill knows that to bring himself back to reality he must rid himself permanently of memories of his mother (la mère). Con's shooting the mare late in the play, however, does not destroy memories, as O'Neill cannot destroy his memories. Rather, that shooting only reenacts once again O'Neill's fantasy killing of his mother, as Con's description of the dying mare makes clear:

> . . . the look in her eyes by the lantern light with
> life ebbing out of them — wondering and sad, but still
> trusting, not reproaching me — with no fear in them —
> proud, understanding pride — loving me — she saw I was
> dying with her. She understood! She forgave me!
> (Yale edition, p. 169)[3]

This is the image of the dying mother we encountered first in *The Great God Brown* and will hear described in its ultimate form in *A Moon for the Misbegotten*. Thus, while Con obviously stands for O'Neill's father in his broader outlines, as Con's struggle with his illusions becomes critical, he stands more and more for O'Neill himself. We are back with O'Neill's old circle of hostility and guilt, even though in this play there is the clear desire to cast off, to exorcise, the memories that initiate its eternal recurrence.

Then there is Sara Melody, in whom O'Neill synthesizes the reactions to their father of both O'Neill brothers. Sara is attractive, intelligent, articulate youth unwilling to accept the illusions of an older generation, especially as those illusions cause others to suffer. Yet also like the brothers, Sara is quite the prisoner of those same illusions, as she comes to realize by the end of the play. For all she tries to fight her similarity to

Con, it keeps breaking out, especially when Con shows signs of admitting what he is. Sara's identification with her father becomes particularly strong as Con finally does precisely what she has been urging him to do — face himself. She panics near the end because she realizes that her father's admitting he is nothing more than a brawling, conniving Irish shebeen-keeper makes her the conniving Irish wench she fears she really is. But she panics still more because she realizes that her father's new vulgarity in speech and behavior are as much a pose as was that of "Major Cornelius Melody." What she really fears, in short, is that both she and her father have *no* basic identity — that they are only what they decide to be for the moment, or conversely, that anything they decide to be is in the last analysis illusory. This same fear is repeated in Sara's thoughts about her lover Simon Harford. She can never resolve the dilemma over whether she truly loves Simon or is only after him for his money because that dilemma is unresolvable. Either alternative is true, or both alternatives are illusions which grow out of feelings of the moment. Sara is like the playwright wondering what is left when everything is revealed as illusion, the playwright who will shortly probe that problem so deeply in *The Iceman Cometh*. Sara is very much the rational part of O'Neill, and as such, like characters representing the rational O'Neill before her (Lavinia Mannon) and after (Larry Slade), carries her logic to inescapably despairing conclusions.

Nevertheless, Sara does not despair. Nora sees to that. "Shame on you to cry when you have love," says Nora to end the play and fulfill her inevitably sentimental function as all-Irish-American Earth Mother.[4] Nora seems most akin to characters who are referred to but who never appear in other plays. It may be Marie Brantome described in *Mourning Becomes Electra* that O'Neill is trying to "bring to life" in Nora. It may also be the mother James Tyrone, Sr. describes in *Long Day's Journey*, the long-suffering Irish washer-woman who was O'Neill's paternal grandmother. This latter idea ties Nora more closely to Con as representative of the more earthy and open paternal side of O'Neill's background, and also allows her to be a version of the ideal mother O'Neill longed for and which he felt his more stable father actually had.

The problem with Nora is that she is just that — an ideal — and ideals tend to fare badly as dramatic characterizations. Nora's unvarying support and her predictable solutions to problems do little to enhance the otherwise convincing power of this play. It may well be that O'Neill, in recognition of this fact, created such later figures as Evelyn Hickman and the elder Mrs. Tyrone only in the descriptions of their husbands or sons. Love represented in the near-saintly qualities of these women is more convincing when treated through memory. A truer representation of love in this play resides in dialogue involving Con himself — dialogue which is as hostile and explosive as it is spontaneous and loving.

Consistent with his practice of including qualities of his own mother even in his Earth Mothers, O'Neill also endows Nora with an overworked sense of guilt and a haunting fear. Here the cause of the guilt is not drugs, of course, but that other O'Neill bugaboo, illicit sex. Nora's guilt is over her premarital relations with Con. It is their special fear of church and priest that especially links Nora and Mary Tyrone. Neither is capable of confession, so terrible do they feel their sins have been. But even in guilt, Nora, unlike Mary, comes through as maudlin and conventional. The absence of a single aggressive reaction in Nora toward any member of her family suggests the limitations of her characterization.

Somewhat as he had with Aunt Lily in *Ah, Wilderness*, O'Neill here creates a second female role more vividly to suggest his mother and her addictive state, a figure who assumes major prominence in this play's sequel. She is Deborah Harford, whose Yankee name and genteel breeding place her directly in the Quinlan-Mannon-Cavan[5] tradition, as the name Melody may be associated with the names O'Neill, Brantome, and Tyrone. Deborah, who comes to forestall or delay her son's marriage into this shanty-Irish family, makes only a single appearance in the play, but it is a memorable one. Like Mary, she is delicate in appearance and exquisite in manner. She is attracted by the swashbuckling Con as the actor James Tyrone had once attracted the delicate Mary. Similarly, Deborah's rejection of Con's advances begins with her recognition of the liquor on his breath, as Mary's rejection of James first grew out of his drinking.

More to the point, however, is Deborah's tendency to withdraw. Here she is most like Mary. Even as she converses with Sara, she withdraws into her private world of dreams, that world she has inherited from her late father, an idealistic old revolutionary who finally found his long-sought "freedom" by withdrawing from all human intercourse into his "little Temple of Liberty," a small, enclosed retreat constructed in the corner of his garden. Deborah's struggles to avoid the same permanent withdrawal into that little Temple in this play and its sequel parallel Mary's struggles to stay out of her spare room, which similarly provides a freedom from life's severities. In addition, Deborah's illusions center on her being the secret mistress of Napoleon — a fantasy paralleling Mary's narcotic memories of her "affair" with the "Count of Monte Cristo."

O'Neill makes some changes in the Mannon-Brantome pattern here which he uses again in *Long Day's Journey* to suggest a basic similarity between his parents despite their more spectacular surface differences.

Deborah's fantasies and withdrawal are presented as eccentricities which actually parallel Con's dreams of glory. Both recite Byron (Deborah in *More Stately Mansions*), both fancy themselves as isolated by their uniqueness, both come by very different routes from similarly humble origins. Immigrant peasant and Yankee lady are seen as living in essentially the same illusory condition — as O'Neill felt his shanty and lace-curtain progenitors both depended on quite similar illusions to maintain their equilibrium. This idea is picked up in *Long Day's Journey* in statements paralleling James's whiskey with Mary's morphine. It should be added, however, that as James never loses his grasp on reality, so Con always is aware of what he is doing. Deborah and Mary, on the other hand, do lose contact with reality, and hence the continuing difference in O'Neill's feelings about his father's difficulties and his mother's.

But the most surprising quality of Deborah Harford in this play is the essential lightness with which O'Neill treats her. That she verges on being a comic figure in her illusions suggests that O'Neill, as in *Ah, Wilderness*, was trying to put his mother into perspective, a perspective lost anew in *More Stately Mansions*, where Deborah becomes a rather terrifying figure. In *A Touch of the Poet*, the bitterness so evident in O'Neill's treatment of the Mannons has become a kind of whimsical, detached amusement. O'Neill has here maintained a distance from his pain which allows him to make all the figures associated with it amusing. Of course, by the same token, the play's emotional penetration of its audience is also less than that of earlier and later plays, though it ranks high even in that regard among American family plays of the twentieth century.

So we have them again — the four figures of *Long Day's Journey*, with Jamie distinctly de-emphasized. The Jamie Cregan who is Con's former military subordinate is like Jamie Tyrone only in that he and the old campaigner seem continually in each other's company. O'Neill has carefully avoided putting any of the real Jamie's personality into him, perhaps for fear of upstaging Con, perhaps because the real Jamie was not so much on O'Neill's mind at the time he wrote this play.

Plots

More important, perhaps, than what O'Neill was doing with the major characters in this comedy is what he seems to be doing with its dramatic action. On the surface, its plot, or plots, again seem to be borrowings, though this time not from anything resembling Aeschylus or Euripides. Instead of high tragedy, O'Neill is working here with various types of low comedy. One of its plots involves an Irish peasant father advising his daughter on how to trap a wealthy suitor into marriage by tricking him into having sexual relations with her. Another is about an Irish peasant humiliating an arrogant aristocrat. O'Neill would naturally be at ease with these plots in that they both come out of that same Irish folkloristic tradition which had already inspired John Millington Synge and Sean O'Casey.[6] As in the past, O'Neill uses ready-made plots as the framework for a great variety of emotional display; but here such plots are little more than humorous folk anecdotes, and the effect shifts from tears and anxiety in the earlier plays to action rich with Irish laughter in this one.

O'Neill's use of low comedy in the plotting of this play may grow in part out of O'Neill's growing sophistication about his art — and about himself. Con's hints that Sara take Simon Harford to bed and the spelled-out intricacy of Sara's efforts to that end have an obviousness about them which seems to suggest that we not take such manipulations seriously. And certainly Con's overwrought description of the revenge he intends to take on Simon's father is intended to evoke a far lighter response from the audience than it does from Con's anxious wife. There is a degree of mock melodrama in the play which evokes responses in us of a mixed variety. We may occasionally be concerned, but we are more often amused. In O'Neill's earlier plays, we were asked to take the characters as seriously as they took themselves. In this play, we are asked not to take them as seriously as they take themselves. Our perspective here is like that of Larry Slade on his tavern-mates in *The Iceman Cometh* — a kind of detached, even paternalistic, certainly amused devotion. Major Cornelius Melody thinks of himself as acting out a heroic revenge plot — something along the lines of *The Count of Monte Cristo* — but his audience knows that what is being re-enacted is actually an old Irish anecdote.

The increase in sophistication O'Neill asks of his audience in *A Touch of the Poet* may represent a further development of O'Neill's emotional and artistic growth. We have already seen something of that growth in the relative lightness with which he treats the chief character standing for his mother in the play, and certainly Con's activities reflect an objectivity regarding his father never before so evident. Con's revenge plot may also be a spoofing of O'Neill's own earlier melodramatic excesses. It may reflect O'Neill's feeling that his earlier plays were basically rather similar to his father's over-stated and over-produced vehicle. O'Neill's middle-period plots embody, after all, many of the same elements as *The Count of Monte Cristo*. The masking and unmasking of *The Great God Brown*, the deceptions and asides of *Strange Interlude*, the conspiracies and pursuits of *Mourning Becomes Electra* may all have been conscious or unconscious corollaries to the story of Edmond Dantes. In writing *A Touch of the Poet* O'Neill may be seeing in himself the pretentious emulator of his father. He may here be recognizing that in part at least he had been seeking to create the kind of stir his father had by using many of his father's methods. Such methods had worked for O'Neill, of course, very much as they had worked for his father. The comic vision comes with acceptance.

The notion of plots and plottings has another ramification as well. Sara plots and schemes a great deal in this play. She plots and schemes to get Simon Harford to marry her against his parents' wishes, and in this context she is oblivious to whether she loves him or not. To gain wealth and position, she says, she will "do anything"; and as a result the tone of her assault on the Harford name and fortune is wrapped in secretiveness and manipulation. Love, she says, has no place in such a package. But Sara does love Simon, and in describing her attempt to seduce Simon, she repeatedly speaks of how in his presence she forgets her schemes and gives way unabashedly to her feelings. What O'Neill implies here, in contrast to his middle period plays, is that when an authentic human relationship occurs, not the fulfillment merely of some previously conceived manipulation, the result is an uncontrollable flow of human emotion. Sara finds that in relation to Simon—and to her father in the final analysis —her immediate feelings must define her and that her plots and schemes only disguise her. Plotting is her means of deception, of herself as well as others, whereas spontaneous, open feeling is her best means of facing herself as well as others. The contrast between Sara's scheming and her outbursts of uncontrived love suggest an O'Neill increasingly aware that excessive plotting—by playwright perhaps as well as character—damages human beings, and that open confession of feeling—by playwright as well as character—saves.

Both the plots of *A Touch of the Poet* and the plottings in it are means by which characters perpetrate illusion. The abandonment of plotting and deceit is the means by which they survive. In this play, we get the first of several instances in O'Neill where the play comments on itself— and on the playwright's earlier work. O'Neill was to use similar material for the same purpose in writing *A Moon for the Misbegotten*.

Dialogue

The final question, then, is the nature of that which saves: the spontaneous, uncontrived responses of its central character toward those closest to him. The dialogue involving Con Melody almost parallels that in the all-but-plotless sea plays. We never see Sara with Simon, so her freely expressed love is merely an idyll as far as the play is concerned. That love is given no stage life because it is not represented in dialogue. The love which has living form on stage is not Sara's, nor even Nora's in her self-demeaning, maudlin expressions of support and affection, but Con's, in his explosive reactions to Nora — and to Sara. Con expresses his love by means of his constant, uncontrollable alternation of verbal abuse and verbal embrace. Typically, whenever Con's aristocratic illusions are questioned by his wife or daughter, he attacks viciously. But each attack is followed by a wave of regret, of apology, and of demonstrated affection. The more the hurt inflicted on him, the greater the attack, and the more sincere the reflex love. The resulting ebb and flow of emotion in Con's speeches seems more studied than what I have been calling the rhythm of kinship in the earlier plays, more part of O'Neill's conscious art. It seems here to be developing into a theatrical *language* of kinship, that language which will become the dominant language of his last plays. The following excerpt establishes a prevailing mood in this play against which all the plottings and deceptions so evident in earlier plays begin to seem paltry:

Melody: . . . I tried my best to educate you, after
we came to America — until I saw it was hopeless.
Nora: You did, surely. And I tried, too, but —
Melody: You won't even cure yourself of that damned
peasant's brogue. And your daughter is becoming as bad.
Nora: She only puts on the brogue to tease you. She
can speak as fine as any lady in the land if
she wants.
Melody: (*Is not listening — sunk in bitter brooding*)
But, in God's name, who am I to reproach anyone with anything? Why don't you tell me to
examine my own conduct?
Nora: You know I'd never.
Melody: (*Stares at her — again he is moved — quietly*)
No. I know you would not, Nora. (*He looks
away — after a pause*) I owe you an apology
for what happened last night.
Nora: Don't think of it.
Melody: (. . .) Faith, I'd a drink too many, talking
over old times with Jamie Cregan.

Nora: I know.

Melody: I am afraid I may have—the thought of old
     times—I become bitter. But you understand,
     it was the liquor talking, if I said anything
     to wound you.

Nora: I know it.

Melody: (*Deeply moved . . .*) You're a sweet, kind
     woman, Nora—too kind. (*He kisses her*)

Nora: (. . .) Ah, Con darlin', what do I care what
     you say when the black thoughts are on you?
     Sure, don't you know I love you?

Melody: (*A sudden revulsion of feeling convulses his
     face. He bursts out with disgust, pushing
     her away from him*) For God's sake, why don't
     you wash your hair? It turns my stomach with
     its stink of onions and stew! (. . .)

Nora: (*Dully*) I do be washin' it often to plaze you. But
     when you're standin' over the stove all day,
     you can't help—

Melody: Forgive me, Nora. Forget I said that.

                              (Yale edition, pp. 41–43)

This passage is a good one because its flow of feeling is entirely natural while at the same time that flow seems carefully accounted for. The
whole range of Con's emotions is present: the anger followed by the guilt
followed by the dependency followed by the pride followed by the love—
and all in turn followed by new irritation and new anger. There is no insult not followed by guilt, no forgiveness not followed by new insult.
Everything said is meant sincerely, while no single emotion is dominant.
Nor is any single emotion consistent with any other emotion. And the insult is never the "liquor talking" as Con is wont to say (along with Sid
Davis, Hickey, the Tyrone men, and Erie Smith); it is always the man
himself. But no less the man himself is the all-out expression of sorrow
and love. As Con, with all his blather, is basically not a hypocrite, there
are few hypocrites among O'Neill's later characters. Everything said in
the heat of emotion is meant, and most things are spoken in the heat of
emotion. Out of feelings stated in such a manner emerges O'Neill's new
language of kinship.

The dialogue is dominated only by Con, however. Nora's patience
can always be anticipated, as can Sara's spite where Con is involved.
Nora's feelings never shift in response to Con, Sara's only occasionally.
Sara has strong feelings, of course, but they are more like those in *Strange*

Interlude, reflected in asides and mini-soliloquies rather than spoken directly to Con, from whom she wishes to disguise her large measure of fellow feeling. In later plays, when O'Neill lets both parties to an emotional exchange go through the sudden shifts Con goes through here, sparks really fly, and concomitantly the sense of kinship is more deeply established. There is some of that between Sara and Con, but it is repeatedly checked by Sara's unwillingness to state her true feelings directly. She is the holdover from the middle period as far as her relationship with Con is concerned. And Nora's responses are all sentimentality. They never vary. It is Con's show throughout, as O'Neill intended it to be.

The basis of such dialogue as I have quoted from this play is found as early as the sea plays, but what one hears in those early plays is only O'Neill's fine sense of the basic rhythms of human communication. In this play we also become aware of a growing understanding of the way closely related human beings seek to communicate — as opposed to the ways they try not to communicate, which had been the central concern of O'Neill's middle period. And by communication alone, we begin to hear the plays suggesting, can man avoid or defer the horror his logical systems must lead him to.

Nevertheless, in spite of the sense of kinship created in this play, the undeniably loving portrait of its central figure, and its unlimited good humor, *A Touch of the Poet* really does end on a despairing note — as O'Neill, despite his efforts to the contrary, seems to have realized in *More Stately Mansions*. It is the same despair which nags at Seth's Shenandoah chanty and the "blessed isles" images in *Mourning Becomes Electra* and which will blossom forth in *The Iceman Cometh*. When one casts out illusion, what replaces it is also illusion — that, or total emptiness. Con's shebeen-keeper posture at the end of the play is every bit as much a pose as that of Major Cornelius Melody, as Sara realizes. The end of the play finds Con a seeming victor and Nora talking about hope through love, but the rational part remains unconvinced. Sara's perspective is finally the same as Larry Slade's. The happy endings of O'Neill's recent plays were beginning to run out, and with the return of O'Neill's gloom in the mid 1930s there were to be no more happy endings, no further attempts to "solve" the human dilemma. But by the same token, only *The Iceman Cometh* ends with a death, and that for quite specific reasons I shall treat in my discussion of that play. In the other plays, the major characters — beaten, tired, almost lifeless — go on living, not in enclosures like Lavinia's mansion, but in the worlds they had already been inhabiting. They go on living possessed of frail new understandings born of the knowledge that they have been in authentic communication with another human being.

More Stately Mansions

Two nine-act plays from the great cycle of which they were both a part intervened between the completion of *A Touch of the Poet* in 1936 and the first draft of *More Stately Mansions* in 1938[7]; and whatever happened to O'Neill during their composition resulted in a return to despair which sentimentally optimistic elements in the unpublished typescript of the play[8] do not allay. *More Stately Mansions* is a play about Simon Harford's failure in marriage, failure in business, and failure in understanding his relationship with his mother — all failures which follow what look for a time like bright prospects in each one of those enterprises.

Philosophically, *More Stately Mansions* points the way directly to *The Iceman Cometh*. The quasi-hopeful implications of Con Melody's rejection of his illusions in *A Touch of the Poet* are squelched in the scene which opens *More Stately Mansions* in the recorded version of its 1964 production in New York. In this scene Jamie Cregan is given a speech which makes clear not only a shift in Con's attitudes before his death but also in O'Neill's. Having tried to believe that man might be better off without his pipe dreams, O'Neill finally gave up the struggle. Says Jamie of Con:

> He could have drunk a keg a day and lived for twenty
> years yet, if the pride and spirit wasn't killed in-
> side him ever since the night that he tried to challenge
> that Yankee coward Harford to a duel and him and me got
> beat by the police and arrested.[9]

By the time he wrote this scene, O'Neill saw Con's "rehabilitation" the way he was to see that of the alcoholics at Harry Hope's saloon, as an experiment in cruel futility. And further, as nothing was left for Con but the quick, grim death O'Neill now envisions for him, so for most of mankind the so-called facing of reality must now be for O'Neill a short road to some form of meaningless self-annihilation. The ability to bear a totally absurd universe is reserved for only the very few — a very few who assume heroic dimensions in O'Neill's last plays.

The fixed, rational view of life's worthlessness in this play, begun with the report of Con's final days, is reinforced and varied through the statements and experiences of each of its central characters, as though O'Neill wished to keep the intellectual certainty of futility before us at all times — lest he slip back into sentimental ways. The Deborah Harford of this play, when she is not off on one of her periodic flights of fantasy, speaks with sobering clarity:

> If life had meaning, then we might properly expect
> its end to have as much significance as — the period at
> the closing of a simple sentence, say. But it has no
> meaning, and that death is no more than the muddy well
> into which I and a dead cat are cast aside indifferently!
>   (Yale edition, p. 30)[10]

These views of Deborah's come to be shared by her son Simon, who perhaps more than any other character in O'Neill's plays suggests the author at his most tormented and his most cynical. Facing his own greed and lust after many years of considering himself an idealist, Simon concludes that the only real "evil" in the world is "the stupid theory that man is naturally what we call virtuous and good instead of being what he is, a hog" (Yale edition, p. 172). Following a pattern previously established by Orin Mannon and John Darling, Simon states that he is planning two books. These two books may stand for the two great periods of O'Neill's playwriting as he may have seen them in 1938: the first hopeful and idealistic, the second, like Orin's, increasingly hard-bitten and dominated by the total certainty of man's bankruptcy of spirit. But Simon goes farther than Orin. He even rejects his second book, nihilistic in its conclusions though it is, because any book at all would imply some lost worth to life, and all worth to Simon now, as to O'Neill, must be illusory.

Reinforcing Deborah's and Simon's explicit statements are the carefully arranged actions of the main characters, which most notably demonstrate the close relationship between making love and making money. Simon discovers the whole of man's rapacity present in himself and his wife. Despite his seeming commitment to ideals, his "touch of the poet," the grasping and treacherous side of Simon's nature must be predominant in the business world. What surprises Simon is not only that his time is increasingly occupied by his business activities, but that he also quite enjoys giving free rein to his rapacious side. He finds further that Sara's nature parallels his own. She seems to turn away from her maternal instincts and her natural altruism, and becomes cruel and manipulative once her acquisitive nature has been aroused. And it is her acquisitive nature, Simon becomes convinced, which is her basic nature, since she seems so adept at handling its demands. Similarly, although Deborah seems honest in her desire to be a good, loving grandmother, she has long been absorbed in fantasies which identify her as more possessive than Sara and quite as willing (though no longer able) to use her sexual attractions to acquire power. What the central characters do in the play, as well as what they say, seems amply to bear out their disquisitions on human corruptibility.

O'Neill's condemnation of the human spirit in this play is also evident in the character of Joel Harford, Simon's tight-lipped brother — a Lavinia Mannon who possesses none of the vitality O'Neill gives that earlier accuser. Joel is tempted sexually, as was Vinnie, but in him lust seems warped and paltry. It is never a sign, as it was in Vinnie, of healthy human impulses fighting their way through. Joel is a self-righteous moralist who considers that since he alone has a clear vision of "the right," he alone may pass judgment on others; and he does so with what he considers surgical precision. O'Neill obviously despises Joel most of all. If Simon stands for an O'Neill committing crimes against others out of a deep disillusionment with life, Joel is the vindictive O'Neill who is far worse because he refuses, or is afraid, ever to expose himself to an authentic human relationship. Joel's is the voice of a dessicated puritanism. O'Neill always hates the judge (in himself as in others) more than he does the sinner.

As usual, autobiography is central to the work. Although O'Neill here totally dismisses the image of his brother Jamie — the puritanical Joel is surely not such an image — his feelings about his late father's career are in evidence early in the play. Simon's late father, the successful Yankee trader, has ended his days near bankruptcy. He had over-estimated his potential and engaged in opportunistic land deals — activities which certainly anticipate those of James Tyrone, Sr. Simon absorbs his father's company, taking on himself the reputation of the Harford name, as by the time this play was written O'Neill has totally overshadowed his father's reputation in his father's own field. O'Neill's feelings about his father are thus rather precisely if minimally represented in *More Stately Mansions*.

Also as usual, the more important action of the play relates to O'Neill's complex of feelings associated with his mother. Following the familiar pattern, Deborah resembles Mary Tyrone physically, and like Mary she has fantasies into which she withdraws when life is too much for her. Deborah's dreams of being a "rich adventuress" in the court of Napoleon parallel Mary's dream of her courtship by the "Count of Monte Cristo," and the "little Temple of Liberty" to which Deborah withdraws certainly parallels Mary's spare room and all the horrors associated with it in O'Neill's mind. Deborah is still more like Mary in the increasing impenetrability of her withdrawals. Deborah senses the oncoming permanence of her condition in terms which precisely express what O'Neill imagines as his mother's state of mind in *Long Day's Journey*. Looking forward to her fate at the end of the play, Deborah says:

> . . . in the end — and I have reached the end —
> the longing for a moment's unthinking peace,
> a second's unquestioning acceptance of one's
> self, becomes so terrible that I would do
> anything, give anything to escape! . . . The
> temptation to escape — open the door — step
> boldly across the threshold.
> . . . .
> It would be so easy for me! Like pushing open a door
> in the mind and then passing through the free-
> dom of one's lifelong desire!
>
> (Yale edition, pp. 28–29)

The fear of a mother's permanent withdrawal is still the context of O'Neill's greatest pain.

But there is a difference between O'Neill's treatment of his old agony in this play and in earlier plays. Here, as in *A Touch of the Poet*, O'Neill seems more detached and self-controlled in dealing with his pain. In *A Touch of the Poet*, that more detached quality revealed itself in lightness and humor. Here there is an underlying scientific, or would-be scientific, tone. Emotions feel numbed in this play, and O'Neill seems bent on examining them in their numbed state with a precision which, ironically perhaps, suggests Joel's precision. O'Neill seems determined throughout most of this play to understand first of all his conflicting fantasies — fantasies associated with the past, and fantasies associated with the present. His fantasies associated with the past, of course, derive from thoughts about his mother — those associated with the present, with thoughts about his problems as husband, father, and provider. The main body of the play reveals first his attempt to reconcile these conflicting fantasies, and finally, in his failure to reconcile them, his resulting panic and despair.

Acts Two and Three in a highly schematic manner dramatize O'Neill's attempt to reconcile his fantasies, then his failure to reconcile them. These two acts are divided into scenes of three types: the first revealing O'Neill's fantasies relating to his marriage,[11] the second his fantasies relating to his mother, and the third his fantasies growing out of his sense of isolation. The first type focuses naturally on Simon and Sara, the second on Simon and Deborah, and the third on Simon responding to

Sara and Deborah as one. The third type deals with thoughts and feelings which represent the author's suicidal despair.

The scenes involving Simon and Sara and those involving Simon and Deborah at first seem simply enough conceived. Unable to sleep with his wife because of the presence of his mother and unable to be happy with his mother because of the presence of his wife, Simon invites his wife to live out his sexual fantasies with him at his office and lives out his childhood fantasies by paying brief visits to his mother in her garden. As part of his sexual fantasies, Sara must play the role of whore, in ritual fashion winning from him all his business holdings in return for her sexual favors, and as part of his childhood fantasies, Deborah must treat him like a little boy. Sara accepts his invitation, thus revealing the immorally acquisitive side of her nature; and Deborah accepts his visits, thus revealing that side of her nature which will not accept the present. That these are O'Neill's conflicting fantasies seems clear. As they had ten years earlier, memories of his mother were ruining O'Neill's sex life, or, conversely, the persistent amorous demands of a wife were interfering with his reveries about an idealized distant past with his mother.

But Simon's (O'Neill's) fantasies are only a part of what these scenes are about — and, in the final analysis, a small part. Simon is indeed tormented by his childhood fantasies to the extent that he cannot have an adult relationship with his wife and by his sexual fantasies to the extent that he cannot treat his mother with mature filial affection. But at the same time, he loves his wife and he loves his mother in ways that have nothing to do with his fantasies. A large part of him wants his wife to be happy — not as an acquisitive whore but as a companion and mother to his children. And a large part of him, the same large part in fact, wants his mother to be happy and fulfilled as an affectionate grandmother. And as with Simon, so with Sara and Deborah. They have natures which exist quite apart from their fantasies. A large part of Sara wants to be loving wife and mother, and a large part of Deborah wants to be affectionate grandmother and wise counselor. These more immediate, down-to-earth qualities in the characters exist side by side with their fantasies right through all these scenes.

At the heart of these scenes is the thought that whatever any character does or says is only one-half of what they are at any particular moment. Simon's sexuality (not his sexual fantasies) is one-half loving desire and one-half greed. And that similarly acquisitive "little boy" half when he is with his mother is one-half genuine desire for love of which he was earlier deprived and one-half a compulsive need for withdrawal, like his mother's. Similarly, Sara's whore/tycoon half is one-half sensible and one-half grasping, and her wife-motherly half is one-half supportive and one-half possessive. By the same token, Deborah's withdrawing half is one-half imaginatively creative and one-half selfish, and her grandmotherly half is one-half supportive and one-half possessive (here like Sara, naturally). Equally important is the fact that all these various halves do not exist in any kind of ironic relationship to their opposites. Each half exists side by side with its opposing half, without commenting on it in any way. Again and again, characters are startled to realize the bifurcations in their responses — but there is nothing to be learned from these bifurcations other than that they exist. Very little hypocrisy is involved in any of these characters. Simon thinks that Sara and Deborah are being hypocritical when they are being affectionate toward one another, but both lines and stage directions make clear that the affection they state is usually genuine. The halvings are always at work in the play. Each half of each response is separate and true, and each half is itself subject, as it were, to surgical bisection. As one examines these scenes more and more closely, one gets the sense of a seemingly endless series of possible halvings.

These halvings are part of the socio-historical message of O'Neill's great, lost cycle, in which he was intent upon developing the theme that all those impulses which brought about the achievements of our national past were at least one part possessive, and that this history of unrelenting acquisitiveness was what was now (in the 1930s) dispossessing Americans. But it is the *other* sets of halves which holds greater interest for me — those qualities which are the opposite of the rapacity and the whoring. Quite contradictory kinds of responses reveal the true state of O'Neill's consciousness in writing this play and the plays that follow it. Sara, early in the recorded production, speaks of admiring her late father for his "defiance of a God he denied but really believed in."[12] It takes a while to appreciate the number of contradictions this idea implies. I only wish to note that the statement includes Con's abiding belief. It is that same abiding belief, I suspect, that underlies the many humane and loving responses and actions in the play — the familial responses of Sara and Deborah, for example, or Deborah's suddenly pushing Simon away from her little Temple at the end of the play. One half a violent gesture of paranoid withdrawal, the latter is also one half the all-out sacrifice of a mother protecting her child from a terrible fate. As I have said, there seems nothing anyone says or does of an evil nature in this play which is not countered by an opposing act or statement. The question comes to be, do these counterings not in the end simply cancel human existence out, reduce it to Samuel Beckett's absolute zero? In this play and its successor, O'Neill vehemently *says* yes, but never quite *means* yes — a division which itself accords with the play's basic duality. Like Con Melody, O'Neill is always defying a faith he denies but never yields.

The Simon who plots and manipulates separate and grotesque relationships with wife and mother is very much the O'Neill of the middle period perceived now with greater objectivity — as, say, William Brown was never perceived. O'Neill *is* Simon, but he is also looking *at* Simon with clinical detachment. This detachment is perhaps most evident in the play's most memorable scene. The scene is of the third type referred to earlier, that which deals with Simon's (O'Neill's) suicidal sense of isolation. To escape his isolation in earlier plays, O'Neill frequently had his central character search for an Earth Mother — a total provider, a bringer of comfort, a figure in all respects, physical and emotional, more powerful than himself. In Act Two, scene three, Deborah and Sara unite to become that figure, a development which reenacts O'Neill's old fantasy. But united, Deborah and Sara become not a blissful fantasy but an image inspiring only terror. The fantasy of mother and wife fused into a single person, which appears in one form or another in many O'Neill plays, becomes here a new center of panic rather than of comfort. Instead of feeling restored, Simon feels completely isolated by this fusion of personalities. He feels shut out by this new image of the Earth Mother even as she embraces him.

In the scene in question (Act Two, scene three), the idea of characters fusing and separating is enacted with characteristic precision as the motherly halves of Deborah and Sara coalesce to master as they isolate the desperate Simon. Each of the scene's three characters, in interior monologue, ruminates over his or her contrapuntal desires and suspicions. All three seem isolated and deeply troubled to begin with, though it is Simon alone who remains in this state throughout the scene. First, Deborah and Sara cease being separate individuals and become a single individual whose existence drives Simon to the edge of panic. They taunt him like harpies, then they confront him "with the calculating coquetry of two prostitutes." Then they break apart, temporarily releasing Simon from the torment they have put him in, though the release is brief, since they will shortly coalesce again to drive Simon over the edge of his abyss. But even now, the torment they inflict as separate individuals is little better than that which they inflicted as a single individual. Simon cannot stand the fusion of mother and wife, but he also cannot stand them as separate, violently conflicting identities — the problem that started his troubles to begin with. Hence the fantasy suicide which this scene intimates and which the final act of the play enacts.

But again, despair and panic pointing toward a fantasy suicide is only half of what this scene enacts. There is here, as everywhere else, the opposing half. Even as the scene dissects its author's overwhelming fear, it also describes the nature of his irrepressible faith. It is a scene that tells us as much about how people survive as about how they do not survive. As I stated earlier, the union of Sara and Deborah may in one sense simply reflect a highly disturbed state of mind, but the two figures are also represented in their "fusion" as quite distinct characters who suddenly find much-needed support from one another. The love they generate in one another feels authentic:

> Sara: (*Thinking — resentfully*) Poor woman! She can't
> read — she's thinking how she'll miss the children —
> alone all day — He'll have me at the office — Alone
> in the past — He'll have her in an asylum in the
> end! — It's a terrible thing he can hate his
> mother so! —
> Deborah: (*Thinking*) She had begun to look upon me as a
> second mother — and I was happy to regard her as
> my daughter — because her strength and health and
> acceptance of life gave me a faith in my own
> living — and now he dares to take that security
> away from me! — to offer me in exchange ghosts
> from the past to haunt me —
> Sara: (*Thinking*) I'm not a thought he moves around in
> his mind to suit his pleasure —
> Deborah: (*Thinking*) If she'd sit with me here as on other
> nights, we'd understand and forgive each other —
> (*They both speak to each other simultaneously:*
> *"Sara" "Deborah" They bend forward so*
> *they can see each other past him and smile*
> *at each other with a relieved understanding.*
> *Deborah speaks with strange gentleness*)
> Yes, Daughter. I ought to have known you guessed
> my thoughts.
> Sara: (*Getting up — with a quiet smile*) I hope you
> guessed mine. May I come and sit with you?
> Deborah: I was going to ask you.
> (*Sara goes around the table and passes*
> *behind Simon, ignoring him, and goes to*
> *the sofa. Deborah pats the sofa on her*
> *left, smiling an affectionate welcome*)
> This is your place, beside me.
> (Yale edition, pp. 122–23)

There is nothing these lines tell us other than that along with their feelings of hatred for one another, Sara and Deborah have feelings of mutual affection — genuine feelings of affection. Simon's is the distorted set of reactions, the "strange" element in the scene despite the use of that word in describing the women. Simon remains in isolation; they do not. His honesty with the audience is honesty only with himself in his spoken inner thoughts. Sara and Deborah communicate honestly with one another, both in their affection here demonstrated and in their hostility. Their coming together and their separating is something more than fantasy. It is also an enactment of the processes of kinship, and the self-defined odd-man-out is the only real sufferer. The alternating hostility and affection between Sara and Deborah makes them as well off as Simon is badly off. The scene tells us finally as much about people in the polyphony of kinship as it does about O'Neill's fantasies and despair.

Kinship is what O'Neill, knowingly or not, seems to be working toward in this play even as he is attempting to certify the folly of any kind of philosophical truth. Simon protests the total meaninglessness of things while others move toward authentic human relationships. Simon insists upon keeping his halves divided—which some would call schizophrenia—while others let their similar halves unite and their opposing halves do battle. In the relationship of Sara and Deborah the matrix of kinship is more systematically presented than in any other previous play. In *More Stately Mansions*, O'Neill seems on the verge of transcending his agony even as he seems most immersed in it. Still, he does not transcend it. O'Neill through Simon continues battering at the interior wall of his old imprisoning circle. Simon's blow to the head near the end of the play, the result of his mother's efforts to protect him from her fate, seems to promise some basic change in his direction—but the blow to the head quickly becomes the old reenactment of O'Neill's original disillusionment. The blow comes from his mother, and thus is O'Neill still trapped by the past. We are back with Orin Mannon, permanently bewildered by the old wound to the head. The state in which O'Neill leaves his hero in *More Stately Mansions* is in fact the worst of human conditions. Simon's fate is like that of Oswald Alving in Ibsen's *Ghosts*. Having avoided suicide or madness—his desire to join his mother in her little Temple could mean either—Simon becomes a vegetable. O'Neill, in his efforts to reach a bedrock level of existence without illusion, has now descended for his central image to that of a semi-conscious invalid needing the literal ministrations of a *nurse*-mother.

In its explicitness, *More Stately Mansions* may be the most informative among O'Neill's plays. Here alone does a figure standing squarely for the author obviously use the study of himself as the basis for his understanding of others. Simon is like Shakespeare's King Richard II in prison "hammering out" the structure of his despair, "peopling his world with little thoughts," descanting on the meaninglessness of existence. Having gone through the pretense of accepting false solutions, O'Neill is philosophically back where he was at the conclusion of *Mourning Becomes Electra*. But whether he would or no, the despair could not erase his strong sense of the emotional pulsations of people in close relationships. Rather than being at the end of his road as an artist, he was actually at the point where he might be ready to combine the two contradictory forces that had dominated all his plays — his despair and his sense of the rhythm of kinship. His skill at writing plays, and his reasons for writing them, were very great. But one more element was needed, a reason to genuinely consider himself a playwright of the largest tragic magnitude. Something was needed to make O'Neill feel that the autobiographical agony and the vision of kinship were of true worth to mankind — and that something may have been his winning the Nobel Prize in 1936.

IV

THE NEW LANGUAGE OF KINSHIP

A FTER THE NOBEL PRIZE, WHAT? Still possessed by his terrible guilt and his still more terrible sense of isolation, still lacerating himself over what he conceived to be his fraud and greed, evidenced in part by his continued disguising of his pain and in part by his popular success in the face of that disguising, O'Neill had now been publicly and officially proclaimed a "great writer." This was the time to be totally honest with himself and with his audiences. In every conceivable sense he had nothing to lose. The conditions of his marital life had gone beyond hope of change, his physical health was declining, the world was on the brink of what seemed apocalyptic catastrophe — yet he was still only approaching the height of his creative powers. The compulsion to *be* the great playwright he had been officially proclaimed must have been overwhelming — and the only way to achieve that pinnacle was to be relentlessly honest about his personal agony, and in doing so to represent the human condition precisely as he felt it.

There is nothing to suggest that O'Neill gave up on his long cycle as a result of winning the Nobel Prize. In fact, he completed most of the actual writing he did on it after winning the Prize, and kept protesting that he intended to return to it. But the cycle was largely conceived before the award, and its purpose seemed endlessly to vary the circle of disguised family guilts and betrayals first explicitly proposed by Orin Mannon's family history. The cycle still had at its essence the masking process which had characterized all O'Neill's earlier works. To be worthy of the Prize he had received meant to transcend his earlier works, and that meant to break out of his circle.

O'Neill's last plays are his most honest and also his most far-reaching. His Miltonic *Iceman* does not "justify the ways of God to Man," but it is forever asking the question whether such justification is possible. And although it always answers that question in the negative, it keeps repeating the question — as though never quite convinced of the negative answer. It also copes with the question by exploring through the language of kinship the process by which men and women manage to survive — a subject examined again minutely in the potent one-act *Hughie. Long Day's Journey* is, of course, the great, long-anticipated autobiographical outpouring; but more significantly perhaps, it employs the language of kinship for the first time within those very relationships O'Neill had so much trouble acknowledging. Finally, there is *A Moon for the Misbegotten*, a play about kinship as redemption. In all these plays, it seems to me impossible not to conclude that O'Neill was finally an affirming playwright, though in none of them did he ever again compromise his monumental honesty. Like his Larry Slade, he kept seeing all sides to every question. His reason kept leading him to the coldly despairing conclusion that life was a stupid, meaningless joke, and his rational honesty made that view the central philosophical statement of all his last works. But his honesty led him equally to a detailed appreciation of the qualities in human relationships which implicitly deny that statement, and his last plays explore the details of that appreciation with even greater impact than they explore the conclusion itself.

8 *The Iceman Cometh*

I AGREE with the frequently expressed assumption that *The Iceman Cometh* is about the need people have for illusions if they are to survive; and I agree that the great conception of salvation through confession, first in Christian terms and later in Freudian, is treated in this play as a dubious panacea for most (though not, as it turns out, for all). Total confession, says the reasoning author of this play, can lead rationally only to seemingly total despair. Among the most important statements made about this play are those which link it to Ibsen's *The Wild Duck.*[1] Nothing in *The Iceman Cometh* states its basic theme so precisely as Dr. Relling's famous observation in Ibsen's play that to "rob the average man of his life-lie" is to "rob him of his happiness." And as Dr. Relling, showing what Hickey would call "the wrong kind of pity," actually nurtures life-lies among his close associates, so Larry Slade nurtures the pipe dreams of his fellow derelicts out of feelings of genuine compassion. For these two uncompromising realists, there is no discoverable truth that can give life genuine meaning.

Little, then, will be added about the play's philosophical conclusions by this study. Nevertheless, many readers and, especially, viewers of the play get the impression that "for some reason" it is not as pessimistic as its stated conclusions would indicate.[2] This response is heard most often among O'Neill's less scholarly admirers, many of them associated with productions of his plays, and less often from academic critics, who tend to be more exclusively concerned with the rational. If one comes at the play primarily from the point of view of O'Neill's abilities as a "thinker,"[3] then it must seem among the most nihilistic pieces ever written. But as one becomes sensitive to its representation of the emotional rhythms in extremely mundane human relationships — which exist in spite of, or beyond, rational conclusion — the play becomes something other than despairing.

My discussion will expand the familiar formula. I shall begin with the dramatic representation of the autobiographical, which is here rich and varied, if still carefully disguised, and conclude with O'Neill's progress in formulating his new language of kinship. The first section will be a treatment again of father, brother, and mother; the last will explore the interplay of illusion and kinship. But the two sections will be bridged by a crucial discussion of Larry Slade, one of the play's two central figures and by far the most articulate spokesman for its rational conclusions. Larry's personal problems, especially in his complex relationship with the hapless Don Parritt, are the expression in this play of the final stages of O'Neill's autobiographical agony. The emotional pain so massively felt is in large measure that which emanates from this likable but most hard-bitten of O'Neill's cynical heroes. Larry is our guide through O'Neill's personal emotional hell and also spokesman for the philosophical despair which seems to underlie this play.

The Autobiographical Agony

Several characters in *The Iceman Cometh* suggest O'Neill's father, and as O'Neill's memories of the old actor were less haunting than those of his mother and brother, so are their dramatic re-enactments here less haunting. We get several images of fathers suggesting O'Neill's: first Willie Oban's father, the big-time racketeer who betrayed his son by his fraud and corruption; later, Hickey's father, the preacher who "could sell those Hoosier hayseeds building lots along the Golden Streets." Then, on stage, there is Harry Hope, who must control even as he is dependent upon a pair of feuding "sons", Pat McGloin and Ed Mosher. To varying extents these figures all suggest O'Neill's feelings about his father, but the play never focuses on those feelings for long or in depth. They are clearly not the feelings which were still haunting O'Neill. Harry Hope, in fact, comes to represent feelings chiefly of accommodation and acceptance.

The Iceman Cometh begins and ends in brother Jamie, who appears in many variations. In fact, he peeps through at us, almost satyr-like, in so many variations that to go into them all would be impossible. Undoubtedly I have not recognized them all. We see him highly distorted, for example, in such remotely related figures as Ed Mosher the circus barker and Hugo Kalmar the anarchist. And he is certainly central to the function of Don Parritt, which I shall treat at length in my discussion of Larry Slade. But in terms of O'Neill's raw, unembellished pity for his dead brother, we see him first in the character of Willie Oban. Willie is the most unfortunate of the derelicts who populate this play. Whereas all the others are probably over fifty, Willie is the most pitiable for being in his late thirties. Like Jamie he is learned, articulate, and brilliantly witty. He is a former attorney, we are told, whose breakdown and total immersion in alcohol came about very suddenly with the discovery that his father was a crook and fraud—a description which closely parallels Jamie's sudden deterioration during his senior year at college. Jamie consistently questioned his father's talents and considered the old man's reputation an empty one. Willie, in his manic (i.e., drunken) moments is also like the Jamie who is the life of the party. Willie amuses his cohorts with wittily obscene songs and literary allusions. And he is also the Jamie we know from the image of terror-stricken withdrawal and final-stage alcoholism in Dion Anthony of *The Great God Brown*. Willie's characterization seems rooted in a compassion for his brother which at times seems uncontrollable in O'Neill. But Willie is far from being the whole Jamie as O'Neill conceived him. Willie is only the Jamie who was cast out by his family, who was consumed with hostility toward his father, who was racked with anguish about and dependency upon his mother, and who was a wonder to his associates in the amount of whiskey he could consume. He is not the Jamie who was to become the embodiment of new understanding in the mature O'Neill.

As an expression of O'Neill's admiration for his dead brother, Jamie's most important representative in the play is Hickey himself,[4] who might be said to represent Jamie at his best, as Willie represents him at his worst. It is indicated early in the play that Hickey has always been able to bring joy and excitement to the saloon-dwellers, a talent which has gone beyond the simple fact that he has always bought the drinks—as Jamie impoverished himself doing. Like his most immediate predecessor, Sid Davis in *Ah, Wilderness*, Hickey's presence has always been that of an eternally bright and spirited crony, a Mercutio who could keep life in a state of perpetual revelry. The Hickey remembered by the derelicts is the mythic Hickey, the Dionysian Hickey, the Hickey who stands for the Jamie so longed for in O'Neill's imagination. Hickey's past reputation cannot be overstated because it explains not only the impact of the false hope he brings in the play but also the true hope he is. The real Jamie never came to save anyone—far be that from the mind of James Gladstone

O'Neill, Jr. — but his very presence was saving because of his brilliant wit and his seemingly endless vitality. And that wit and vitality, which O'Neill had felt constrained to eliminate from his reverential treatment of Jamie in *Lazarus Laughed*, is the essence of this false, but finally true, savior in *The Iceman Cometh*. Obviously, I shall have more to say on this subject.

Hickey also parallels Jamie in the complexity of his feelings toward the most important woman in his life. Hickey has persistently betrayed his ever-forgiving wife as Jamie persistently betrayed his ever-forgiving mother. Hickey's murder of Evelyn and his sudden awareness of the implications of that action parallel Jamie's whole complex of frenzied hostility and guilt regarding his mother's death as described and lived through in *A Moon for the Misbegotten*. In that later play, Jamie's guilt has been aroused to hysterical proportions by the fact that his mother awoke (or so he imagined) immediately before her death, saw him drunk, and died immediately afterward. He decides this is what killed her, and to compound his guilt, he keeps killing her symbolically through his nightly relations with the whore on the train. Hickey's grotesque corollary to this story is that he actually did kill his wife. As in *Mourning Becomes Electra*, a real murder stands as metaphor for the murder O'Neill felt his brother and himself to be guilty of. But the more important point is that Hickey, like Jamie in the later play, has the capacity finally to suffer openly and volubly for his crimes against his wife-mother; and it is that capacity which gives him heroic stature in *The Iceman Cometh*, as it will later give Jim Tyrone heroic stature in *A Moon for the Misbegotten*. Characters who stand for O'Neill's own brooding, negative cynicism never achieve such stature because theirs is an abstract, held-in penance. For a man to be a hero in O'Neill he must actively and emotionally, not simply intellectually, face his ghosts. Their ability to do this is what makes Hickey and Jamie superior to Simon Harford and Larry Slade — though the latter finally also emotionally faces his in private.

It is surprising in any discussion of an O'Neill play to think of the image or images of his mother taking second place. But they do here, largely because no character representing his mother, or anyone's mother, actually appears on stage. Yet the agony associated with his mother remains central. The figures who stand for her are many and tend to parallel each other. They are the remembered wives and mothers who either are dead or have disappeared, or in one case who is permanently incarcerated.[5] The most important of these remembered women are three very differently described matrons. The first is Bessie Hope, dead these twenty years (O'Neill's mother had been dead nearly that when he wrote the play), and blessed in memory to Harry, another drunken shebeen-keeper. Actually, Bessie's memory serves only to insulate Harry from the real world. His feelings about her are in fact ambivalent. The real Bessie, Larry tells us, was a persistent nag from whom Harry took refuge in life by means of the bottle. Bessie hardly anticipates Mary Tyrone in personality, but she was, like Mary, obsessed with proprieties she felt her husband was insufficiently attentive to. The chief theme involving Bessie is Harry's fear that he might betray her memory, a fear which supports the shaky stability of his existence. Harry uses this fear to protect himself from the realities of the present, which was one manifestation of O'Neill's struggle with his guilt many years after the events that set it off.

Second, there is Rosa Parritt,[6] whose parallels with O'Neill's mother are clearer. As O'Neill's mother was betrayed by a son in California, causing hysterical anguish both in that son and in a second son in New York, so Rosa was betrayed by a son in California causing hysterical anguish both in that son and in a former lover in New York. The "Movement" Rosa heads is also related to the always-abiding theme of betrayal by and of a mother. Rosa is obsessed with her Movement to the point that it has dominated her life. Because of it she has all but abandoned both her son and her lover. It thus parallels Mary's addiction. Rosa's obsession is rooted, Parritt tells us, in her desire for freedom, which recalls Deborah Harford's obsession with her "little Temple" and certainly parallels the freedom brought by Mary's morphine: freedom from life's sorrows and responsibilities. Along with her Movement are Rosa's lovers, who also parallel Mary's narcotic withdrawals in that they cause Rosa to repeatedly turn away from those who genuinely love her and whom she genuinely loves. Rosa, we are told, has felt much guilt toward the men she feels closest to, as does Mary. Parritt reports that when she had time to think about him, she acted "as if she wanted to make up for something, as if she felt guilty."

But Rosa's Movement stands not only for Mary's addiction. It also stands for the altogether opposing pipe dream of family life itself. Rosa has been a good leader, serving her followers, or children, as both provider and protector. Thus, even as the Movement represents Rosa's escape from responsibility, it also represents her fulfilling of it as the nurturing, providing mother. As Rosa the sinner betrays her loved ones Larry and Parritt, so Rosa the saintly is betrayed by them. What O'Neill suggests here is the seemingly endless recurrence of betrayal and betraying, his old circle. Which comes first, the betrayal or the betraying, again is of no consequence. Rosa Parritt represents the most agonizing of O'Neill's dilemmas still smoldering inside him, only half understood.

Finally, the third remembered matron is Evelyn Hickman. Evelyn parallels Rosa not only as nurturer and provider, but also in her obsession with an ideal which draws her away from reality. Her ideal, her "Movement," of course, is her certainty that Hickey will reform. But we are brought to perceive Evelyn in a very different way than we do Rosa. Rosa, despite her betrayals by son and lover, never seems really victimized. Described with remarkably few concrete details of appearance or behavior, she is never made quite vivid. She seems in the descriptions of Parritt and Larry always vaguely self-contained and in command. We feel we ought to have compassion for her in her suffering, but somehow we do not. The clearest impression we ever get is of her being bossy, and that tends to antagonize us, as does her unfaithfulness. Hickey's description of Evelyn, on the other hand, makes her seem ever the victim. What we are told places her directly in O'Neill's growing line of long-suffering wife-mothers, ever patient and ever-forgiving — and she is thus at all times the betrayed mother, never the betrayer. And the betrayal this time takes the form, as in *Mourning Becomes Electra*, of actual murder. As Rosa Parritt's personality, or what we learn of it, suggests O'Neill's abiding vindictiveness, Evelyn's suggests his equally abiding guilt.

While all three images of O'Neill's mother, then — Bessie Hope, Rosa Parritt, and Evelyn Hickman — reveal the persistence of O'Neill's favorite haunt, in this play he was to come to grips with that haunt as never before. We must turn now to Larry Slade, who represents O'Neill himself in his most critical of struggles with the past, a struggle out of which is born the vision of the final plays.

Larry Slade

No character in O'Neill, including the illustrious Hickey, arrives so fully prepared for as does Larry Slade. To understand him at all well, one must go back to *Days Without End*, where the central character was divided into two separate dramatic personalities, the youthful dreamer John and the cynical nihilist Loving. John conformed in personality to many other youthful dreamers in O'Neill (Stephen Murray, Juan Ponce de Leon, Robert Mayo, Jim Harris, and the early unmasked Dion Anthony), and undoubtedly represented O'Neill's basic self-image during the years he wrote his earlier plays. This hero was inherently a believer, whether or not one takes his conversion seriously. He was melancholy, like his predecessors, but his melancholy never yielded to hard-bitten cynicism. He was deeply troubled, but he was always the poet who sought for mystical affirmations in both man and nature. Loving, on the other hand, was an image of the hero O'Neill felt himself increasingly drawn to. He spoke with the voice of the rational O'Neill who had reached the conclusion that life was altogether without meaning or purpose. Loving was also free of doubt, self-contained, and absolutely convinced in his cynicism. That O'Neill felt increasingly drawn to him is suggested in part by Loving's resemblance in despairing tone and manner to Lavinia Mannon and Simon Harford.

Following directly from Lavinia and Simon, Larry Slade seems the ultimate voice of O'Neill's rational despair, the culmination of his steady move toward hard-bitten nihilism. Larry's philosophical observations are a seemingly endless series of variations on the single theme that life is hopeless and meaningless, that death is best, that "best of all," says Larry, "is never to have been born." But again we must go back to *Days Without End* to realize that this nihilism is not all there is to Larry. John and Loving in the earlier play really only constituted two halves of a single individual — an inherently believing half and an inherently unbelieving half. In the characters who were not artificially cut into those halves — Lavinia and Simon — we saw similar halves at war within a single individual. In John Loving, the John half just barely won out over the Loving half, and John emerged sentimentally triumphant. But in Lavinia and Simon, one might say the Loving half triumphed. These characters yielded more and more to their savagely morose cynicism. Finally, in Larry Slade the yielding seems complete. He seems the total nihilist from the start.

But not so. As John was always troubled by his "Loving," his unbelieving other half, the Loving that culminates in Larry Slade is always troubled by his "John." The divided nature remains — and will remain. As there was always a hard-bitten cynic struggling against the dreamer in O'Neill's earlier heroes, so there is always a dreamer fighting the nihilist in Larry Slade. Larry keeps revealing his compassion and understanding in the play — not in the manner of Loving but in the manner of John. Thus is the aura of uncompromising nihilism in *The Iceman Cometh* never quite convincing. It is always being compromised by Larry's emotions and Larry's actions — though never by Larry's mind. In earlier plays, O'Neill had been trying to believe but kept being disturbed by the doubt cast by his reason. In this play, O'Neill is trying not to believe but keeps being disturbed by his instincts.

The chief difference between Larry and the nihilists who precede him is that through Larry, O'Neill for the first time really digs at the roots of his sickness. Through Larry, he breaks the circle of hostility and guilt which has dominated just about every play we have dealt with. To understand how O'Neill does in fact triumph over his past in this play, we must look at Larry's relationship with Don Parritt, and we must assess the significance of Parritt's suicide near the close of the play.

Except in his seething guilt, which finally drives him to take his own life, Don Parritt is endowed with little personality. He is unlike all the other characters in the play, each of whom possesses some quality or trait capable of exciting an affectionate human response. Parritt has no such quality or trait. O'Neill seems to want us to hate him as characters in the late plays hate what they refer to as "the dead part" of themselves. Parritt is the embodiment of unalloyed guilt, that guilt which O'Neill felt had totally destroyed his brother and was in the process of destroying him. Parritt's experiences parallel Jamie's, though his guilt may be seen interchangeably as that of either brother. Like Jamie, Parritt betrayed a mother in California, and like O'Neill he refused to *face* what he had done. Parritt has used his reward money to take up with a whore the way Jamie took up with the blonde on the train. Like both brothers, Parritt has continued to act out his resentment of his mother even as he is tortured by ever-increasing guilt. Finally, like Jamie, Parritt has come East to seek the comfort that O'Neill coldly denied Jamie and that Larry here denies Parritt. But throughout, we never have any sympathy for Parritt. Lacking the humanity each of the other characters possesses, he leaves us cold. Larry feels guilt toward Parritt, but it is a guilt which continually slips back into disgust. There is no real compassion associated with Parritt, and there is no hope. That is, in the O'Neill who writes the play there is no pity for the suffering he has known, and thus there can be no hope. There is only the feeling, which Larry repeatedly gives utterance to, that he cannot escape the past.

There is also an unreal quality in the relationship between Larry and Parritt. Their exchanges, even as Parritt's state becomes hysterical, seem repetitious, exaggerated, and strangely unspontaneous. The two are like figures living out some awful horror in a dream. And so they are. What we see re-enacted is indeed a dream — O'Neill's central nightmare. Larry and Parritt first live out the old agony of O'Neill's rejection of Jamie. Submerged in O'Neill's immediately preceding plays, that agony is allowed to surface as never before in *The Iceman Cometh*. Should he have comforted Jamie by offering him reassurance — or should he have advised him to kill himself for committing that worst of human crimes, mother-betrayal? The latter is also the lingering question in O'Neill about his relationship with himself. (He had long since forgiven Jamie.) Larry is fundamentally

guilty because of his own rejection of Rosa Parritt, as O'Neill was fundamentally guilty over his rejection of his mother. Parritt the mother-
betrayer is only a reflection of Larry the "mother"-betrayer. And so with
the thoughts of suicide in both characters. Since O'Neill's despair, probably already concerning his mother, actually did bring him to attempt suicide at Jimmy-the-Priest's in 1912, we are with Larry and Parritt at the
center of O'Neill's torment in 1939, Larry the present-day O'Neill considering Parritt the O'Neill of nearly thirty years before. Should he not finish
the job now that he failed to finish then? What we see and hear on stage is
an exploration of O'Neill's struggle with that question. But O'Neill is doing something more. By unrelentingly putting that struggle on stage, he is
also for the first time attempting to cast out his life's greatest terror.

To more fully understand the Slade-Parritt relationship is to understand the nature of its dialogue, which for all its talk of literal kinship is
the very opposite of kinship dialogue. It concentrates on a past full of betrayal and guilt which Larry tries to evade Parritt's interpretation of, and
Parritt concomitantly tries to deceive Larry about. In other words, it concentrates on Larry as the O'Neill who is still trying to face his emotional
past and on Parritt as the "image of that horror" — the craven, spiteful
youth who tried to escape his pain and could not. Their dialogue is naturally full of the qualities which characterized the dialogue of O'Neill's
middle period: the deception and counter-deception, the manipulation
and resistance to manipulation, the accusation and counteraccusation,
the cry for pity and the mask of indifference. If we consider the two, like
John and Loving, as two sides of a single person, then the dialogue becomes inner dialogue, that of someone deciding whether or not to commit
suicide. The deception then becomes self-deception, the manipulation
self-manipulation, the accusation self-accusation, the cry for pity self-
pity, and the mask of indifference the attempt to protect oneself. The pain
is always there, the one constant, and that pain results in the periodic explosions of intense feeling between these two which culminate in Larry's
final imperative:

> Go! Get the hell out of life, God damn you, before I
> choke it out of you! Go up — !
>
> (III. 720)

And so Parritt, the seeming descendant of all O'Neill's earlier self-
tormenters, finally does go up, and by means of some extreme spasm of
self-torment, which we never see on stage since the adult O'Neill thank-

fully never brought himself to that extreme a spasm, manages to throw himself off. But Parritt is not really the descendant of anybody. He has none of the human qualities of O'Neill's earlier heroes, being only the faceless embodiment of their unbearable guilt. It is *Larry* who is the true heir to O'Neill's earlier suicides and would-be suicides, and it is Larry—not Parritt—who throughout is O'Neill. The figure we remain with at the end is not that remote image of O'Neill's horror leaping from the fire escape, but the highly immediate and familiar, perpetually agonizing figure of the real self-tormenter Larry Slade, who is those earlier heroes grown older and on the brink of being wiser. What happens late in *The Iceman Cometh* is that O'Neill manages somehow to throw himself off that fire escape without literally doing so. If my idea that Parritt, as his name implies, has no truly separate identity, then the thought of his fallen crushed body has something of the unreal effect of the smothered baby in *Desire Under the Elms* many years earlier. When we reach out in our minds to pick that body up, what we find is a pile of rags. The fall reduces Parritt to the imaginary ghoul he really is. The whole emphasis throughout is on Larry and how Larry reacts. Part of Larry's reaction to Parritt's suicide is, of course, the renewed commitment to nihilism I shall shortly discuss, but another part is his sense of immense relief, the relief of a man who has hurled some terrible weight off his shoulders—some weight that plummets down like that of a body falling from a fire escape. Parritt's suicide thus becomes finally a metaphor for O'Neill's triumph over suicide.

The Larry Slade-Don Parritt relationship and its conclusion constitute a very real psychological exorcism for O'Neill. Like other relationships in O'Neill's plays, this one has embodied, in thin disguise, all the elements of his years of nightmare regarding his mother, his brother, and his ever-recurring self-hatred—the agony, in short, one stage of which had led him to a suicide attempt in 1912 and which made him suicidal throughout his life. Yet in this relationship he dramatizes all those suicidal urgings in such a way that they seem not likely to return; and, in fact, there are no suicides amid the emotional tumult of O'Neill's last three plays. Furthermore, this action is more than merely the effective therapy that is implied. O'Neill has also made this experience highly effective drama through his by now superbly developed talent for transforming his most hidden feelings into people, events, and conversations. Few who encounter the play fail to be haunted by Larry Slade and Don Parritt and their mysterious relationship to the past. Some feel so devastated by this part of the play's action that they turn away from the play altogether, but that result is the risk run by any authentic tragedy. To empathize with the purgation implicit in this action is to recognize that authenticity.[7]

But there remains much more to be said about Larry Slade. We must also consider that seemingly reinforced nihilism which closes the play, and to do so we must look at the nature of his cynicism throughout. We must compare his condition before and after Parritt's leap. Throughout the earlier portions of the play, Larry is spokesman for "the big sleep." He has, he says, through experience become disillusioned with life, and he has withdrawn "into the grandstand of philosophical detachment" to patiently await a much-desired death—with drink in hand. But the falsely rational quality of his attitudes convinces few. Especially do Rocky and his tarts know that Larry's cynicism is at least half blarney, that if he really hated life as much as he says he does, he would have killed himself long ere this—a sentiment which is echoed by the all-knowing Hickey. And the depth of Larry's nihilism is even rendered suspect in what he says to Parritt. Claiming to be totally objective, Larry lets slip remarks indicating that his supposedly detached rejection of life is really intensely subjective, emotionally rooted in personal disappointment, the result of some deep psychological trauma. A passage often cited as the essence of Sladean nihilism actually gives this subjectivity away quite unexpectedly:

> Honor or dishonor, faith or treachery are
> nothing to me but the opposites of the same
> stupidity which is ruler and king of life,
> and in the end they rot into dust in the
> same grave. All things are the same meaning-
> less joke to me, for they grin at me from
> the one skull of death. So go away. You're
> wasting breath. *I've forgotten your mother.*
>
> (III. 649. Emphasis added)

Despite Larry's intent that these remarks have a universal context, the last sentence reveals that he is really only feeling sorry for himself. He has not forgotten Parritt's mother. His suffering, like Parritt's, grows out of a bad experience with a woman who was close to him and not out of some thorough, detached assessment of all facets of human existence.

So Larry's nihilism in the play at first has the sound of much popular and largely superficial early twentieth-century debunking of Victorian optimism and has something of the ring throughout of the sophomore's lament. It is, like so much barroom cynicism in all ages, a substitute for the crying towel—as the other derelicts at Harry Hope's seem instinctively to know. The Larry we first encounter, though a good deal more hard-bitten, has not really advanced that much from the lovelorn Smitty of the sea plays. The world is indeed a dark and dreary place, but largely, to quote Jamie quoting Swinburne, because "she would not hear." Larry is not at first even a match for the earlier Loving, because Loving is intended only as the essence of pure negation, while Larry is always revealing the hurt child underneath the ultra-cynical mask. (He is both John and Loving.) O'Neill wants us to see Larry's nihilism at first as only an expression of his unresolved guilt and fear because he wants us to understand that a genuine change takes place in Larry following Parritt's suicide, a change born of O'Neill's own casting out of his ghosts. And it is the change which John Loving does *not* go through in the pseudo-exorcism which concludes *Days Without End.*

O'Neill's sentimental endings to plays in the 1930s — *Days Without End, Ah, Wilderness,* and *A Touch of the Poet* (with reservations) — are all intended to leave their heroes triumphant following some life-redirecting struggle. Their heroes all go off newly awakened to the meaning of life. The ending of *The Iceman Cometh,* on the other hand, is as un-sentimental as O'Neill can make it. It deals with a new awakening not to the meaning of life but to the meaninglessness of life. The hero now emerges with a bright new sense of the true nihilism. Larry Slade, whose name implies the bed-rock reality he claims to have reached earlier, finally reaches that bed of rock through his encounter with Parritt. He reaches what to his reason seems the core of knowledge that everything in his previous life—his decisions, ideas, opinions, tastes, aspirations, goals —had been tied up with his personal agony, and that without that agony there genuinely does seem to be nothing. There seems no meaning to life whatsoever; and Larry "from the bottom of his coward's heart" can say for the first time and mean that he is a "true convert to death." Larry's great purgation has left him empty, at one with an infinite nothingness. This is the play's real nihilism, and it is what makes O'Neill in this play an early dramatist of the absurd. This time, we are persuaded, O'Neill has really given up.

Or has he? I am reminded by Larry's statements as opposed to Larry's actions at the close of the play of perhaps the greatest of all twentieth-century absurdist plays, Samuel Beckett's *Waiting for Godot.*[8] At the close of each act of the Beckett play, the two leading figures agree to "go," but they do not go. Instead, they remain in place. Where they will *go,* and what they will *do,* it seems implied, will be forever precisely where they have *been* and what they have been doing. In the same manner, Larry, having just recommended and experienced a suicide, says he has become a true convert to death — which might suggest that he too intends to commit suicide. But he does not "go." He remains essentially in the same posture he has been in throughout the play, and there is nothing to indicate really that he will do anything else. He will keep doing the things he has been doing, and he will await death. In short, he will do what all people do, though he will now do it free of illusion. It is, then, what he has been doing which begins to assume importance. It is what Larry has been doing — not thinking, but doing — which is essential to this play's transcendence of the absolute nihilism it seems to preach; and what Larry has been doing has a great deal to do with the process of human kinship.

His relationship with the shadowy Parritt aside, Larry's relation-ships with everyone else in the play, even Hickey, are close and trusting. He has a separate, distinct, and total relationship with each member of Harry Hope's band which makes him an eminently welcome figure to them even as they treat him roughly and refer to him as "the old fooloso-pher." He does not use people, and he is not used by them. He is instead directly and honestly involved with them, his "grandstand" remarks not-withstanding. Jimmy Tomorrow speaks for the group, I think, when he calls Larry's bluff. "You pretend a bitter, cynic philosophy," says a mo-mentarily objective Jimmy, "but in your heart you are the kindest man among us." (III. 600.) And what has happened to Larry at the end is not likely to stop him from continuing to be the kindest man among them. What Larry condemns in himself as "the wrong kind of pity" is not pity at all but a deep instinct for quickly recognizing and respecting the feelings of others — whether or not these feelings grow out of or proliferate illu-sions, which they probably do. Larry's basic attitudes are those of quiet acceptance and the willing capacity to forgive. He has an instinctive faith in human decency which his words, when confronted by his actions, can never convince us has been destroyed.

Larry Slade, in ways which the lines make clear better than do the stage directions, is a nurturing figure at Harry Hope's saloon.[9] He is less "in the grandstand" than anyone else in the play and always will be. His rejection of all causes and ideals only makes him more in touch with his fellow human beings than most people are. His responses, even when he is on the defensive as he frequently is earlier in the play, indicate the na-ture of his relationship with others, as do their responses to him:

Margie: (*sneering*) De old wise guy!
Pearl: Yeah, still pretendin' he's de one exception, like
      Hickey told him. He don't do no pipe dreamin'!
      Oh, no!

Larry: (*sharply resentful*) I —! (*Then abruptly he is drunkenly good-natured, and you feel this drunken manner is an evasive exaggeration*) All right, take it out on me, if it makes you more content. Sure, I love every hair of your heads, my great big beautiful baby dolls, and there's nothing I wouldn't do for you!

Pearl: (*stiffly*) De old Irish bunk, huh? We ain't big. And we ain't your baby dolls! (*Suddenly she is mollified and smiles*) But we admit we're beautiful. Huh, Margie?

Margie: (*smiling*) Sure ting! But what would he do wid beautiful dolls, even if he had de price, de old goat? (*She laughs teasingly — then pats Larry on the shoulder affectionately*) Aw, yuh're aw right at dat, Larry, if yuh are full of bull!

Pearl: Sure. Yuh're aces wid us. We're noivous, dat's all.

(III. 635)

The crucial point in this exchange is that at which Larry's flattery gets through to Pearl and Margie, and their tone toward him veers sharply. He has fed their illusions, of course ("the wrong kind of pity"), but they recognize his flattery well enough, and the feeling he evokes in so doing is genuine — "you're aw right at dat, Larry. . . ." Not his flattery, which O'Neill calls an evasive exaggeration, but the authenticity of the attention he focuses on them gives them reassurance, and for that he will always be "aces wid" them. As for the "evasive exaggeration" of the stage direction, Larry's flattery is the only exaggeration he is guilty of. His first response is not at all exaggerated: "All right, take it out on me, if it makes you more content." His ability to "take it" is evidence of his relative strength and stability. The tarts' feeling for him is first evoked by his willingness to let himself be their punching bag, then flowers with the attention he focuses on them. What Larry says half fits the stage direction "evasive"; but, true to the divisions in human response explored in *More Stately Mansions*, it is also half authentic altruism. And the halves are really indistinguishable here. Larry gives even as he evades, and once his reason for evading is gone, as it is at the end of the play, his giving will be more complete than ever.

Larry's relationship with Pearl and Margie here seems a special one, but so is his relationship with each one of Harry's clientele. I do not speak of his particular sense of guardianship in the case of Hugo Kalmar, which is tied to Larry's past and seems one more kind of compassion for himself. I speak rather of his unpremeditated communication at very basic levels with all those "misbegotten" individuals who have nothing to do with his past. The long-awaited Hickey brings them joy for special occasions and is much to be celebrated; but it is Larry who has more to do with their everyday lives. They are dependent on Larry, and far more than he might wish to admit it, he is dependent upon them. If he is "aces wid" them, they are certainly aces with him. In complete contrast to his relationship with Parritt, his relationships with them are free of any kind of serious deception or manipulation. And the ever-present defensiveness and hostility are but the inevitable and necessary indication of the totality of those relationships.

A larger understanding of *The Iceman Cometh* must recognize that its nihilism does not debate its kinship. This idea is most evident in the character of the *bona fide* nihilist Larry Slade, whose confrontation with himself in the suicide of Parritt frees him from all past fears, beliefs, and aspirations and also frees him to be more fully the nurturing figure he really has been all along, while trying to deny it. Washed clean of what Martin Buber calls "the rot" in human relationships,[10] Larry is ready at the end to engage more fully with each of his "misbegotten" tribe, as we have seen him from the beginning engage them haltingly but always lovingly. At the end, Larry is for the first time in tune with the present, which is what the play celebrates, whether it wants to or not — the present, which always constitutes one or another of the fierce struggles to survive that attest how precious man considers life regardless of its inevitable disillusion. The real ground of this play is these present struggles lived out not primarily by Larry so much as by the play's minor characters in their pairings and groupings. More than any other O'Neill play since the sea plays, *The Iceman Cometh* is as much about society as it is about himself.

The Language of Kinship

Perhaps Beckett's *Waiting For Godot* is a good play to return to in seeking more completely to understand *The Iceman Cometh*. If it is clear that Beckett is a brilliant exponent of the nihilism which Larry's casting off the burden of his past brings him to, it is also clear that *Waiting For Godot* is a play which comprehensively describes the forms and textures of human kinship in the face of that nihilism. The play deals with the relationships among the individuals in two pairs of characters. Much that these characters say, like much that Larry says, deals with the bankruptcy in the twentieth century of all philosophical and religious systems; and much else that they say deals with their mutual dependency upon one another. Vladimir and Estragon, the central pair, make clear that the only certainty they have in life, aside from their appetites and the inevitability of death, is the complex interaction of their feelings toward each other. Their conversations are in the main aggressive and mutually challenging, but when hurt or seriously challenged, each tends to lose confidence and seek comfort from the other, who generally provides it. Their exchanges are rapid-fire and are all — the tone of the dialogue leaves little doubt — rooted in their illusions. The only thing not illusory in what they say is the emotion which underlies it, and that emotion is half-destructive, half-supportive. Most important, there is great joy in this play. Its mood is never really dark for all that its themes are, and there is little question that the two central figures take genuine pleasure in one another's company. Their wait for some externally delivered meaning for life is futile, but their lives themselves do not feel futile. And this absence of futility seems inextricably linked to their total and freely acknowledged interdependence.

In discarding all beliefs and systems as illusory, Beckett in *Waiting For Godot* leaves man with only the bedrock reality of his human relationships. The real terror in the play is that of isolation. A moving, almost sentimental, view of human interdependency is the second of the two pairings, that between the authoritarian Pozzo and the hapless Lucky. Pozzo's cruelty and arrogance of the first act are reversed in the second, where Pozzo, now blind and helpless, is altogether the charge of the still-serving Lucky. Their relationship remains constant regardless of who at the moment happens to possess that greatest of all illusions, power. One might say of the play's second act, where all the characters become figures of great endurance and instinctive understanding, that *Waiting For Godot* envisions the workings of human kinship about as precisely as any play of the twentieth century.

Far more complexly presented, *The Iceman Cometh* is also a play about the possibilities of human kinship in the face of enervating twentieth-century nihilism. O'Neill's use of the phrase "the misbegotten" to describe Harry Hope's clientele parallels in mood and purpose the Chaplinesque quality of Beckett's heroes. They are, of course, not *misbegotten*, no more than any who endure the human condition. Or perhaps we are all misbegotten in the twentieth century, if to be otherwise means that we must adhere to traditional beliefs and values. Like Beckett's characters, O'Neill's, in their rejection and poverty, live at the bedrock of reality and must strain if they are to maintain the life-preserving illusions which the more fortunate among us keep up more easily but are still very much indebted to. And also like Beckett's characters, O'Neill's establish the dramatic shape of their interdependence through their dialogue — in O'Neill as in Beckett, dialogue which is essentially characterized by its endlessly varied rhythm of alternating hostility and affection. Through his minor characters and their groupings, O'Neill in *The Iceman Cometh* makes a giant step toward the full expression of his language of kinship.

To begin with, Harry Hope expresses in his monologues the oscillations of feeling which are for O'Neill the essence of kinship. In the earlier plays, those oscillations were most apparent in the voluble Irishmen — Driscoll, and Paddy, and Mat Burke — who first captured the ebbs and flows of kinship in rhythms which were like those of the sea on which they lived. O'Neill presented their capacity to give uninhibited voice to the split-second changes in their moods as a great natural gift, and this gift he later passed on in purest form to Con Melody and later still to Harry Hope. The sharply contradictory feelings of people living in close proximity are heard and felt in almost every speech of the volatile Harry. We encounter them first in his savage attack on the unfortunate Willie Oban. Early in Act One, Harry attacks Willie for singing so early in the morning and threatens to send him to his miserable room because of the noise; but when Willie "dissolves into pitiable terror" at the prospect, Harry immediately relents. Without warning, he becomes ostentatiously charitable toward Willie and instead attacks Rocky for refusing the poor lad a drink. Then, equally without warning, he relents toward Rocky — and so in turn each member of the group first feels the sting of Harry's voluble abuse, then is abruptly forgiven and rewarded with a drink. The antiphony of loudly expressed, altogether contradictory emotions which constitute the core of Harry Hope is the core of kinship in this play.

Harry's speeches in the second act follow the same pattern. Sober, to defy Hickey, he arrives at his much-anticipated sixtieth birthday party with what he calls "a real grouch on" and proceeds to roast everyone in turn:

> Cut out the glad hand, Hickey. D'you think I'm a sucker?
> I know you, bejees, you sneaking, lying drummer! (*With
> rising anger, to the others*) And all you bums! What
> the hell you trying to do, yelling and raising the roof?
> Want the cops to close the joint and get my license
> taken away? (*He yells at Cora who has stopped singing
> but continues to play mechanically with many mistakes*)

Hey, you dumb tart, quit banging that box! Bejees, the
least you could do is learn the tune!

(III. 654)

But as soon as he sees how much he has hurt them, Harry's hostility melts:

Listen, all of you! Bejees, forgive me. I lost
my temper! I ain't feeling well! I got a hell of
a grouch on! Bejees, you know you're all as welcome
here as the flowers in May! (*They look at him with
eager forgiveness. Rocky is the first who can voice it*)
Rocky: Aw, sure, Boss, you're aces wid us, see?

(III. 660)

He is aces with them, and they with him, and all is well — until the next
volley, which follows very soon.

The progression of Harry's feelings is relatively clear and represents
O'Neill's paradigm of human feeling generally. Harry does what is necessary to maintain his illusions — that is, he drinks. Any attack upon the insulation of those illusions — statements by others or the intrusion of sobriety
— enrages him. To regain his insular position, he attacks the intruder, usually the person last addressing him, whether or not that is the real intruder. He attacks explosively and, on the surface at least, viciously. But
almost before the attack is over, Harry becomes aware of the person he is
addressing, and that awareness immediately translates itself into compassion and regret. His instincts are thus both to protect himself (his illusions) *and* to nurture. Both instincts are expressed freely and fully, neither
is ascendant over the other, and neither is relinquishable in the face of the
other.

And so the process is established for the others. Beginning with
some hurt or imagined hurt, some assault or imagined assault upon a
character's fortress of illusion, often merely the result of that character's
waking up sober, the character lashes out with an attack on his neighbor's
most sacred territory — whether or not the neighbor is the offender. And
the neighbor replies in kind. In the normal state of affairs — that is, the
state of affairs early in the play — this takes the form of some crudely comical insult exchange from which the parties quickly recover. But occasionally, the attacks and counterattacks develop into torrents before the forgiveness sets in. The volleys of abuse may in fact threaten violence, but in
the normal state of things the hostility subsides before harm is done. One
party, realizing the hurt he or she is inflicting, becomes sorry or apolo-

getic, the other party returns in kind, and a harmony is reestablished — a harmony of mutually-respected pipe dreams.

To understand how things are *in the beginning* — that is, before Hickey's arrival — we must consider the arrangement of the characters which opens the play. At the very beginning, we have Larry as narrator, serving as a kind of god to his own nihilism, "creating" his world of the misbegotten. One by one, Larry introduces the newly arrived Parritt to the residents at the saloon. Larry does so "with sardonic relish," says O'Neill, "but at the same time showing his affection for them." (III. 593). The first characters we meet are the worst off in that they are the most isolated. The brilliant Willie Oban, the most pitiable, sits alone and communicates only in alcoholic extremes of biting wit and haunting fear. He is very badly off, but since he does manage communication of a sort, he can barely manage to survive. Following Willie, just a little better off by virtue of a special though enigmatic relationship with Larry, is the old bomb-thrower Hugo Kalmar, the arrogant East European revolutionary whose pipe dream is to be a member of the aristocracy. Hugo's articulation of the pain that sobriety and the necessary facing of reality brings with it is the most poignant in the play. Because he is so articulate, he later describes for us most precisely what the others feel in response to Hickey's "saving" message.

Only a little better off than Willie and Hugo is one of the play's most brilliant and prophetic characterizations, that of the black gambler Joe Mott. A descendant of Brutus Jones, Joe is certainly the American black as the American white establishment has forced him to be, though his name suggests that he may also stand for other racial and religious minorities as well.[11] Desperately isolated, full of indignation, he capitulates not so much because of his personal ghosts, though they exist, as out of a necessity bred by the inescapable vulnerability America has forced upon its racial minorities. He is linked at first with the urban Italian-American pair Rocky and Chuck, but the link is an unwilling one on both sides, and their "reconciliation" is particularly debasing to Joe. His relations with the white African pair, Lewis and Wetjoen, who stand in part for the black man's earlier tormentors, seem more promising from the start and develop to the point where in the end Joe actually joins (or should one say, rejoins) their "table." Joe is better off than Hugo or Willie. He moves boisterously and genially among the groups, but he evokes perhaps the greatest compassion of all in his outburst against white society in Act Three. The individual afflicted by his inner fears (Willie) and the individual afflicted by a repressive society (Joe) are seen as essentially in the same condition.

Then there are the groups at the other tables, each a community made up of a pair of individuals accompanied by a single individual. Usually the members of the pair are better off than the single individual at the table because they feel less isolated, though all are better off than the most isolated Willie, Hugo, and Joe. At one table are paired the former British Army captain, Cecil Lewis, and the Afrikaans farmer, Piet Wetjoen — the old Boer War team — in residence with the former war correspondent Jimmy Cameron (Jimmy "Tomorrow"). Jimmy is only a step removed from Willie, Hugo, and Joe in the extent of his isolation. At another table sits the Irish-American team of Harry Hope and his pair of sponging cronies Pat McGloin, the corrupt policeman, and Ed Mosher, the former circus . barker. The similarity in pattern between this table and the first is obvious enough, but so too is the dissimilarity. Among other things, O'Neill consciously avoids symmetry and system in this play. Quite unlike the spineless Jimmy of the first table, Harry is boss at the second by virtue of his position and his verbosity. McGloin and Mosher never emerge as far from the background as do the earlier pair, Lewis and Wetjoen. Then, behind the bar, is a pair without accompanying single partner, Rocky and Chuck, whose battles approach violence and whose reconciliations are deep and convincing. And at another table, in the adjoining bar, are the whores, Margie and Pearl, who are joined sporadically by the more isolated Cora. Margie and Pearl are also in a pair-single relationship with the pimping Rocky, who joins their table at crucial moments; and Cora is seen often in tandem with Chuck, the sole man-woman pairing on stage in the play.

The essential pattern of kinship is evident in all these groups. Hostility among them is always associated with some kind of interference with pipe dreams, reconciliation with a return to those dreams, a return which it is important to say is in no way isolating but is instead unifying. These people are closest to one another when most comforted by their illusions and farthest from one another when they are most insecure about their illusions. As the overall effect is unschematized, these relationships are quite difficult to illustrate, but one passage may serve to convey the quality of much of the first act, the "beginning" state of things before Hickey arrives. When we first meet them, each character is at his most desperate because he has just waked up sober and, of course, hung over:

> (. . . at the middle table, Captain Lewis and
> General Wetjoen are as wide awake as heavy hangovers
> permit. Jimmy Tomorrow nods, his eyes blinking.
> Lewis is gazing across the table at Joe Mott, . . . The
> expression on Lewis's face is that of one who can't
> believe his eyes)

Lewis: (*aloud to himself, with muzzy wonder*) Good God!
    Have I been drinking at the same table with a bloody
    Kaffir?

Joe: (*grinning*) Hello, Captain. You comin' up for air?
    Kaffir? Who's he?

Wetjoen: (*blurrily*) Kaffir, dot's a nigger, Joe. (*Joe
    stiffens and his eyes narrow. Wetjoen goes on with
    heavy jocosity*) Dot's joke on him, Joe. He don't
    know you. He's still plind drunk, the ploody Limey
    chentleman! A great mistake I missed him at the
    pattle of Modder River. Vit mine rifle I shoot damn
    fool Limey officers py the dozen, but him I miss.
    De pity of it! (*He chuckles and slaps Lewis on his
    bare shoulder*) Hey, wake up, Cecil, you ploody fool!
    Don't you know your old friend, Joe? He's no Kaffir!
    He's white, Joe is!

Lewis: (*light dawning — contritely*) My profound apologies,
    Joseph, old chum. Eyesight a trifle blurry, I'm afraid. . . .
    No hard feelings, what? (*He holds out his hand*)

Joe: (*at once grins good-naturedly and shakes his hand*) No,
    Captain, I know it's mistake. Youse regular, if you
    are a Limey. (*Then his face hardening*) But I don't
    stand for "nigger" from nobody. Never did. In de old
    days, people calls me "nigger" wakes up in de hospital.
    I was de leader ob de Dirty Half-Dozen Gang. All six
    of us colored boys, we was tough and I was de toughest.

Wetjoen: (*inspired to boastful reminiscence*) Me, in old days
    in Transvaal, I vas so tough and strong I grab axle
    of ox wagon mit full load and lift like feather.

Lewis: (*smiling amiably*) As for you, my balmy Boer that
    walks like a man, I say again it was a grave error
    in our foreign policy ever to set you free, once we
    nabbed you and your commando Cronje. We should
    have taken you to the London zoo and incarcerated
    you in the baboons' cage. With a sign: "Spectators
    may distinguish the true baboon by his blue behind."

Wetjoen: (*grins*) Gott! To dink, ten better Limey officers,
    at least, I shoot clean in the mittle of forehead
    at Skion Kopje, and you I miss! I neffer forgive
    myself!

                                        (III. 598–600)

What we have here is a complex interplay of emotions involving
three characters. Each character is in the process of moving from hostility
to good will, though since the artificial symmetry that characterizes much

of the dialogue in *More Stately Mansions* is missing, that emotional movement is more difficult to trace. Captain Lewis, his pipe dream of racial superiority briefly threatened by his finding himself awake, sober, and in the company of a black, is quickly reconciled with Joe but enters upon a familiar refrain of abuse and counterabuse with Wetjoen. As old war enemies, Lewis and Wetjoen have established a kinship which is deeper than that between Lewis and Joe. Thus their hostility is more severe and their reconciliations more pronounced. But the tone of the hostility at this point is still no more than the jesting camaraderie characteristic of most fraternal relationships. The hostility is not yet the virulent sort we shall encounter later. My quotation stops at this point because to go on with the ensuing outflow of good will among these figures would take too long. But following the lines quoted, and as the effects of the first morning drink take hold, each character in the room gives a recital of his personal pipe dream, in the course of which Lewis and Wetjoen exchange the warmest, most mutually respecting utterances. The emotion, previously jestingly hostile, now becomes sentimentally affectionate. We know, of course, that the hostilities will resume, but so too will a return to the harmony follow the hostilities.

All this — the hostility and the good will — grows out of the illusions these characters are striving to preserve, but that is not the main point. The main point is that the emotions themselves are authentic and the continuing rhythm of their oscillation, albeit with variations, is assured. Though these figures live at the bottom of civilized human existence, as Larry tells us, they freely feel all the emotions that cluster around hurt and resentment countered by all the emotions that cluster around forgiveness and reconciliation. In short, they feel what everyone feels, their drink serving only to intensify both sets of feelings. This is the point that Hickey misses in his reforming zeal. He fails to see that from the start the illusions these people protect are their means of communication, and that throwing off their illusions will result in nothing more than the perpetual hell of isolation. He also fails to recognize, both in the other characters and in himself, the necessary alternation of hostility and affection. Like most reformers, he wants to cast all hostile reactions out of them, as he supposes he has cast all hostile reactions and all guilt out of himself. Hickey is seeking a utopian existence, and O'Neill now opposes utopias of any sort.

Hickey has in the past served an important purpose in Harry Hope's world. In the past, he has represented a break from the ordinary. But the break has not been a change, really. Hickey has been an extension of the nickel rotgut, more highly charging the pipe dreams and delaying longer the inevitable morning afters. He has allayed the tedium of the old ebbs and flows for a while, and thus has genuinely served to make the saloon-dwellers happier. This time Hickey arrives "saved," he believes, and determined to "free" others from their destructive pipe dreams as he feels he has been freed. But in his efforts to get the others to face themselves, he only does more penetratingly what they have been doing all along in their barroom aggressiveness. He attacks their pipe dreams, and the effect is to make what had usually been said under the protective canopy of raillery become serious. As this happens, real portents of violence begin to be heard. The central pairs begin to disintegrate. There cease to be the regular returns to the reciprocal acceptance that binds them. Moreover, the characters begin to gang up on one another, which we have not seen them do before. The idea of a scapegoat comes into being. We see groups under pressure to "face" their illusions attacking their weaker members as a means of reassuring themselves.

The sickness Hickey comes to cure is for most simply the fear of disappointment and failure all flesh is heir to. To admit one's pipe dreams and to confront one's fears is for Harry Hope and company as for Relling's "average man" only to be made miserable, hopeless, and alone. The rehabilitation Hickey seeks is not possible. Illusion and kinship for most people go hand in hand — which is not to call kinship an illusion. Kinship is authentic. Most people simply need illusion as a catalyst in achieving it. But there are heroes in the fold, and a hero in O'Neill's later plays is one who can in fact "face his ghosts," who can live without illusion and in kinship with others. O'Neill is explicit about this in every play from *A Touch of the Poet* on. I suggested earlier that Larry's stature is larger than the others because he does cast out his fears and his armor of protective illusion, and he has the strength not only to survive but to continue helping others to survive. Hickey is larger yet, in ways we must now examine. Like Larry he lives out a terrible ceremony of emotional exorcism, but Hickey does so aloud, in public, for others to see and learn from. Larry's agony in the Parritt affair is treated throughout as a personal matter, as are his reactions to Parritt's suicide. No one knows, or will ever know, the significance of that falling body but Larry, not even an audience unfamiliar with O'Neill's life and earlier works. But everyone can know and understand what happens to Hickey. Hickey is wrong in what he tries to do for the others, but he is not wrong finally in what he does for himself.

Hickey, misled and misleading, nevertheless finally transcends all others in this play because he most openly and clearly brings together its two affirming energies: the energies of confession and kinship. Con-

fession we have encountered in the many personal confessions throughout O'Neill's works, and kinship we have encountered in the dialogue of
genuinely communicating people ever since the *S. S. Glencairn* series.
But we have rarely encountered them together as we do in the character of Hickey. We have never heard a confession like the one we hear
from Hickey, and we have encountered no embodiment of the spirit
of human kinship, with all its ebbs and flows starkly in evidence, to
rival his. O'Neill through Hickey goes beyond the nihilism of Larry
Slade.

Hickey's great confession anticipates Jamie's in *Long Day's Journey*
and *A Moon for the Misbegotten* in that he lives out what he is confessing
as he confesses it. Hickey starts intending to confess "everything," and
ends up confessing more than he thought was there to confess. In the
practiced manner of the brilliant raconteur that he is, he builds up slowly
to the story of how he came to kill his wife out of love. He thinks he is admitting all the foulness that is in him by recounting the many times and
ways he betrayed his wife, always to return and be forgiven. He confirms
what he believes to be the totality of his confession by asserting that he
came finally to hate her forgivings and her belief in him. But these are all
realizations bred by Hickey's not very strong reason, and the "freedom"
he thinks he has achieved by murdering his wife is the muddled pseudo-
freedom rationalized confessions lead to. Hickey is not free until the last
phrase of his long confession because though he states that he hated his
wife, he has never really come to grips with the reality of that hatred.
Even his admission that he killed her to spare her his betrayals is a ration-
alization. He killed her because he hated her, pure and simple — and only
in reliving this hatred does he understand it for what it is: "Well, you
know what you can do with your pipe dream now, you damned bitch!"
He actually has these hateful feelings as he expresses them. But even in ex-
pressing them, the realization is not complete. He must also relive the
equally potent feelings of the love which completes his kinship, and this
takes place immediately following his famous explosion. As his hatred
was great enough to result in his act of ultimate violence, so is his love for
her large-scale and authentic:

> No! That's a lie! I never said — ! Good God,
> I couldn't have said that! If I did, I'd gone
> insane! Why, I loved Evelyn better than any-
> thing in life.
>
>   (III. 716)

And he means it.

Throughout his adult life, Hickey's love and hate had lived inside him — twin feelings, neither of which could ever affect the other. This twinning of opposite, mutually exclusive, feelings is what O'Neill's dialogue of kinship has been revealing and will reveal further about all close human relationships. Who really cares about the cause of Hickey's hatred — the guilt, the envy — or of his love either, for that matter? The facts are simple, that the hate was terribly real, and the love equally so. Only the failure to *recognize* these twin truths breeds the violence: to recognize that authentic love cannot in fact even exist without an accompanying hate. Hickey's tale is an extreme one, but it is through extremes that tragedy has always communicated.

Hickey's doom is the sole tragic irony in this play — because for all the joyous, mock-hypocritical exploitation of his false "insanity" by the pipe dreamers, Hickey has in fact been insane, as many are insane. He has at a crucial moment lost touch with reality, not because he hated his wife, but because he never acknowledged the inevitability of that hatred. He did not perceive reality because he could not perceive the irreconcilable extremes which govern man's inescapably contradictory nature. The result was the burst of violence by which true tragedy brings things home to us. Hickey is himself ready to die for his crime, not out of guilt so much as for his failure in perception. Like Shakespeare's Gloucester in *King Lear*, he really was blind when he thought he could see. The ever-cerebral Larry, thinking as much of the still-living symbol of his own agony, Parritt, as of Hickey, hopes that "the Chair" may "bring him peace at last," but the Hickey led out by the police is already and for the first time actually at peace with himself. He has grown in a moment of deep, sudden recognition, and his growth adds to his already mythic stature. The "lord of misrule" has become tragic hero. No longer the "average man," he must *see* where others cannot.

Though Larry Slade is stage center at the end of the play, it is the departed Hickey the end of the play celebrates.[12] Hickey's spirit of old — Hickey the bringer of fellowship and good will — governs the saturnalia in which all take part but the benumbed Larry. Hickey has failed in his misguided mission, but he has succeeded in bringing about that kind of release he has always inspired. The celebration we witness at the close of the play is a celebration of the essential Hickey, the Hickey of his previous visits. It is a full, vital expression of the joyful pole of kinship, as the

morning after will be the most abysmal expression of its inevitable opposite. The flow of feeling from individual to individual is true, even if it *is* a
flow three parts whiskey to one part fellowship. The cacophony which
dominates these final festivities, resulting from each person literally "singing his own song" is an altogether welcome dissonance which tells us that
the kinship we have encountered here is real. This clash of songs is one of
the few musical images we ever get from O'Neill, but it is a fitting one.
The sound is not pleasant, but it is the sound of release — and that is the
most satisfying sound of all in the plays of Eugene O'Neill.

In the midst of the festivities Larry sits alone and "stares oblivious to
their racket" — a counter-image, but no more than that. Larry's responses
at the end of the play are, as they have always been, cerebral — and cerebral response can lead only to despair in *The Iceman Cometh*. But the
party which goes on around him is as much a part of this scene as Larry's
ashen detachment. Larry's nihilism cannot be denied, but even Larry acknowledges, by his continuing existence and his abiding loyalty to his
"misbegotten" cohorts, that there will be a morning after and that he will
have duties to perform. Unlike Parritt, Larry does not *go*.[13]

9 *Hughie*

Hughie SEEMS A BY-PRODUCT OF *The Iceman Cometh* in that it concentrates on two figures who would fit in perfectly well around one of
the back-room tables at Harry Hope's. In *Hughie*, however, the dialogue
does not dramatize an ongoing relationship of the kind we see at Harry's
but rather how such a relationship comes to pass. It is a brief play enacting a passage from chaos to kinship. Though the play is almost pure monologue, both characters in it are equally important. And the monologue
in question is mostly confessional monologue, bearing much similarity to
Hickey's long confession in *The Iceman Cometh*. Only after Erie Smith's
long and rambling summary of his seamy past and of his crushing sense of
loss at the death of his friend, a confession which is deeply affecting but
cannot change the fact of Erie's emotional and moral bankruptcy, does his
kinship with the Night Clerk suddenly and unexpectedly find its terms.
Thus, as in *The Iceman Cometh*, the two processes in this play which relieve man of his misery and quiet his panic are confession and kinship —
and the greatest of these here, as there, is kinship.

The events of O'Neill's past are still important here, though as in all
the last plays, they are secondary to the vision of human kinship the play
evolves. Erie is like Hickey before him — and Willie Oban (all have names
ending in the familiar "ie" sound) — primarily a dramatic representation of
brother Jamie, this time with emphasis on the "Broadway sport" image
which will be stressed again in *A Moon for the Misbegotten*. This Jamie is
primarily a gambler, though his alcoholism is in ample evidence; and he
has known the company of a long string of "tarts," some of whom, he admits, were pretty "raw babies." Jamie's educated wit is not shared by Erie;
but Erie is certainly as articulate as Jamie, and he is able to bring to pass

157

his saving kinship chiefly because he is quick of tongue. Erie is also like Jamie in being perpetually down on his luck. Whether his bad luck is the result of his vices, or his vices the result of the bad luck — quite the condition of James Tyrone, Jr. — Erie is never able to get up off the floor. For all his mastery of words, he is, like Jamie, first and last the perennial "loser."

Erie's being a loser, of course, is primarily associated with his past, a past which is treated more obscurely than Hickey's but in which certain particulars make the identification with Jamie inescapable. Erie's reference to "a blond movie doll on the train" from Tia Juana with whom he came "all the way in a drawing room" explicitly anticipates Jamie's confession in *A Moon for the Misbegotten*, though it is not put in the same context of frenzied guilt. So, too, do Erie's references to other "dolls," one of whom took him "to the cleaners." Erie is, he admits, "a sucker for blondes," as is the retrograde Jamie who takes senseless revenge at his mother's death. And that mother herself is also represented in *Hughie*. She is figured in Erie's references to the late Hughie's wife, who rejected Erie as "a bad influence" on her husband as Jamie was rejected as a bad influence on O'Neill. Erie, Jamie-like, has tried valiantly to win that proper lady around, though equally Jamie-like, he remains vindictive toward her to the end.

What O'Neill again wants chiefly to emphasize in this play is his admiration for his late brother, and this he does through the story of the horseshoe of roses Erie has sent to Hughie's funeral. The main themes here are familiar: the all-out generosity of Erie's Jamie-like affection and the sacrifice he is willing to undergo to express it. The supposedly tight-fisted, cheating gambler is, under his Broadway facade, a generous and loving figure. He anticipates the Jamie of *Long Day's Journey* in giving all he has, dangerously increasing his own vulnerability, out of love for "his brother." Erie literally endangers himself by borrowing money from gangsters to pay for Hughie's roses without the means to pay it back.

O'Neill himself also makes his appearance in the play. He is certainly the Hughie who found Erie's gambling and loose women "romantic" and whose wife/mother was "narrow-minded about gamblers."[1] At striking moments he is also Erie himself — as when Erie speaks of turning away Hughie's troubled concern about his wife. "Believe me, Pal," says Erie, "I can stop guys that start telling me their family troubles." This seems a fairly explicit allusion to O'Neill's oft-alluded-to indifference to Jamie following their mother's death.

But on the whole, *Hughie* is a play devoted to Jamie and to kinship. Like all the final plays, it is not alone about hauntings but about the triumph over hauntings; and the figure O'Neill envisions doing the triumphing is the figure representing his brother. Erie's very name suggests that the theme of haunting here should not be taken seriously. It is like that of the "eerie" tale, the ghost story intended to be laughed at. Erie's boasts and posturings, which are the evasions of his pain, are essentially clownish, and we are invited to be amused rather than terrified. Unlike the earlier plays, we here in no way identify with this hero in his fear.

But we do identify with him as he seeks and finds kinship. O'Neill explores more intensely in this play even than in *The Iceman Cometh* the conditions of man's survival in the absence of philosophical direction. Erie at one point describes the state which existed between Hughie and his wife, which Erie greatly envied, in the following terms:

> Hughie and her seemed happy enough the time
> he had me out to dinner in their flat. Well,
> not happy. Maybe contented. No, that's boosting
> it, too. Resigned comes nearer. . . .
>
> (*Later Plays*, p. 279[2])

The crux of O'Neill's outlook on life in this period of his writing is implicit in these lines. He clearly lets Erie envy Hughie's relationship with his wife, but he quickly stifles Erie's temptation to sentimentalize that relationship. The critical word here is "resigned." It is a pivotal word standing precisely between the bearable and unbearable in human existence. It is a word which O'Neill can use without fear of falling into his earlier happy ending syndrome while still affirming man's instinct to endure. It is altogether tied in with the concept of kinship since what Hughie and his wife are *resigned* to is each other; and what Erie feels the loss of so terribly in the death of Hughie and is seeking to find again is no more than such resignation, even on the very small scale the Night Clerk might provide.

Erie, of course, has never found kinship with a woman, as Hughie did. The worst thing about the real and imagined "dolls" he keeps referring to is the mechanical quality of his relationships with them. They mutually exploit one another in their sex, then part — and this kind of exploitation, as O'Neill has already indicated and will again, is the most isolating of human relationships. The theme of the later *A Moon for the Misbegotten* is that kinship between man and woman is finally the most powerful of any, but that play amply attests how hard that kind of kinship is to come by. Here we have Erie's report on the kinship between Hughie and wife, but we directly encounter kinship only as it may develop between man and man, in an a-sexual relationship. Sex is a complicating, if not insurmountable, problem in the achievement of kinship for O'Neill — and here, as in *The Iceman Cometh*, he chooses largely to ignore it.

The other half of the pair in this play is the enigmatic Night Clerk, a figure less dynamic than Erie in being less voluble, but a figure no less important. O'Neill seems, intentionally, to have created in him a thorough resistance to rational understanding — either ours of him, or his of life. He comes about as close to being a twentieth-century embodiment of the ancient allegorical figure of Chaos as any in modern drama. Certainly all the images his mind spills out in senseless sequence and great profusion are chaotic in the extreme. For reasons we are not made party to, he is consumed with thoughts of mass destruction. He considers the dying "lucky," but we are presented nothing specific relating to why he might hate life — other than that he is bored. He is haunted by no past that we know of.

Early in the play, the Night Clerk seems happy living among his chaotic fantasies and neither listens to what Erie is saying nor says anything of significance to him. It comes, then, as something of a surprise when late in the play he suddenly acknowledges that he is lonely. He should be lonely, of course, but loneliness has never seemed to cross his mind, so secure has he seemed in his featherbed of futility. We finally discover, however, that he is human after all. In admitting his loneliness, he joins the rest of O'Neill's later characters. Up to the point at which the admission is made, he has referred to Erie only as "Mr. Smith" and thought of him only as "492" (Erie's room number); but with the admission of loneliness comes his acknowledgment of Erie's presence, then the acceptance of Erie's nickname, and finally, human contact.

Erie's agonizing appeal for communication with the Night Clerk works through all the stages of Erie's past, his pain, and his illusions. When we first see him, he is at the same low point as are the denizens of Harry Hope's saloon shortly after Hickey's unsuccessful therapy. He is hung over, of course, and going up to his room will mean hours of sleepless horror followed by nightmares more terrifying still. His illusions, which he as a gambler calls his "luck," are shot; and he can find no means by which to reawaken them. Previously, when he had been in such a condition, he had had a ready-made context in which he might rebuild those illusions. He could live out a make-believe gambling ritual (in which he was always the winner) with his late lamented friend. But Erie cannot reach the new Night Clerk. Even though this one looks like a reincarnation of the old one, and even has the same name, Erie cannot break into the cocoon of absurdity in which the new Night Clerk lives. It is not that Erie fails to try. He works through their similarities in age and background, their mutual interest in follies girls, their mutual interest even in gambling itself — a theme which as the play progresses is subtly winding its way slowly through the density of the Night Clerk's drab and violent imagination. But there is no signal to bring them together — no code word. The Night Clerk's responses continue to parallel Harry's "Who the hell cares?"

As Erie fails to get the response he needs, his monologue begins to fall back upon itself and becomes a withdrawal not unlike the Night Clerk's own. He gets farther and farther away from the still abstracted Night Clerk, so far in fact that he all but misses the code word when suddenly it is spoken:

> **Night Clerk:** . . . Do you by any chance know — Arnold
>   Rothstein?
> **Erie:** *(his train of thought interrupted — irritably)*
>   Arnold? What's he got to do with it? He
>   wouldn't loan a guy like me a nickel to save
>   my grandmother from streetwalking.
> **Night Clerk:** *(with humble awe)* Then you do know him!
> **Erie:** Sure I know the bastard. Who don't on Broadway?
>   And he knows me — when he wants to. He uses me
>   to run errands when there ain't no one else
>   handy. But he ain't my trouble, Pal. My
>   trouble is, some of these guys I put the bite
>   on is dead wrong G's, and they expect to be paid
>   back next Tuesday, or else I'm outa luck and have
>   to take it on the lam, or I'll get beat up and
>   may be sent to the hospital.
>   (*The Later Plays*, p. 289)

Erie goes on to talk about his run of bad luck and his increasing despair. It is he, this time, who will not allow the Night Clerk to break in.

> **Night Clerk:** *(pleadingly)* Just a minute, Erie, if you
>   don't mind. *(With awe)* So you're an old friend
>   of Arnold Rothstein! Would you mind telling me
>   if it's really true when Arnold Rothstein plays
>   poker, one white chip is — a hundred dollars?
> **Erie:** *(dully exasperated)* Say, for Christ's sake,
>   what's it to you — ? *(He stops abruptly,
>   staring probingly at the Clerk. There is a pause.*

Suddenly his face lights up with a saving revela-
tion. He grins warmly and saunters confidently
back to the desk) Say Charlie, why didn't
you put me wise before, you was interested in
gambling?

(*The Later Plays,* p. 290)

The name Arnold Rothstein is actually spoken, and repeated, by the Night Clerk himself. It is Erie now who is lost in his trance and "will not hear." But the Night Clerk is persistent and the message gets through — just barely. Erie's confidence (his "luck") returns with the kinship implied by their new relationship. He is "saved," says O'Neill not insignificantly. They begin what will become their nightly crap game in which Erie, with his loaded dice, is the invariable winner, and from which both find protection from the abyss. The Night Clerk, Hughes, becomes the new Hughie, and Erie becomes the high roller in a game that will restore him to life.[3]

One thing becomes abundantly clear as we see the beginnings of this kinship develop. The words "illusion," or "life-lie," or even "pipe dream" have very little meaning — as they did not finally in *The Iceman Cometh.* Neither of the two characters in the least believes in the fantasy he is creating. There is no assumption that the crap game will be authentic. Erie gives Hughes the money to make the bet, and Hughes knows that Erie's dice are loaded. So there can be no thought that either of these characters is fooling himself or the other. They are only creating the form or container in which their kinship may live and thrive. Nothing has happened to convince Hughes that mass destruction is not bliss; and nothing has happened to convince Erie his luck will return. But now their responses, focussed on their two-man game, have been made part of a living order. They are now a team, free to express (through their game) their wildest dreams to one another and be heard, free to utter their deepest agonies to one another and be heard. We are too early in the relationship to actually begin to feel the rhythm of their kinship, the hostility which will alternate with the newfound affection, but it will be forthcoming, as we know from Erie's story of his relationship with Hughie. This play is more concerned with the conditions of kinship than with its actual processes, and those conditions have been carefully and feelingly laid out.

Hughie anticipates the rash of quasi-philosophical two-character plays of the decades succeeding it. Like Beckett's pairs in *Waiting for*

Godot, Erie and Hughes need only the relationship their make-believe provides for them to know kinship and to survive. They are also not unlike the pair in Edward Albee's one-act *Zoo Story,* a play which is also about establishing the conditions for kinship. But in Albee's play, kinship comes to pass only in the instant before death. It is, implicitly, not really available to people in life. The kinship of Jerry and Peter is created only in the ancient stoic ritual wherein one recognizes his truest friend as he who can be persuaded to hold the sword on which one may thrust oneself. No on-going contact is made between the characters in Albee's play because there is none to be made except in the mutual acceptance of death. *Hughie,* on the other hand, is a play about the defeating of death. Downtrodden and unhealthy as they are — Erie is like Jamie certainly well on his way to an alcoholic's demise — O'Neill's pair enacts the establishment of a relationship which will allow them to live, and by living justify existence. The relationship between Erie and Hughes will survive as long as the frailties of their physical beings will permit — which may not be very long, as in the case of the late Hughie, but which makes no difference whatsoever to what the play is about. In discovering their kinship, the characters have been transformed from dust into life. They are not happy, they are not contented — but they are *resigned.*

10 Long Day's Journey Into Night

IN TALKING ABOUT *Long Day's Journey*, as in talking about *The Iceman Cometh*, one must begin, not end, with its despair. This play grows not out of O'Neill's autobiographical agony, but out of his triumph over that agony, a triumph which is obvious in the very fact of the play's searing explicitness—especially regarding Mary Tyrone. The whole point about her addiction is that in this play it is no longer seen as the most shameful of horrors. Mary's affliction and her accompanying guilt are treated here with a detachment made all the more effective by being anything but clinical. But O'Neill's objectivity has come at a price, the price paid by Larry Slade in his great struggle and victory. The price is the loss of all illusions and the inevitable sense of universal emptiness that accompanies such a loss. The "night" that this play, and O'Neill's entire creative career, has been a "long journey into" is one of now-uncynical disbelief in everything. At the end of the play there are no rights and wrongs, goods or evils, ups or downs, panics or manias—only the image of four beings linked together around a faintly lit electric light in an illimitable ocean of darkness.

There are, as in *The Iceman Cometh*, two stages in the despair of this play. First there is the cynicism born in both sons by the deprivation of motherly affection when it was crucially needed. That their mother is a "dope fiend," a "hop head," is only their adult shame. The real failure has been Mary's withdrawals themselves, quite apart from the social stigma attached to her addiction. And the play's most poignant utterance of this fact is Jamie's in his quotation from Swinburne's "A Leave-Taking" near the end: "Yea, though we sang as angels in her ear, She would not hear." The needed love withheld, the sons have come to know feelings of intense bitterness which are expressed typically in their cynical humor. Jamie observes that he has been made a "cynical bastard" by his mother's repeated "leave-takings." He reveals through his reference to her addiction as "a game" the real source of his renowned iconoclasm. His gambling and drink are simply extensions of her narcotic. Still more explicitly does Edmund see his mother's condition as the source of his despair. Learning of her addiction, he says, "made everything seem rotten." The psychologist O'Neill has learned, of his brother and himself, that their negative feelings about life resulted quite simply from a very early, critical deprivation of mother-love — a deprivation which was followed in their adolescence by rational disillusionment with their addicted mother and by shame before society at the evidences of her condition.

But the "night" of the play's ending goes beyond despair — as do all O'Neill's last plays. Jamie's evoking of Swinburne also speaks of a state of despondency "without fear":

> Let us rise up and part; she will not know.
> Let us go seaward as the great winds go,
> Full of blown sand and foam; what help is there?
> There is no help, *for all these things are so,*
> And all the world is bitter as a tear.
>
> (Yale edition, p. 173. Emphasis added[1])

It is the acceptance of *fact* that is so important about this quotation. It is O'Neill's acceptance of his, and man's, incapacity to direct his life by moral ideals. Whatever life is, it is — and man's only means of survival is to live it. We move away from moral decision-making, away from hope, away from disappointment, away even from the irony which is tied to the failure of ideals — and we move toward an acceptance of life rooted in its processes. And the main process associated with that acceptance is the relating of humans to one another, a process which it has been Mary's sole real failure to have been so little a part of. This play is primarily about human isolation, seen mostly through Mary, and human kinship, seen mostly through the men. It is a play which sees in human kinship man's sole means of survival in the vast night that both man's reason and his ideals have led him to.

There is not a single scene or episode in which the basic rhythm of kinship is not heard or felt in this play.[2] Even in the frenzied second and third acts — where we see the characters pulling away from one another in torrents of deception, suspicion, and recrimination — there are recurrent outbursts of the most genuine if anguished love. The love exists in and may be expressed by any of the three men, but it must come first from Mary, who turns the flows of kinship on and off in these acts as her fears and affections dictate. When she is haltingly and desperately able to admit her awareness of her condition, or Edmund's, the feelings of kinship are immediately apparent. But such admissions by Mary are invariably followed by panic and withdrawal. Nothing is more isolating for the men than her persistent "stubborn denials" of the facts regarding her affliction and her son's illness. The alternation of these denials with Mary's outbursts of affection and appeals for sympathy constitute the basic rhythm of kinship in the middle acts of this play, but as those outbursts and appeals are highly repressed and increasingly hopeless because of Mary's progress into her narcotic state, so the sense of isolation in these acts is the most intense in the play. The rhythm of kinship is always present, but in these most desperate scenes of the play, it is overwhelmed by the bitterness of deception and hurt.

Kinship in this play largely derives from what we see and hear not in its middle acts but in its opening and closing acts. And it is now more a true language rather than merely a recurrent rhythm of kinship we are talking about since O'Neill seems so consciously and primarily concerned with the emotional ups and downs his dialogue traces. In the opening act we hear a language of everyday kinship, while in the last we hear the language of a far deeper kinship elicited by severe emotional pressure. It is that opening language I wish to examine first, and to examine in a way I have not heretofore employed.

In discussing O'Neill's dialogue, I have followed the customary procedure of making interpretive observations and supplementing them with appropriate illustrations aimed at suggesting the rhythm. So many emotional variations are packed into the dialogue of these later plays, however, that the number of illustrations which might really be needed to show the complexities is precluded by the amount of time and space available. Nevertheless, to do justice to O'Neill's art, I believe that in one instance an extended passage should be included which might, regardless of length, more fully suggest the emotional shifts and changes typical of the dialogue generally in these plays. I would like therefore to examine two episodes from Act One from the point of view of the emotional interactions and variations they contain. The first is the family scene in which Edmund tells the anecdote about Shaughnessy's pigs — that anecdote which is enlarged and made central to the first half of *A Moon for the Misbegotten* — and the second is the extended exchange which follows between Jamie and James. I shall not discuss these episodes in the abstract but shall instead seek to annotate them with indications of the sharply varying emotions underlying their dialogue. Both episodes evoke a sense of the close kinship which exists among these people — the second, in the sharpness of its anger and the bitterness of its recriminations no less revealing of the closeness than the first, with its mutually enjoyed joke. In fact, the hostile scene may be more revealing of that closeness because the subjects discussed are critical to the family's survival.

To begin the first of the two episodes in *Long Day's Journey* then, Jamie and Edmund enter laughing from the dining room to interrupt James's and Mary's opening conversation:

> **Mary:** (*turns smilingly to them, in a merry tone that is a bit forced*) I've been teasing your father about his snoring.
>
> (*To Tyrone*)
> I'll leave it to the boys, James. They must have heard you. No, not you, Jamie. I could hear you down the hall almost as bad as your father. You're like him. As soon as your head touches the pillow you're off and ten foghorns couldn't wake you.
>
> (*She stops abruptly, catching Jamie's eyes regarding her with an uneasy, probing look. Her smile vanishes and her manner becomes self-conscious*)
> Why are you staring, Jamie?
>
> (*Her hands flutter up to her hair*)
> Is my hair coming down? It's hard for me to do it up properly now. My eyes are getting so bad and I never can find my glasses.

Mary's concern for her hair is the first overt evidence of her return to her addiction.

> **Jamie:** (*looks away guiltily*)
> Your hair's all right, Mama. I was only thinking how well you look.

Jamie, in fear and suspicion, reveals his feeling with his eyes, but uncharacteristically he disguises his fear.

> **Tyrone:** (*heartily*)
> Just what I've been telling her, Jamie. She's so fat and sassy, there'll soon be no holding her.

James puts up his usual "front."

> **Edmund:** Yes, you certainly look grand, Mama.
> *(She is reassured and smiles at him lovingly. He winks with a kidding grin)*
> I'll back you up about Papa's snoring. Gosh, what a racket!
>
> **Jamie:** I heard him, too.
> *(He quotes, putting on a ham-actor manner)*
> "The Moor, I know his trumpet."
> *(His mother and brother laugh)*

Jamie parodies his father.

> **Tyrone:** *(scathingly)*
> If it takes my snoring to make you remember Shakespeare instead of the dope sheet on the ponies, I hope I'll keep on with it.

James, hurt, counterattacks.

> **Mary:** Now, James! You mustn't be so touchy.
> *(Jamie shrugs his shoulders and sits down in the chair on her right)*
>
> **Edmund:** *(irritably)*
> Yes, for Pete's sake, Papa! The first thing after breakfast! Give it a rest, can't you?
> *(He slumps down in the chair at left of table next to his brother. His father ignores him)*

Edmund, hurt on behalf of Jamie, overreacts. This is typical of the brothers' relationship with their parents.

> **Mary:** *(reprovingly)*
> Your father wasn't finding fault with you. You don't have to always take Jamie's part. You'd think you were the one ten years older.
>
> **Jamie:** *(boredly)*
> What's all the fuss about? Let's forget it.
>
> **Tyrone:** *(contemptuously)*
> Yes, forget! Forget everything and face nothing! It's a convenient philosophy if you've no ambition in life except to —

James, in turn, overreacts, his anger having accumulated over the years.

> **Mary:** James, do be quiet.
> *(She puts an arm around his shoulder — coaxingly)*

You must have gotten out of the wrong side of the bed this morning.
(*To the boys, changing the subject*)
What were you two grinning about like Cheshire cats when you came in? What was the joke?

Mary in this scene consistently demonstrates her mastery of the maternal art of peacemaking, one of the many admirable qualities her addiction denies her.

Tyrone: (*with a painful effort to be a good sport*)
Yes, let us in on it, lads. I told your mother I knew damned well it would be one on me, but never mind that, I'm used to it.

Jamie: (*dryly*)
Don't look at me. This is the Kid's story.

Edmund: (*grins*)
I meant to tell you last night, Papa, and forgot it. Yesterday when I went for a walk I dropped in at the Inn —

Mary: (*worriedly*)
You shouldn't drink now, Edmund.

Edmund's and Jamie's mutual delight in this tale is very much part of the emotional ambience of their closeness, as is Mary's motherly care.

Edmund: (*ignoring this*)
And who do you think I met there, with a beautiful bun on, but Shaughnessy, the tenant on that farm of yours.

Mary: (*smiling*)
That dreadful man! But he is funny.

Tyrone: (*scowling*)
He's not so funny when you're his landlord. He's a wily Shanty Mick, that one. He could hide behind a corkscrew. What's he complaining about now, Edmund — for I'm damned sure he's complaining. I suppose he wants his rent lowered. I let him have the place for almost nothing, just to keep someone on it, and he never pays that till I threaten to evict him.

James's attack on Shaughnessy is born in part of the hostility he still feels toward Jamie and in part on his Con Melody-like aristocratic pretensions. In his heart James admires the Irishman and shares his contempt for the arrogant rich.

Edmund: No, he didn't beef about anything. He was so pleased with life he even bought a drink, and that's practically unheard of. He was delighted because he'd had a fight with your friend, Harker, the Standard Oil millionaire, and won a glorious victory.

Mary: (*with amused dismay*)
Oh, Lord! James, you'll really have to do something—

Tyrone: Bad luck to Shaughnessy, anyway!

James's carping reactions here form a counterpoint to the family's enjoyment—and their kinship.

Jamie: (*maliciously*)
I'll bet the next time you see Harker at the Club and give him the old respectful bow, he won't see you.

Edmund: Yes. Harker will think you're no gentleman for harboring a tenant who isn't humble in the presence of a king of America.

Tyrone: Never mind the Socialist gabble. I don't care to listen—

Mary: (*tactfully*)
Go on with your story, Edmund.

Edmund: (*grins at his father provocatively*)
Well, you remember, Papa, the ice pond on Harker's estate is right next to the farm, and you remember Shaughnessy keeps pigs. Well, it seems there's a break in the fence and the pigs have been bathing in the millionaire's ice pond, and Harker's foreman told him he was sure Shaughnessy had broken the fence on purpose to give his pigs a free wallow.

Mary: (*shocked and amused*)
Good heavens!

Mary, "shocked and amused," is contributing to a harmony they will shortly lose.

Tyrone: (*sourly, but with a trace of admiration*)
I'm sure he did, too, the dirty scallywag. It's like him.

Edmund: So Harker came in person to rebuke Shaughnessy.
   (*He chuckles*)
A very bonehead play! If I needed any further proof that our ruling plutocrats, especially the ones who inherited their boodle, are not mental giants, that would clinch it.

Tyrone: (*with appreciation, before he thinks*)
Yes, he'd be no match for Shaughnessy.
    (*Then he growls*)
Keep your damned anarchist remarks to yourself. I won't have them
in my house.
    (*But he is full of eager anticipation*)
What happened?

James's sense of identity with Shaughnessy breaks out, but he quickly stifles it. The positive response represents his instinct toward kinship with
his family.

Edmund: Harker had as much chance as I would with Jack Johnson.
Shaughnessy got a few drinks under his belt and was waiting at the
gate to welcome him. He told me he never gave Harker a chance to
open his mouth. He began by shouting that he was no slave Standard
Oil could trample on. He was a King of Ireland, if he had his rights,
and scum was scum to him, no matter how much money it had stolen
from the poor.

Edmund's rendition of the story's detail suggests both his joy and ability
in conveying its quality as well as reporting its facts. The story is a good
deal simpler than Edmund's sophistication in the telling of it.

Mary: Oh, Lord!
    (*But she can't help laughing*)

Edmund: Then he accused Harker of making his foreman break
down the fence to entice the pigs into the ice pond in order to destroy
them. The poor pigs, Shaughnessy yelled, had caught their death of
cold. Many of them were dying of pneumonia, and several others had
been taken down with cholera from drinking the poisoned water. He
told Harker he was hiring a lawyer to sue him for damages. And he
wound up by saying that he had to put up with poison ivy, ticks, po-
tato bugs, snakes and skunks on his farm, but he was an honest man
who drew the line somewhere, and he'd be damned if he'd stand for a
Standard Oil thief trespassing. So would Harker kindly remove his
dirty feet from the premises before he sicked the dog on him. And
Harker did!
    (*He and Jamie laugh*)

The family is in complete, if temporary, harmony. This excerpt continues
in a similar vein. Edmund then "withdraws" in reaction to renewed carping by James, which is followed by exchanges in which Mary reveals her

anxiety over the seriousness of Edmund's illness. Then follows the James-Jamie sequence, which begins in mutual hostility growing out of Mary's refusal to accept facts.

> Jamie: (*shrugging his shoulders*)
> All right. Have it your way. I think it's the wrong idea to let Mama go on kidding herself. It will only make the shock worse when she has to face it. Anyway, you can see she's deliberately fooling herself with that summer cold talk. She knows better.
>
> Tyrone: Knows? Nobody knows yet.
>
> Jamie: Well, I do. I was with Edmund when he went to Doc Hardy on Monday. I heard him pull that touch of malaria stuff. He was stalling. That isn't what he thinks any more. You know it as well as I do. You talked to him when you went uptown yesterday, didn't you?
>
> Tyrone: He couldn't say anything for sure yet. He's to phone me today before Edmund goes to him.
>
> Jamie: (*slowly*)
> He thinks it's consumption, doesn't he, Papa?

The two are briefly brought together by their mutual concern for Edmund,

> Tyrone: (*reluctantly*)
> He said it might be.
>
> Jamie: (*moved, his love for his brother coming out*)
> Poor kid! God damn it!
>   (*He turns on his father accusingly*)
> It might never have happened if you'd sent him to a real doctor when he first got sick.

but the subject of doctors quickly separates them.

> Tyrone: What's the matter with Hardy? He's always been our doctor up here.
>
> Jamie: Everything's the matter with him! Even in this hick burg he's rated third class! He's a cheap old quack!
>
> Tyrone: That's right! Run him down! Run down everybody! Everyone is a fake to you!

As James's attacks on Jamie center on Jamie's failures, Jamie's on his father center on the older man's supposed miserliness, especially concerning health care, and on his real estate speculations.

> **Jamie:** (*contemptuously*)
> Hardy only charges a dollar. That's what makes you think he's a fine doctor!
>
> **Tyrone:** (*stung*)
> That's enough! You're not drunk now! There's no excuse —
>   (*He controls himself — a bit defensively*)
> If you mean I can't afford one of the fine society doctors who prey on the rich summer people —

The pattern now is one of straight attack and counterattack dealing with oft-repeated motifs.

> **Jamie:** Can't afford? You're one of the biggest property owners around here.
>
> **Tyrone:** That doesn't mean I'm rich. It's all mortgaged —
>
> **Jamie:** Because you always buy more instead of paying off mortgages. If Edmund was a lousy acre of land you wanted, the sky would be the limit!
>
> **Tyrone:** That's a lie! And your sneers against Doctor Hardy are lies! He doesn't put on frills, or have an office in a fashionable location, or drive around in an expensive automobile. That's what you pay for with those other five-dollars-to-look-at-your-tongue fellows, not their skill.
>
> **Jamie:** (*with a scornful shrug of his shoulders*)
> Oh, all right. I'm a fool to argue. You can't change the leopard's spots.

These attacks, like most attacks in O'Neill, build in intensity until something happens to stop them. Someone may turn violent, as Edmund does later and Jamie and James both almost do on several occasions. Someone may get hurt sufficiently to weep or in some other way appeal to the other's sympathy. Or some subject may get introduced which appeals to the sympathy of both. In each case, the hostility is broken and feelings of good will are set free. The pattern of kinship is thus completed. What follows reveals both the breakdown of hostility through the appeal for sympathy by the more vulnerable character in a particular exchange *and* the breakdown of hostility through mutual affection for another individual, Edmund or Mary.

Tyrone: (*with rising anger*)
No, you can't. You've taught me that lesson only too well. I've lost all hope you will ever change yours. You dare tell me what I can afford? You've never known the value of a dollar and never will! You've never saved a dollar in your life! At the end of each season you're penniless! You've thrown your salary away every week on whores and whiskey!

Jamie: My salary! Christ!

Tyrone: It's more than you're worth, and you couldn't get that if it wasn't for me. If you weren't my son, there isn't a manager in the business who would give you a part, your reputation stinks so. As it is, I have to humble my pride and beg for you, saying you've turned over a new leaf, although I know it's a lie!

Jamie: I never wanted to be an actor. You forced me on the stage.

Tyrone: That's a lie! You made no effort to find anything else to do. You left it to me to get you a job and I have no influence except in the theater. Forced you! You never wanted to do anything except loaf in barrooms! You'd have been content to sit back like a lazy lunk and sponge on me for the rest of your life! After all the money I'd wasted on your education, and all you did was get fired in disgrace from every college you went to!

Jamie: Oh, for God's sake, don't drag up that ancient history!

Tyrone: It's not ancient history that you have to come home every summer to live on me.

Jamie: I earn my board and lodging working on the grounds. It saves you hiring a man.

James's hostility subsides, replaced first by self-pity,

Tyrone: Bah! You have to be driven to do even that much!
   (*His anger ebbs into a weary complaint*)
I wouldn't give a damn if you ever displayed the slightest sign of gratitude. The only thanks is to have you sneer at me for a dirty miser, sneer at my profession, sneer at every damned thing in the world — except yourself.

Jamie: (*wryly*)
That's not true, Papa. You can't hear me talking to myself, that's all.

then by self-pity on Jamie's part.

Tyrone: (*stares at him puzzledly, then quotes mechanically*)
"Ingratitude, the vilest weed that grows"!

But James quickly renews the hostilities.

> **Jamie:** I could see that line coming! God, how many thousand times—!
>   (*He stops, bored with their quarrel, and shrugs his shoulders*)
> All right, Papa. I'm a bum. Anything you like, so long as it stops the
> argument.
>
> **Tyrone:** (*with indignant appeal now*)
> If you'd get ambition in your head instead of folly! You're young
> yet. You could still make your mark. You had the talent to become
> a fine actor! You have it still. You're my son—!
>
> **Jamie:** (*boredly*)
> Let's forget me. I'm not interested in the subject. Neither are you.
>   (*Tyrone gives up. Jamie goes on casually*)
> What started us on this? Oh, Doc Hardy. When is he going to call
> you up about Edmund?

Another brief break in the hostilities,

> **Tyrone:** Around lunch time.
>   (*He pauses—then defensively*)

but James will not desist.

> I couldn't have sent Edmund to a better doctor. Hardy's treated him
> whenever he was sick up here, since he was knee high. He knows his
> constitution as no other doctor could. It's not a question of my being
> miserly, as you'd like to make out.
>   (*Bitterly*)
> And what could the finest specialist in America do for Edmund,
> after he's deliberately ruined his health by the mad life he's led ever
> since he was fired from college? Even before that when he was in
> prep school, he began dissipating and playing the Broadway sport to
> imitate you, when he's never had your constitution to stand it.
> You're a healthy hulk like me—or you were at his age—but he's
> always been a bundle of nerves like his mother. I've warned him for
> years his body couldn't stand it, but he wouldn't heed me, and now
> it's too late.

In persistently defending the Doctor, James is really defending himself.
His tone here anticipates his long confession of Act Four.

> **Jamie:** (*sharply*)
> What do you mean, too late? You talk as if you thought—

Tyrone: (*guiltily explosive*)
Don't be a damned fool! I meant nothing but what's plain to any-one! His health has broken down and he may be an invalid for a long time.

Jamie: (*stares at his father, ignoring his explanation*)
I know it's an Irish peasant idea consumption is fatal. It probably is when you live in a hovel on a bog, but over here, with modern treatment —

Now it is Jamie who seems unwilling to desist — his antagonism having been built up through years of his mother's suffering, his father's seeming callousness, and his own frustrations.

Tyrone: Don't I know that! What are you gabbing about, anyway? And keep your dirty tongue off Ireland, with your sneers about peas-ants and bogs and hovels!
      (*Accusingly*)
The less you say about Edmund's sickness, the better for your con-science! You're more responsible than anyone!

Jamie: (*stung*) That's a lie! I won't stand for that, Papa!

Jamie is on the defensive again. While both are still on the attack, they are actually, and not very subtly appealing for sympathy — which will be forthcoming.

Tyrone: It's the truth! You've been the worst influence for him. He grew up admiring you as a hero! A fine example you set him! If you ever gave him advice except in the ways of rottenness, I've never heard of it! You made him old before his time, pumping him full of what you consider worldly wisdom, when he was too young to see that your mind was so poisoned by your own failure in life, you wanted to believe every man was a knave with his soul for sale, and every woman who wasn't a whore was a fool!

Jamie: (*with a defensive air of weary indifference again*)
All right. I did put Edmund wise to things, but not until I saw he'd started to raise hell, and knew he'd laugh at me if I tried the good ad-vice, older brother stuff. All I did was make a pal of him and be ab-solutely frank so he'd learn from my mistakes that —
      (*He shrugs his shoulders — cynically*)
Well, that if you can't be good you can at least be careful.
      (*His father snorts contemptuously. Suddenly Jamie becomes really moved*)

That's a rotten accusation, Papa. You know how much the Kid means to me, and how close we've always been — not like the usual brothers! I'd do anything for him.

Jamie's truculence completely gives way, replaced by self-pity, then by affection for Edmund.

> Tyrone: (*impressed — mollifyingly*)
> I know you may have thought it was for the best, Jamie. I didn't say you did it deliberately to harm him.

Mutual feelings of concern and love for Edmund are expressed,

> Jamie: Besides it's damned rot! I'd like to see anyone influence Edmund more than he wants to be. His quietness fools people into thinking they can do what they like with him. But he's stubborn as hell inside and what he does is what he wants to do, and to hell with anyone else! What had I to do with all the crazy stunts he's pulled in the last few years — working his way all over the map as a sailor and all that stuff. I thought that was a damned fool idea, and I told him so. You can't imagine me getting fun out of being on the beach in South America, or living in filthy dives, drinking rotgut, can you? No, thanks! I'll stick to Broadway, and a room with a bath, and bars that served bonded Bourbon.

but the Broadway theme sets off new explosions.

> Tyrone: You and Broadway! It's made you what you are!
>   (*With a touch of pride*)
> Whatever Edmund's done, he's had the guts to go off on his own, where he couldn't come whining to me the minute he was broke.
>
> Jamie: (*stung into sneering jealousy*)
> He's always come home broke finally, hasn't he? And what did his going away get him? Look at him now!
>   (*He is suddenly shamefaced*)
> Christ! That's a lousy thing to say. I don't mean that.
>
> Tyrone: (*decides to ignore this*)
> He's been doing well on the paper. I was hoping he'd found the work he wants to do at last.
>
> Jamie: (*sneering jealously again*)
> A hick town rag! Whatever bull they hand you, they tell me he's a pretty bum reporter. If he weren't your son —

(*Ashamed again*)
No, that's not true! They're glad to have him, but it's the special stuff that gets him by. Some of the poems and parodies he's written are damned good.
(*Grudgingly again*)
Not that they'd ever get him anywhere on the big time.
(*Hastily*)
But he's certainly made a damned good start.

(Yale edition, pp. 20–26, 29–36)

Jamie's precise zig-zagging of emotion in these four utterances is a paradigm of the feelings of both characters throughout the exchange: from (1) attack to (2) sympathy, to (3) attack again, and (4) back again to sympathy. All the feelings are genuine, none pretended.

The two segments quoted are obviously quite different in mood. The Shaughnessy episode is comic, the James-Jamie exchange serious. The tone of the first segment suggests the "everyday" kinship I spoke of earlier; the second, prompted by emotions under increasing stress, foreshadows the dialogue of the last act. But the progression of feeling in both episodes is of the same order. Hurts and frustrations of long standing breed hurtful comments until a full-scale pattern of attack and counterattack ensues. Then, at some point, the deep sympathies among these people emerge to reassert the basic kinship among them. Though the hostility may give rise to responses approaching violence, the hostility itself never destroys the kinship so long as it is part of this all-important rhythm, as it is throughout all the scenes of this play in which more than a single member of the family is present.

What destroys the kinship is never hostility but withdrawal. Edmund withdraws toward the end of the first episode in a miniscule version of his mother's withdrawals. That withdrawal relieves the pressure on him for the moment, but for the long run it is the harbinger of the loneliness that all O'Neill's characters find the greatest of all terrors. Significantly, it is implicit in these episodes that while Jamie is alienated from his mother and has withdrawn from her in response to her withdrawals from him, he never withdraws from his father, no matter how virulent the attacks become. His kinship with his father is secure. On the other hand, Edmund's responses suggest a habit of withdrawing from his father when the going gets rough, while he stays in touch with his mother up to the very edge of her "leave-taking." Thus, Edmund is in closer kinship with his mother than are the other members of the family; but since Mary ultimately denies kinship with everyone, Edmund is the one most left out in the cold. Ultimately, he must establish genuine ties with his father, which he does in the final act.

Before turning to the all-important last act, however, let me examine the middle acts in greater detail. The emotional pattern of Edmund's conversations with his mother must be looked at because they describe the way in which kinship is destroyed in the play, and thus make the kinship the men are able to establish in the last act the more significant. These mother-son conversations are spaced at regular intervals, the first coming late in Act One, the second late in Act Two, and the third late in Act Three. The first takes place just as Mary's relapse is beginning to become apparent, the second constitutes a kind of eleventh hour appeal by Edmund spoken on behalf of all three men, and the third is made up chiefly of Edmund's report that his illness is indeed consumption. In each confrontation, Edmund tries to get his mother to face a fact: in the first, the fact that her affliction has embarrassed the family socially; in the second, the fact that the affliction has recurred; and in the third, the fact of his illness. In each instance, Mary struggles to accept, but then she rejects —totally and uncompromisingly. This pattern constitutes the basic rhythm of their conversation—the movement between her acceptance of the fact, which creates a tentative bond between them, and her cold rejection of the fact, and concomitantly of Edmund. Edmund meanwhile encourages and supports her as she struggles to accept the facts—then hurts her, first by innuendo, later by outright assault, as she coldly denies them.

The second-act encounter between Edmund and Mary is the most frustrating for both because it is here that he tries hardest to get through to her and she comes closest to accepting herself—that is, of reasserting her kinship with him and with the others:

> . . . I don't blame you. How could you believe me—
> when I can't believe myself? I've become such a liar.
> I never lied about anything once upon a time. Now I
> have to lie, especially to myself. I've never under-
> stood anything about it, except that one day long ago
> I found I could no longer call my soul my own.
>
> (Yale edition, p. 93)

In lines following these, Mary ties that acceptance closely to her religion, which, to O'Neill, in spite of his nihilism, is clearly more acceptable than

the morphine. Mary's religion may be thought of as an illusion, but all
O'Neill seeks, in this play as in *The Iceman Cometh* and *Hughie*, is the illusion which will permit the two people to remain in touch with one another, and religion would more than adequately fulfill this function. But
Mary's illusions when she is under the influence of her drug deny rather
than in any way perpetuate her relationships with others. Despite her im-
passioned pleas and her half-acknowledgments, in the end there is always
the "blank denial": "I don't know what you're talking about!" And Edmund must feel for the thousandth time the loneliness of the small child
deserted by his parents followed by the bitterness of the adolescent who is
reacting against that desertion. Despite the clamorous sounds of battle
between James and Jamie, their kinship is always there; whereas the deep
affection between Edmund and Mary, which is so penetrating when it
comes through, always ends by being stamped out — by a withdrawal in
words first and then in fact. By the third act, the desertion which is the effect of Mary's denials becomes so pronounced and Edmund becomes so
frustrated that he turns from innuendo to direct attack, and he utters the
killing phrase which has been one chief source of O'Neill's many matricide
fantasies in his earlier plays:

> It's pretty hard to take at times, having a dope-fiend
> for a mother! (She winces — all life seeming to
> drain from her face, leaving it with the appear-
> ance of a plaster cast. . . .)
>
> (Yale edition, p. 120)

At this point, all contact ceases. Mary cannot accept Edmund's attempts
to right things with his ensuing apologies.

The middle acts of *Long Day's Journey*, which quite possibly by intent are the closest in feeling to the plays of O'Neill's middle period, are
melodramatic. In addition to the Edmund-Mary exchanges we have just
looked at, we also see the men spying on Mary, Mary deceiving and evading, and all the characters wearing a variety of masks. Jamie "discovers"
for his crestfallen brother and father the "truth" about Mary's backsliding,
and Mary grows increasingly suspicious about what the men suspect.
Even the dialogue between Edmund and Jamie now concentrates on
themes of suspicion and intrigue. But the melodrama is really a facade. It
is not action seriously intended to grip us with its suspense. We are never
in any doubt that Edmund is actually ill or that Mary has returned to her
morphine, and we are never in any doubt that son and mother will both

have to be hospitalized. What we are really seeing is all the members of
the family acting melodramatic in the face of unalterable facts and dam-
aging their kinship in the process. Individuals start to abuse, exploit, and
gang up on one another, as they do in the middle acts of *The Iceman
Cometh*, rather than confront one another in whole human terms. Mary
and James use Edmund's illness in attacking each other, the sons gang up
on their father, James's increased bully and bluster hide his deepening
pain.

It is in the later stages of these middle acts that Mary makes her his-
trionic progression, or retrogression, from nervous mother to hardened
addict. But here we must be extremely careful to recognize the effect
O'Neill wishes to achieve. What we see on stage in Act Three is melodrama, yes, but not the kind of frightening melodrama we witnessed in
Strange Interlude, when Mrs. Evans spoke vaguely and mysteriously of a
mad sister wasting away in an upstairs room. There O'Neill was in the full
grip of his fears concerning his mother. Here, having triumphed over
those fears, he wishes to elicit understanding and compassion; and the
scene which is most important to that understanding and compassion is
the one in which Mary, increasingly drugged, makes her long, rambling
speech to Cathleen the tipsy servant girl. In this speech Mary, like James
an act later, develops the motifs relating to her past, and we come to understand her as Edmund later comes to understand his father. These motifs have to do with her lost dreams: of becoming a nun, of becoming a
concert pianist, of marrying a swashbuckling hero. They creep into her
conversation early in the play, she keeps returning to them in her increasingly rambling monologues, and she withdraws into them as the drug
takes possession of her. But what is most important about her Act Three
"confession" to Cathleen and her "mad scene" late in Act Four is that the
effect has been reduced to size. Mary is only an ill, troubled woman drift-
ing away from reality, not the central figure of a nightmare, as are so
many earlier characters who represent O'Neill's mother. We are asked to
have perspective on her illness, not be absorbed by it. That is as far as
O'Neill goes with the memory of his mother in this play. He will not in
this play, as he has so often in the past, seek to reestablish a kinship with
his mother which he never reestablished in his life. But he can present his
mother honestly and objectively, plead for our compassion, and go on to
other matters.

By the end of the play, of course, Mary has totally withdrawn, but
even then the effect is hardly intended to horrify. She appears in pigtails,
like a young girl, and Jamie quite aptly compares her to Ophelia, whose
"mad scene" should elicit extreme compassion but never the horror which

accompanies other mad scenes in literature. The feelings which accompany Mary's appearance in the final scene of this play are finally not those terrified ones underlying the scenes in earlier plays which anticipate that appearance, scenes such as Mrs. Keeney wildly playing the organ in *Ile* or Ella Downey attacking her husband with a knife in *All God's Chillun.* Mary in Act Four is an extremely sensitive woman whose fear and loneliness have become intensified by a drug. In Act Four, as in Act Three, we feel sorry for her and we feel sorry about the fear and dismay she creates for her husband and children; but in no way do we feel drawn into the web of her "madness," as Simon Harford feels drawn into his mother's "little Temple." We need no longer identify with a character representing O'Neill's mother, as O'Neill no longer needs to identify with her. The figure created to represent his mother here is in fact finally lost to him. The long guilt has subsided; this play is not primarily associated with O'Neill's mother. It is the men, not the woman or even the memory of a woman, who finally create the full impact of this work. It is the men who in their kinship of Act Four keep the light burning in the night that this has been a long day's journey into.

As I observed earlier, at no point during this play does the basic rhythm of kinship entirely disappear. Even at their most acrimonious and duplicitous in Acts Two and Three, the characters periodically burst into expressions of undeniably authentic affection. But these portions of the play provide little hope of survival. Mary's denials and the mutual distrust are too intense for the expressions of love to complete the kinship. There is always a desperation, even in the affection, which portends a calamitous conclusion of the sort we have known in most other O'Neill plays. The last act comes, then, as a change of pace for O'Neill, anticipated only in the small-scale *Hughie. The Iceman Cometh* enacts much of the same triumph over the past that this play does and dwells extensively on the rhythms and sounds of human kinship, but *Iceman* still contains a suicide and a murder. O'Neill there must still make actual violence a metaphor for his psychological state. In *Long Day's Journey*, O'Neill abandons such metaphors. Its ending is hardly a happy one, certainly not in the sense of sentimentality or escape. But that ending is also far from being the all-out denial of life that some would have it. The overall tone of the last act becomes quite different from that in Acts Two and Three — and even from that in Act One. It is a tone suggestive of man's capacity to survive under the worst emotional circumstances.

Opening the last act, a drunken Edmund confronts a drunken James, taking over, as O'Neill did in real life, his brother Jamie's various postures and attitudes. With biting, cynical wit, Edmund attacks his father for his miserliness and for his treatment of Mary over the years. James in turn counterattacks, criticizing Edmund's cynicism, his avant-garde tastes, and his own undeniable but hardly avoidable complicity in bringing about Mary's condition through his birth. But the bond between father and son is stronger than the antipathy. There is no impulse toward withdrawal on Edmund's part here. The flow of their affection begins with their mutual awareness of the perilousness of Edmund's condition and becomes stronger with their mutual anxiety over Mary as she paces back and forth in her spare room above their heads. Finally, their bond comes to be expressed in poetic terms. Though James disparages what he considers to be the "morbid" sentiments of Edmund's quotations from Dowson and Baudelaire, he is obviously moved by what he hears — the blend in these poets of philosophic pessimism with a confidence in the value of human contact. Concomitantly, James's allusions to Shakespeare suggest to Edmund the essential similarity of much in Shakespeare to the sentiments of his favorite poets.

Edmund's attacks on his father early in this scene are more vitriolic than any attacks made in the play — even Jamie's. James's desire to economize on Edmund's hospital costs provokes Edmund to say that his father's attitudes make him "want to puke"; and he ends by calling James a "stinking old miser," directly paralleling his calling his mother a "dope fiend" a few hours earlier. But the difference is that whereas following that earlier attack, Edmund flung himself out into the night and the fog asserting his right to the isolation that ultimately kills, here he remains with his father, ready to give as good as he gets; and as a result Edmund finds a kinship with James greater than any he has previously known. Edmund's virulent attacks lead James into the long autobiographical statement out of which Edmund comes to understand his father better.

Edmund has heard all the facts in James's long account before, the facts of James's poverty-stricken childhood and of the ups and downs of the old actor's career; but he has never felt about them the way he is brought to feel this night, when his sensibilities have been intensified by his advancing illness, his drink, and his mother's deteriorating condition. I suggested earlier that James's "confession" is not basically different from Mary's in Act Three. Like Mary, James dwells on experiences of his childhood and adolescence in sincere if exaggerated terms; and he similarly dwells longingly on his frustrated ambitions — notably to have been "a great Shakespearean actor." But unlike Mary, James makes his confession *to* someone, with the clear understanding on his part that that person is listening — which is hardly Mary's state in regard to Cathleen. James speaks as powerfully and sincerely as he can in order to bring the perspective of someone close to him into focus with his own, and he achieves that purpose. James's drunkenness is thus not the equivalent of Mary's narcotic state, as some have felt it to be, because he is always aware of the communal nature of what he says. Like his sons, James is always conscious of the presence of a listener, a consciousness which is heightened by his inebriation rather than reduced. Like the pipe dreamers at Harry Hope's, James is carried away by what he is saying, but at the same time is bound emotionally to the person he is saying it to, in this case the close friend and alter ego who happens to be his son. If James is ever the old actor in his long oration, he nevertheless speaks out of love for his son and out of need for love in return.

Edmund feels the love and the need to return it. He feels he should make a statement of his own dreams and aspirations which will assure his father of the similarity in their feelings. O'Neill here is in the position of having to determine what he would have said in frankness to someone close to him at the age of twenty-four and put it in a play written when he was over fifty, a play which was itself a much deeper and larger "confession" than any Edmund might here deliver. He solves his problem by refitting Paddy's oft-varied speech from *The Hairy Ape*, that lyrical description of the beauties and harmonies of the sea which obviously grew out of O'Neill's own experience on shipboard. Accurately simulating the romanticism of his young adulthood, O'Neill here allows the speech to culminate in the great Emersonian mystery. Recalling the beauty of nights at sea, Edmund says: "For a second you see, and seeing the secret, are the secret." O'Neill thus makes the yearning for unity between man and nature the sum and substance of Edmund's "confession." He is saying through Edmund's speech that the experiences of his young adulthood had taught him to feel things powerfully and authentically. But O'Neill has gone past the romanticism of his youth. The kind of experience that James talks about in his confession, that Jamie will shortly talk about, and that Eugene O'Neill in his early fifties has come to know constitutes truer experience in this play. O'Neill has not altogether forsaken the old romanticism of Edmund's confession, but he treats it in this play more in terms of man's need for authentic human contact than in terms of vague, if powerful, yearnings about the mysteries of nature.

Having established the kinship between Edmund and his father in what is the longest single scene in any published O'Neill play, O'Neill turns finally to the kinship, deeper still, between Edmund and his brother. The relationship between Edmund and Jamie conveys both a detailed sense of the nature of close human relationships and of the penalties such relationships must involve. The key figure here is Jamie — who becomes the chief focus of O'Neill's vision in all his final works. Jamie's massive contradictions are central both to his character here and to the way O'Neill comprehends life in these plays. Jamie is a hardened alcoholic, but his drunkenness never leaves him out of touch with reality. His drunken weeping, O'Neill observes, always "appears sober." He fornicates, but he treats whores with genuine grace and compassion. He is the cause of wit in others, yet he alone possesses a genius for getting others to think seriously about their lives. He cynically insists that money is the only thing worth having, yet he is utterly indifferent to financial gain. His language is blasphemous and at times vulgar, yet he best of any character expresses the joy of existence. He loudly announces his contempt for mankind, yet his commitments to anyone he is close to, and some he is not so close to, are authentic and uncompromising. He is indolent, yet in emotional terms, no one works harder. As a material provider, especially for himself, he is a total failure, yet as an emotional provider, he is a total success. He is, in short, the means by which O'Neill is finally able to honestly celebrate man.

It is clear that the brothers have the kind of understanding most brothers who are very close have. They speak in a kind of code, and they seem to read responses as much in each other's eyes as from what they hear each other say. They are always more together than apart, even when hostilities approaching violence break out between them; and the very subjects which excite those hostilities are the subjects which draw them closest together. Their father is always the first subject of their discontent, yet they share an instinctive love for "the Governor" which parallels that of the pipe dreamers for Harry Hope. They suspect and resent one another to the point of Jamie's letting slip that he just might like his sick brother out of his way, yet their mutual compassion and Jamie's concern about "the Kid's" illness are extreme. Their most intense feelings are about Mary. They quarrel most violently about her, yet it is their mutual concern for her that makes them most interdependent in their love. Theirs is a relationship which O'Neill sees as one involving the closest human kinship.

One of the means by which the brothers express their kinship in this play is the poetry they mutually love and quote. Again, O'Neill turns to his favorite nineteenth-century poets, this time emphasizing Kipling, Wilde, and Swinburne. The importance of the poetic quotations in this play cannot be over-stressed. O'Neill cites these poets in a time (the early 1940s) when their popularity was in decline, when the mode of the moderns (Pound and Eliot) was just cresting, when pain and joy were feelings to be intellectualized by means of tonal complexity and obscure symbolism. O'Neill instinctively could not intellectualize his feelings, and his was a pessimism communicated not through images of dessication, of "wastelands," but through direct, raucous outbursts of rage and disillusion. Kipling suits Jamie because his poetry approaches life's disappointments with bitterness that is directly and boldly stated. Wilde and Dowson write poems about people who actively engage in life, are desperately vulnerable and show their feelings freely — people who in Jamie's quoted Kipling "'ave tried 'em all." The very least that can be said of this poetry is that it is vital, and it is to vitality that O'Neill, sick with his "old passion," made his primary commitment throughout his canon. Thus, vitality is the most important word to be associated with the Jamie who becomes O'Neill's keystone in his final plays.

Jamie, breaking into verse as easily as he downs his drinks, concentrates mostly on familiar topics with Edmund in their midnight conversation: booze and women, of course; their father; their mother; Edmund's illness; and finally Jamie himself, a subject less familiar as a topic of conversation. They begin with the usual comments about their father, Jamie launching the familiar attack on his miserliness, with the now genuinely forgiving Edmund in the unusual role of the old man's defender. Since Jamie knows that James is on the porch overhearing their conversation, much of Jamie's drunken vitriol is really meant to directly insult his father. But James is not really the chief subject on Jamie's mind. He turns quickly to his evening's activities — booze, of course; then women. Jamie's tale of his experience at Mamie Burns's bordello is the most important element in this scene, up until his great confession, because it reveals much about Jamie which is never otherwise revealed in this play. It tells of his relationship with someone other than a member of his family, someone he is not close to, and subtly prepares us for what we will later see of his relationship with someone he is close to, his brother. What we see in both cases is Jamie's unique version of what constitutes authentic human giving.

Beginning in the spirit of sniggering cynicism young men universally and meaninglessly reserve for their discussions of sex, the story blossoms into a parable of Christian love — resist that phrase as Jamie might. It is a story that is brief enough to allow Jamie to recount it in his own words:

> Mamie began telling me all her troubles. Beefed how rotten
> business was, and she was going to give Fat Violet the gate.
> Customers didn't fall for Vi. Only reason she'd kept her
> was she could play the piano. Lately Vi's gone on drunks
> and been too boiled to play, and was eating her out of
> house and home, and although Vi was a good-hearted dumbbell,

and she felt sorry for her because she didn't know how the
hell she'd make a living, still business was business, and
she couldn't afford to run a home for fat tarts. Well,
that made me feel sorry for Fat Violet, so I squandered two
bucks of your dough to escort her upstairs. With no dis-
honorable intentions whatever. I like them fat, but not
that fat. All I wanted was a little heart-to-heart talk
concerning the infinite sorrow of life. . . .
She stood it for awhile. Then she got good and sore. Got
the idea I took her upstairs for a joke. Gave me a grand
bawling out. Said she was better than a drunken bum who
recited poetry. Then she began to cry. So I had to say
I loved her because she was fat, and she wanted to believe
that, and I stayed with her to prove it, and that cheered
her up, and she kissed me when I left, and said she'd fallen
hard for me, and we both cried a little more in the hallway,
and everything was fine, except Mamie Burns thought I'd
gone bughouse.

(Yale edition, pp. 159–60)

Not only Mamie Burns but a large section of his audience might also
assume that Jamie had "gone bughouse," but that bughouse is the essence
of Jamie Tyrone. It constitutes altruism in the most earthy terms O'Neill
can conceive, and which he repeats, with considerable variation, in *A
Moon for the Misbegotten*.[3] In that play, Jamie really does love Josie
Hogan, of course, but who is to say that what he does for Fat Violet here
is not also one kind of human love? Jamie is certainly no do-gooder. He
has simply experienced a genuine feeling for his obese companion, an uncomplicated desire to make her happy which has resulted in satisfaction
quite different from the satisfaction he went to Mamie's seeking. And
even that earlier satisfaction was not sexual only, because he has already
told us that he went to find a "motherly bosom" to weep on. Having gone
to find motherly affection and sexual release, he attained more than either
by giving love—both in sexual and non-sexual terms. The story of Fat
Violet is a story of the essential Jamie, and to understand that it is created
out of the same impulses that led O'Neill to create the character of Lazarus is to begin to understand O'Neill's vision of his brother.

In keeping with the rhythm, of course, Jamie turns cynical once
more and talks about being the lover of the fat lady at the circus. The harmony between the brothers is then broken as Jamie issues his virulent attack upon their mother and Edmund physically assaults him. This action
is followed in turn by the inevitable regrets and apologies, and they in

turn by new grounds for attack and counterattack. This time, all Jamie's old resentment of Edmund for being the favored son comes out, and Edmund is brought even to the point of suspecting that his brother might really wish his death. But always, there follow the reversals: the mutual remorse, the apologies, and the peacemaking in drink. The feelings of both brothers fluctuate wildly in this scene — the attacks increasing in intensity, the reconciliations becoming ever more profound. Finally, the reality of Edmund's possible death becomes too much for Jamie, and he feels the need, as he calls it later, to go "to confession." He must purge himself of all his accumulated guilt toward his brother, and in so doing give "all he has to his Brother."

Jamie's confession is the only genuine confession in this play because it deals with life as it *is* more than with life as it *was* — which so possessed both Mary and James in their confessions. Though Jamie's confession alludes to the past, its world is the present, and the play is a play about the present. The theme of Jamie's statement is that envy has always made him a corrupting influence on his brother. He might, he says, one day do his brother real harm — but despite this he not only loves his brother but regards him as "all I've got left!" There is nothing that has not already been touched on in Jamie's statement, but, like James, he lives his feelings out so vividly that Edmund feels them fully and most painfully:

Jamie: . . . Want to warn you — against me. Mama and
        Papa are right. I've been a rotten bad influence.
        And worst of it is, I did it on purpose.
Edmund: (*uneasily*) Shut up! I don't want to hear —
Jamie: Nix, Kid! You listen! Did it on purpose to
        make a bum of you. Or part of me did. A big
        part. That part that's been dead so long. That
        hates life. . . . Never wanted you to succeed
        and make me look even worse by comparison.
        Wanted you to fail. Always jealous of you,
        Mama's baby, Papa's pet! (*He stares at Edmund
        with increasing enmity*) And it was your being
        born that started Mama on dope. I know that's
        not your fault, but all the same, God damn you,
        I can't help hating your guts — !
                            (Yale edition, pp. 165–66)

Jamie relives each of his earlier emotions precisely as Hickey did, but Jamie is ahead of Hickey in knowing his own nature as Hickey did not until the very end of his confession. What Jamie knows, of course, is that there are two sides of his nature and always will be—one "dead" and therefore murderous, the other alive, and therefore capable and in need of both giving and receiving love. This division has been evident in every character throughout the play, but in being as explicit and as emotional as he is here, Jamie gives the idea new meaning.[4]

The special qualities of Jamie's speech are the intensity of his feelings and the diction he uses to communicate them. When Mary McCarthy said some years ago of *The Iceman Cometh* that you "cannot write platonic dialogue in the language of *Casey at the Bat*," she was saying something quite important about the later O'Neill.[5] She was wrong, of course—you can write platonic dialogue in any language at all—but by associating O'Neill's language with the lingo of American baseball she did identify an important ambience of the language used by the Jamie-figures in all these plays. (She might have come still closer with horse-racing.) It is a wide-open, early twentieth-century urban slang which when tied to the intelligence, the extremely acute sensibilities, and the education of a character like Jamie Tyrone produces sounds and images of a uniquely American hero:

> Oscar Wilde's "Reading Gaol" has the dope twisted.
> The man was dead and so he had to kill the thing
> he loved. That's what it ought to be. The dead
> part of me hopes you won't get well. Maybe he's
> even glad the game has got Mama again!
>
> (Yale edition, p. 166)

It is the juxtaposition of Oscar Wilde and the racetrack dope sheet, the identification of his mother's affliction as a deadly "game," that so characterizes Jamie. This is a man who can quote Latin in sentences which are otherwise spoken in the diction of the "Broadway sport," who can mock Shakespeare even as he is intensely sensitive to the very lines he is mocking, who is "all show biz" even as he pours out the deepest pain of his soul.

Jamie's confession reveals man at both his gut-level worst and transfigured best—unsentimentalized and unadorned, yet capable of giving as much as it is possible to give to another person. And that is a great deal. Jamie warns of his certain propensity to harm his brother even if that warning loses him the one thing in life which makes him capable of going on—his brother's love. The warning reveals love which risks the sacrifice of one's own emotional life support system. Jamie gains great dignity in his confession, a dignity often lacking in the central figures of modern drama while essential to the heroes of ancient drama, heroes who had to face terrible truths about themselves which others had not the stature to face. It is a dignity which grows out of the strength to be completely self-knowing and the strength to admit that self-knowledge to others. Created out of the same antiphony of brashness and guilt, blasphemy and penitence, mockery and self-condemnation which is the voice of Jamie in all O'Neill's later plays, Jamie Tyrone transcends that everlasting rhythm of hate and love by recognizing it, comprehending it, and taking the risk of passing his comprehension on to his brother — even if the message be misunderstood and earn him his brother's permanent distrust. Jamie's legacy is O'Neill's legacy: "Greater love hath no man than this, that he saveth his brother from himself" (Yale edition, p. 167).

Thus has this play transcended the unashamed autobiographical statement it set out to make. It is more than simply the story of the "four haunted Tyrones." It is a story of how past fear and disappointment become so crushing a part of the present. It is a story of the massively destructive effects of prolonged self-imposed isolation. And it is a story of man's potential for redemption in kinship. The play does not end with Jamie's great paraphrase of the line from the Mass, probably because O'Neill was determined to the end to eschew Messianic conclusions. The concluding statement of the play is instead a scenic image: a tableau of family disintegration and family unity in one — the men assembled in awe around the unhearing Mary, with Jamie reciting Swinburne and Mary delving ever deeper into the "little Temple" of her memories. No easy conclusions, positive or negative, are to be drawn from this tableau, but Jamie has already said what is to be said. The larger vision of the play frees man to live in that it frees him to love and reciprocate love — in the way men and women do those things, by attacking and defending, appealing and succoring. Only the fears associated with the past destroy kinship — and those fears are what father and son, brother and brother, clear away briefly in their deep encounters late in this play. *Long Day's Journey* is the most far-reaching of O'Neill's dramatic explorations of what it is to be a human living among humans.[6]

11 A Moon for the Misbegotten

A *Moon for the Misbegotten* is a play about finding peace — not the peace at the bottom of a whiskey bottle found by Harry Hope and company, but peace rooted in human kinship of the closest kind. It is a play about forgiveness and self-forgiveness, both of which seemed so hard to come by in the earlier O'Neill. And it is a play about the close of life, though no one dies in it and there is no violence whatsoever in its conclusion. It feels like an autumnal play, a play which looks toward death without fear or bitterness. It may be more than happenstance that O'Neill set *The Iceman Cometh* in July, *Long Day's Journey* in August, and *A Moon for the Misbegotten* in September. The first two are far more full of anguish and the torrid heat of summer, the last of "mellow fruitfulness." That O'Neill was in a Keatsian mood when he wrote the play is suggested by quotations from that poet in it; and they are quotations which emphasize death as a natural, inevitable process. Nothing could be further from the tone of this play than the panic associated with Parritt's suicide. This play is tragedy concluding in a tone of reconciliation and lyrical sadness.[1]

The problems posed by the play in the context of this study are so varied that a somewhat rigorous organization needs to be imposed on my discussion. I shall attempt to make the many observations I wish to make in three stages: the first dealing with its plots, the second with Josie Hogan, and the third with kinship. The first section will concentrate on humorous Irish anecdotes centering on an Irish tenant farmer and his daughter, the second on the generation of the most remarkable woman O'Neill ever created, and the third on the equally remarkable love brought into being between that figure and the play's hero, James Tyrone,

Jr. Of autobiographical motifs as such there is finally little to say.[2] Based on recollections of O'Neill's long-dead brother, on his personality rather than necessarily on actual situations, the play goes beyond the facts of O'Neill's life in communicating what it does about the nature of close human relationships. With *A Moon for the Misbegotten*, O'Neill has completely transcended his personal past (at least insofar as his plays are concerned).

Plots and Plottings

The "plots" of this play, the story of James Tyrone, Jr. excepted, are the work of Phil Hogan.[3] Phil is more than the last in the long line of O'Neill stage Irishmen stretching back to the volatile Driscoll. He is a stage leprechaun, an incorrigible meddler and practical joker. But he is also a wise and loving father to his daughter, the only one of his children who is a match for him. His sons obviously have not been. In other words, while we ultimately realize that he is a deep and complex character in his own right, his primary function throughout most of the play is that of comic plotter and manipulator. A descendant of the clever servants in earlier drama, who engineer most of what actually happens in the plays in which they appear, Phil engineers most of what actually happens in *A Moon for the Misbegotten*. The events of the play are built around two comic actions, both involving Phil's comic manipulations. The first manipulation is the humiliation of Harder, the Standard Oil millionaire. Though Jim Tyrone actually lays the groundwork for this action, it is Phil's show throughout. True to his Irish peasant tradition, Phil loves humiliating the rich and the proud; and he achieves his end here in comedy which is probably the lowest and surely the most farcical of any in the O'Neill canon. O'Neill's version of the proud lord's downfall shows the rich man actually wallowing in a pigsty to the accompaniment of Phil's crudest sarcasm.

Phil's second manipulation, which he does not pull off successfully, is intended to get his daughter married to the "wealthy" James Tyrone, Jr. This second trick is as old as the first. It is known throughout folklore in countless variants on the theme of "how to catch a rich husband," though it may be better known in popular American culture under the guise of stories about travelling salesmen, farmers' daughters, and shotgun weddings. In these legends, the father must either conspire with his daughter, or he must manipulate her into giving up her supposed virginity in return for a lifetime of financial security. The fun for centuries of audiences and readers has been that of watching the suitor, himself involved in a deception of both girl and father, getting his "just rewards." Phil's situation fits the traditional one at the start. He both conspires with and manipulates his daughter; and that daughter is, as we are surprised to learn late in the play, indeed a virgin.

But Phil's second manipulation never reaches its anticipated conclusion. Jim and Josie are never "discovered" in bed together, and Phil's attempt to manipulate his daughter into a profitable marriage is broken off by developments Phil has no way of anticipating. This failure is the point of the play. Despite its seeming emphasis on traditional low comic intrigues, we, like the eavesdropping Phil, are startled to learn about two-thirds of the way through that such intrigues have nothing whatever to do with what this play is really about. We are startled to learn that the play's deeper subject has little to do with plottings and deceptions, with tricks and intrigues of any sort — only with confessions of the most hidden secrets and the baring of the deepest guilts. The play is not, after all, a situation comedy, and America's most serious playwright is still at his most serious.

To understand what O'Neill is doing in this play, we must again, as we did in considering *A Touch of the Poet*, call attention to O'Neill's use of deception and intrigue in earlier plays. Having recognized at some point along the line that the plottings and deceptions of his middle period resulted largely from his compulsion both to reveal and disguise his personal suffering, O'Neill in the thirties began to employ comic rather than serious intrigue. The melodrama of *Strange Interlude* and *Mourning Becomes Electra* gave way in the main to the manipulations of Con Melody, who is surely Phil Hogan's ancestor in his Irishness and his trickery regarding his daughter. O'Neill no longer felt the need to be melodramatic. His sense of intrigue could be treated in a lighter vein. No longer quite so much ruled by his fears and guilts, he could take plots and intrigues less seriously. He could become more open to life without deceptions and more accepting of it. That acceptance is finally evidenced by O'Neill's total subordination of intrigue in *A Moon for the Misbegotten* — even comic intrigue, which, having taken up so large a part of the play, is summarily dismissed once Jim and Josie begin really to communicate with each other.

It had of course been an early twentieth-century commonplace that without intrigue there was no drama, but turn-of-the century dramatists well before O'Neill had questioned that commonplace. Ibsen, Strindberg, and Chekhov — all of whom were, like O'Neill, products of a tradition which demanded deception and intrigue as central to drama serious or comic—yearned to get away from that demand in their efforts to probe more deeply into life. And O'Neill acknowledged two of those playwrights as his chief creative models.[4] It is then as a commentary upon the theatrical heritage he is rejecting as well as upon his own shift in personal psychological perspective that O'Neill in this play knowingly tricks his audience. Out of a Phil Hogan streak in his own nature, O'Neill carefully manufactures a mood for his audience suitable to Phil's Irish comic intrigues, and then pulls the rug out from under that audience. The suitor who appears is no stock character to be used in the manipulations that fill out the standard comic plot, but a tortured introvert who becomes the one *bona fide* tragic hero of all O'Neill's later drama. Shortly after the middle of the play, comic intrigue—all intrigue—gives way to psychological exploration through strong, utterly open emotional interchange and confession which probes more deeply into the human spirit than O'Neill had ever gone before.

Early in the play, Jim Tyrone comes to the Hogan home to be entertained—there is no doubt of that. One small part leprechaun himself, he comes expecting to find tricks and verbal games to pass the long hours until the tavern opens. And he finds them. Even before the action involving Harder, he and Phil engage in a series of set comic exchanges which, while they cover a broad variety of subjects, are in form taken directly from the American music hall stage. Josie recognizes the ritual when she laughingly refers to their dialogue as "that old game between you." But the Tyrone we see in Act One is but the tip of the tip of the iceberg. Less than one-tenth of his being is giving itself to the repartee and the by-play—even as he stifles his laughter while secretly witnessing the discomfiting of millionaire Harder. Always, the large mass of him below the surface—and never far below it—is fixed unwaveringly upon his pain, his guilt, his fear. With all his efforts to escape into the kind of entertainment Phil provides, Jim never escapes, nor does he ever for an instant deceive himself. Even as he is audience to and participator in a pair of comic intrigues, he is living through a personal hell; and it is this hell which ultimately sweeps aside the intrigues and everything associated with them.

The details of Jim's story, divorced from their emotional implications, seem baldly simple when compared with the complexity of detail in Phil's scheming. The mother of a middle-aged man dies of a stroke while the two are visiting California. The man feigns great emotion while drowning himself in drink, and on the way home to New York with his mother's body he nightly hires the services of a prostitute. He arrives home too drunk to walk off the train or even attend the funeral. No ma-nipulations, no intrigues — no suspense really, except that about when Jim will finally blurt out his tale. But the impact of the emotional pain that underlies the story obliterates all that has gone before — as O'Neill seems to have intended his later drama to obliterate his earlier. The impact transforms Josie Hogan, as even her own confession does not, from hy-persensitive self-pitier into the most unselfish of givers. It finally even shames the leprechaun Phil into open revelation of his own unspoken fears and guilts. And it brings these changes without being maudlin.

Before going into Jim's great confession, however, and its larger im-plications, we must first more closely consider the unusual character to whom it is spoken. I refer, of course, to Josie Hogan — who is described so precisely at the beginning of the play, who is brought to life so brilliantly in the play, and who is so important to the play's final vision of human kinship.

Josie Hogan

Josie Hogan lives on stage with all the complexity and authenticity of O'Neill's most affecting characters, yet it is uncertain how O'Neill came to create her in the detail and with the understanding that he did. Not that the O'Neill brothers in their youthful days were unacquainted with buxom Irish colleens, but they probably knew so many and their identi-ties would be so obscure that any attempt at specific identification would be pointless — as well as quite foreign to the purposes of this study. Josie's power and uniqueness must be explored from sources other than O'Neill's biography.

The way to approach Josie Hogan is to consider her in contrast to earlier characters who grow out of the same impulses she does. There is nothing new about O'Neill's desire to create his "Mother Earth" or about his custom of seeing that figure as a virginal (or at least temporarily *chaste*) whore. What he sought was the all-out, volatile frankness of whores he had known without what was to him the complicating sexual-ity that went with the frankness. But he had never been able to create such a figure both movingly and convincingly. Josie's most obvious predecessor in the 1920s was the whore Cybel in *The Great God Brown*.[5] But Cybel is a marionette whose contradictory responses are only that — contradictory. She emerges (partly as a result of O'Neill's use of masks in the play) not as a complex human being but as a being wooden and undeveloped in both her artificially separated phases. Far more convincing as Earth Mother is Cybel's predecessor, the whorish Abbie Cabot with her "horrible mixture of lust and mother love" in *Desire Under the Elms*. But Abbie is only an Earth Mother so long as she and Eben yearn for one another. Once that yearning is satisfied, she begins to reenact the crimes and terrors of O'Neill's real mother, and her Earth Mother function all but disappears.

His failure to successfully represent his Earth Mother in Cybel or Abbie made O'Neill turn away from the *whore,* important as the qualities associated with that word continued to be for him, and concentrate for some time on purely maternal figures. But here his failure was greater still. Miriam in *Lazarus Laughed* is more a marionette even than Cybel; Charlie Marsden in *Strange Interlude* is quite unconvincing as a maternal protector; and Mrs. Fife in *Dynamo* indicates O'Neill's own recognition of the grotesqueness of his demands. He could tell about a Marie Brantome in *Mourning Becomes Electra* as the once fetching (whorish) nurse-maid become long-suffering provider, but he could not bring such a figure to dramatic life. Similarly, Nora Melody, like Marie Brantome partially rooted in O'Neill's highly vague impressions of his paternal grandmother, is dramatically realized only in part. Long-suffering she is, and troubled by an earlier sexual wrong-doing — but she manifests none of the real conflict between the sexual and the maternal O'Neill began with in Abbie and Cybel, and seemed determined to return to.

The best earlier sketch for Josie Hogan is Sara Harford in *More Stately Mansions.* She is one of O'Neill's most genuinely arousing figures sexually, her maternal qualities are adequately developed, and she is genuinely confused about the implicit contradictions between these two facets of her nature. But in the end, *More Stately Mansions* is not a play about Sara. Not only is her confusion suddenly dropped in the play's final scene, but the entire thrust of that scene is toward the complex involvement of son and mother. Sara is reduced to being another marionette, a source of comfort with no personality of her own. Josie, in contrast, not only possesses a personality of her own from the start, but comes in the last act of *A Moon for the Misbegotten* to understand that personality.

Having put his Earth Mother on the shelf, as it were, while he traversed his personal hell in *The Iceman Cometh* and *Long Day's Journey,* O'Neill still sought her as the one woman who could be loved, and could love, without fear or guilt. He sought a woman who would express feeling free of modesty or a sense of propriety, as a whore might, yet also free of the coldness and disgust he associated with coarse sexuality. An image of such a woman appears fleetingly in *Long Day's Journey* — not Jamie's

"fat Violet," who is the gross and vacuous real-life version of O'Neill's renewed dream (another Mrs. Fife in "her fashion," poor Vi) — but in the
"enormous trull" of Edmund's quotations from Baudelaire: the giant
harlot who was for Baudelaire mistress, mother figure, and goddess.[6] In
the same volume out of which Edmund does most of his quoting from
Baudelaire is another poem, "La Géante," which precisely fits the image
O'Neill wants to create in Josie. Baudelaire's "giantess," in the Arthur Symons translation O'Neill apparently knew by heart, is pictured as a great
passive "Queen" about whom the author lives "like a voluptuous cat." The
ultimate notion of the peace she brings him is figured in his culminating
desire not for sexual union (which by that time unquestionably bored
him) but: "To sleep listlessly in the shadow of her superb breasts, / Like a
hamlet that slumbers at the foot of a mountain."[7]

These lines suggest better than anything else the kind of comfort
provided by O'Neill's Josie Hogan. Josie is "so oversize," says O'Neill,
"that she is almost a freak." Her "sloping shoulders are broad, her chest
deep with large, firm breasts, her waist wide but slender by contrast with
her hips and thighs." Yet she possesses no quality whatsoever of the "man-
nish" for all her physical strength. And it is in the shadow of "her superb
breasts" that Jim Tyrone spends the first peaceful night he has known in a
long time. Through the image reminiscent of Baudelaire, O'Neill seeks to
suggest the immense instincts of such a woman — a nurturing capacity
great enough to restore life, however briefly, to a mortally wounded hero.
Josie is O'Neill's "all-woman." Her greatness resides in her ability (1) to
take and to return in kind all that the interior horrors of those who love
her may prompt them to throw at her, (2) to maintain her individuality at
all times, (3) to love in dimensions comparable to her physical size,[8] and
(4) to love deeply only someone as strong as herself. All these qualities
constitute O'Neill's final Earth Mother.

But Josie is more than solely an Earth Mother. She comes across as
someone a good deal more immediate than a goddess, and therein lies the
real genius of her characterization. She is possessed of terribly mundane
fears and illusions which are far more familiar and convincing than those
of her predecessors. That her physical dimensions symbolize her great
emotional and moral strength does not take away from the fact that her
size has been the cause of great emotional suffering to her, and the source
of her illusions. Her unusual build is accompanied by a fear born of that
characteristic — a universal fear, shared by men and women alike, that
such a physical idiosyncrasy might deprive her of love. As a result, Josie,
who does everything large-scale, must compensate for her gargantuan
size by enticing men in the fashion of a whore; but once sure of their de-

sire, she must cast them off, both because she is herself offended by off-hand sexual encounters and because she is quite naturally waiting for someone to love. The only thing really unusual about Josie is that her physical strength makes the casting off so convincing to its recipients and so comical.

Finally, with Jim's help, Josie transcends her fears. She is able to enter into the kind of relationship with him which dictates that she can no longer hide from herself. That relationship of course involves anger, nearly violent at times, and it involves great resistance—emotions expressed on a scale only Josie can provide. But once Josie has mastered her gargantuan weakness, she is able to help Jim through his much fiercer struggle. Her strength in listening to Jim's confession and giving him the love he needs following it is, like all things about her, also gargantuan. It is in the long midnight interchange between Josie Hogan and Jim Tyrone that O'Neill's culminating image of human kinship emerges.

The Language of Kinship

As in *Long Day's Journey*, the language of kinship in *A Moon for the Misbegotten* roughly falls into two general categories: the kinship of everyday conversation, and the deeper kinship which comes to exist between characters who are under great emotional stress. We get variations of the everyday kinship early in the play in dialogue first briefly between Josie and her brother Mike, then between Josie and Phil, then between Phil and Jim; and we get the deeper kinship in the dialogue between Jim and Josie late in the play. The early, everyday kinship is not unlike that emanating from the rituals of family conversation early in *Long Day's Journey*. Phil and Josie reveal their closeness in their highly explosive attacks upon one another in Acts One and Two, attacks which are of course invariably followed by explanations, apologies, and forgiveness. But though this kinship is genuine, it is not complete. Through these exchanges we come to know that Phil is trying to manipulate Josie and that Josie is protecting herself with her brazen pose. The emotional rhythms of their dialogue, the anger and forgiveness, keep bringing them together, but at the same time their mutual deceptions keep separating them, as deception has separated people throughout O'Neill. Thus, while we know that Phil and Josie are close, we are not satisfied that their relationship is secure.

With Jim's entrance, we encounter another ritual of everyday kinship: a corollary to much we heard in *The Iceman Cometh* and *Hughie*, though the characters involved here are far more self-knowing. Phil and Jim begin their "old game," their exchanges that come directly out of early twentieth-century vaudevillian two-man comedy routines:

> (*Tyrone turns his attention to Hogan. He winks*
> *at Josie and begins in an exaggeratedly casual manner*)
> Tyrone: I don't blame you, Mr. Hogan, for taking it easy
>   on such a blazing hot day.
> Hogan: (*Doesn't look at him. His eyes twinkle*) Hot,
>   did you say? I find it cool, meself. Take off your
>   coat if you're hot, Mister Tyrone.
> Tyrone: One of the most stifling days I've ever known.
>   Isn't it, Josie?
> Josie: (*Smiling*) Terrible. I know you must be perishing.
> Hogan: I wouldn't call it a damned bit stifling.
> Tyrone: It parches the membranes of your throat.
> Hogan: The what? Never mind. I can't have them, for my
>   throat isn't parched at all. If yours is, Mister
>   Tyrone, there's a well full of water at the back.
> Tyrone: Water? That's something people wash with, isn't
>   it? I mean, some people.
> Hogan: So I've heard. But, like you, I find it hard to
>   believe. It's a dirty habit. They must be
>   foreigners.
>   (*The Later Plays*, pp. 326–27)[9]

There seems to be the most blatant deception in this kind of ritual, but it is mock deception, as their insults are mock insults. This is a ritual rooted in pure humor. It provides a convenient vent for the hostilities of the participants without ever causing us to doubt in the slightest the authenticity of their good will. It is also vastly entertaining. In their quickness and self-awareness, Jim and Phil are, here as well as in other situations described in the play, "the cause of wit in others." Like Shakespeare's Falstaff, they create kinship through the wide-open satire implicit in their mock battles. In mimicking real conflict and real deception, they give listener and audience alike a release from their pettinesses and outrages, and draw them closer together in shared appreciation, laughter, and finally participation.

In the father-daughter kinship of Phil and Josie, then, and in the man-to-man kinship of Phil and Jim, the earlier portions of this play create an ambience of well-being in spite of life's difficulties. This sense of

well-being disappears, however, first in the plottings and deceptions of
Phil Hogan, however well meant, then in the dark cloud of Jim Tyrone's
agony. And to recover it a deeper kind of kinship is called for, a kinship
which develops in the relationship of the play's gargantuan lovers.

James Tyrone, Jr. is the hero of this play—its chief sufferer and its
chief provider of kinship. The first thing that must strike us is that his
name is not *Jamie*. He is known only as James Tyrone, Jr., or Jim Tyrone.
Having written the play before he expected the Tyrone family to be identified, O'Neill may have been attempting to conceal his brother's identity
by the change, but anyone at all familiar with the O'Neill family would
easily know whom Jim Tyrone represented. There seems something more
to the change than the effort to disguise. In Jim Tyrone, O'Neill has created another character out of the well-known characteristics of his brother
—the brilliant wit, the Broadway cynicism, the extraordinary intelligence, the compulsive gambling, the devastating alcoholism—but here
the figure created has somehow gone beyond that brother's earlier manifestations. In dropping the diminutive "ie," O'Neill may be suggesting
that, unlike his predecessors, the James Tyrone, Jr., of *A Moon for the
Misbegotten* has become a full-fledged hero. He now has greater capacity
to suffer, greater capacity to grow, and greater courage in the face of death.

It is in part his special grace with words that makes Jim Tyrone such
a winning figure. He reveals his strength in a seamless blend of American
dialects which run a gamut from racetrack to vaudeville stage to remembered poetry:

> You can take the truth, Josie—from me. Because you
> and I belong to the same club. We can kid the world
> but we can't fool ourselves, like most people, no matter
> what we do—nor escape ourselves no matter where we
> run away. Whether it's in the bottom of a bottle,
> or a South Sea Island, we'd find our own ghosts there
> waiting to greet us—"sleepless with pale commemorative
> eyes," as Rossetti wrote. . . . The old poetic bull, eh? Crap!
> (*The Later Plays*, p. 382)

Jim's lines are rapid-fire, charged with poetry and song; they change
key and direction without warning; they sound slightly inebriated even
when he is not (though he usually is). His poetic quotations are often extremely resonant. For the play's central figure to enter with a mock-heroic
statement in Latin on the subject of the barrenness of Phil's farm is brilliant wit, pure and simple. For him to call to mind Rossetti's "pale, com-

memorative eyes" in bringing Josie to face herself is to evoke all the ghosts of O'Neill's imagination from the terror-stricken mothers of the early twenties to the already hinted-at haunting mother of this play. And the Broadway cynicism of his inevitable follow-up — "The old poetic bull, eh? Crap!" — is the mark of the hostility which is essential in the language of kinship.

The deepest kinship in the play, in O'Neill, emerges from the dialogue of Jim Tyrone and Josie Hogan; and in this case that kinship has been noted before, though never so labeled. The Swiss critic Rolf Scheibler recognizes the essential movement of the dialogue throughout Jim's and Josie's long night's emotional journey. He identifies five episodes, or "scenes," of conversation between them:

> The scenes follow a rhythm of alternating tension and re-
> laxation. When Tyrone is cynical, Josie is offended. She
> either replies with some bitter remark or hides behind her
> mask, and now it is he who is offended. There follows a
> short quarrel, but as soon as it reaches a certain degree
> of tension, one of the two lovers will break it off in a
> moment of contrition. . . . But all such attempts at sooth-
> ing the other already contain the germ of a new squabble. . . .
> The cyclic structure of the dialogue makes the
> speeches appear almost illogical and fortuitous, and en-
> dows them with a rising and ebbing rhythm.[10]

Scheibler also observes the sources of both the affection and the hostility which constitute the "rising and falling rhythm" he so accurately identifies. Jim and Josie are drawn to one another because both are large, courageous, and articulate people. The amount of love they have to give is outsize, and so too is the amount they need. But the hostility is, as it must be, of the same proportions. Josie's grows not only out of Phil's deception but out of her deeper fear that Jim, like the others, has no real love for her — only sexual desire — while Jim must see Josie as he sees all women he is attracted to, as a sex object, and all sex objects for him resolve themselves into the "whore on the train."

The special nature of Jim's feelings about Josie in this regard needs to be explored further. Having been unable before to create so powerful an image of human kinship where sexual attraction was involved, O'Neill finally confronts the necessity of including this complicating component. Earlier he had tried to deal with the problem in the relationships between Abbie and Eben Cabot and between Sara and Simon Harford, but could only concentrate with fierce intensity upon the awesome contradictions implicit in their sexuality. He could not get beyond that "horrible mixture of lust and mother love." Here, without begging the question, he acknowledges the impossibility of the mixture when the characters are in the grip of their deepest fears. There can be no doubt of the authenticity of Jim's and Josie's sexual attraction to one another; but sex has become so inseparably bound to the essentially non-sexual terrors and guilts of both that it cannot flow freely, especially in a context which finds each jolted into sudden release of those terrors and guilts. Jim's attraction to Josie gets immediately confused by his association of sex with all his earlier revengeful debaucheries, especially his use of sex with the "blonde pig" as a means of seeking such dreadful revenge upon his mother for dying. Josie's gets confused with her comparable attempts to use her sexuality to humiliate men who refuse to want her for herself — masking from herself the damage she has been doing to the sensibilities of her frustrated suitors, her father, and herself in the process. Therefore, their sexuality — in terms which obviously grow out of O'Neill's experience — instead of becoming a means by which they express their affection, becomes rather a means by which they express their hostility.

But that it does so finally does not matter. O'Neill here transforms his old theme of distorted sexuality into the basis of that hostility which is one pole of human kinship. Not sexual desire itself, but the large-scale corruption of that desire becomes one facet of the "dead part" of Jim Tyrone which alternates with his equally large live part to make him a human being of more than human proportions. It is tempting for some, seeing the play purely in psychological terms, to see disturbed sexuality as central to it.[11] This attitude does as much harm to it as did the Detroit police chief who in 1947 insisted on "moral" grounds that certain words and phrases be deleted.[12] In fact, both Jim's and Josie's problems about sex represent magnified versions of universal distortions of the sex drive in human beings, and in the play these distortions are a part of what tends to isolate these humans from one another. What brings them together is their love, and that includes in generous measure their *un*distorted sexual attraction.

What Scheibler does not stress sufficiently is what in their kinship Jim and Josie give to one another. In *The Iceman Cometh*, Hickey brought a truth which had to be made a falsehood because the majority of men could not live with it. The men and women at Harry Hope's had to protect their pipe dreams even while they knew them for what they were. In *Long Day's Journey*, Jamie acknowledges a truth about himself which must test to the limit his relationship with a brother who is all he has left;

and the full impact can be felt only when it is recalled that in real life that brother did betray the real Jamie's trust. Jamie thus could "save his brother from himself," but could not save himself from his brother. In neither *The Iceman Cometh* nor *Long Day's Journey* is the Jamie figure entirely successful in saving those he wants to save. In *A Moon for the Misbegotten*, Jim Tyrone saves Josie. What he does for her should not be underestimated. Although it takes up less stage time than Josie's gift to Jim, its implications for the future are greater, since Josie will live on. Jim's physical condition makes him beyond hope of rehabilitation, but Josie has a long life before her, and Jim brings her into permanent contact with that life.

To briefly review Jim's treatment of Josie, it must be recalled that Josie has the well-established habit of defending her shyness and modesty by seeming loose, hard, and bitter — a front which is not uncommon in modern society. Jim, seeing through the "bluff" from the start, insists that she talk to him as the frightened but immensely sensitive person she really is. Her responses toward him are complicated, of course, by Phil's intrigue; but basically and instinctively she is relieved at not having to "play the tart" with Jim — especially because she feels so genuinely drawn to him.

But Jim's insistence and his admonitions about her hard language do not penetrate far enough. Because he needs her, and because her defenses continue to prevent him from reaching her entirely, he must eventually present her with a vision of herself that she can accept. True to form, he does this with rough but deeply sympathetic directness:

> You don't ask how I see through your bluff, Josie. You
> pretend too much. And so do the guys. I've listened to
> them at the Inn. They all lie to each other. No one
> wants to admit all he got was a slap in the puss, when he
> thinks a lot of other guys made it. You can't blame them.
> And they know you don't give a damn how they lie. So —
> Josie: For the love of God, Jim! Don't!
> (*The Later Plays*, pp. 382–83)

Since Jim speaks out of love, which he also tells her of as directly as he here reports the facts about her behavior, Josie is able to make her confession. Her behavior has been intended only to perpetuate the illusion that she is attractive to men. She *is* a virgin.

The main fact about Josie is that all she needed was to have someone come along to help her, and someone did. Her kind of ailment is common. It cripples only when allowed to go unrelieved too long. Where Jim is concerned, however, the important fact is that once freed of her own ghost, Josie is able to help him confront his; and his is much more terrible. It is axiomatic that Jim was critically damaged long before the episode surrounding his mother's death ever took place. To be convinced of that, one need only consider why a 44-year-old alcoholic would be on-the-wagon and so dependent upon his mother in the first place. Eschewing any talk of dope fiends or madness, O'Neill leaves us in no doubt that Jim's troubles go way back. He makes us sense, without ever saying so directly, that Jim's earlier deprivation of his mother's love and deep, gnawing guilt about some earlier treatment of her made his behavior at her death only the tip of the iceberg. So great has been the deprivation, and so deep the guilt, that the resultant wounds in Jim have gone beyond hope of recovery. As the alcohol has killed him physically, the past has killed him emotionally. He cannot live. But he can be forgiven, and it is forgiveness of a very large order that he seeks.[13]

Jim Tyrone's confession gets about as close to the heart of psychological suffering in an individual sane enough and strong enough to endure such suffering at its worst as any I know in modern drama and film.[14] Jim begins, like the Jamie of Long Day's Journey, by acknowledging the "poison" which seems to him at the root of his nature, both in his alcoholism and his revengeful determination to debase women through sexual encounter: "Believe me, Kid, when I poison them, they stay poisoned!" But he goes farther. Through the story of his mother's death, he rehearses as never before all the stages of his — and O'Neill's — personal agony. It is Jamie's story but certainly O'Neill's feeling throughout. Jim tells of refusing to face the pain of his mother's death by refusing to "feel" it — of only pretending an emotional response. Then he tells how the real feelings emerged on the train, feelings which are in part panic but in greater part rage — the temper tantrum rage of a small child who insists he will get revenge on his parents for some real or imagined desertion. It is revenge he seeks through his fifty-dollar-a-night whore "with a come-on smile as cold as a polar bear's feet." (Jamie's inimitable diction is in high gear throughout his confession.) But with the revenge, of course, comes the guilt, more devastating than ever, the guilt for which he has taken the alcoholic revenge on himself which is already fatal.

Jim Tyrone's confession takes us deeper than any of the earlier confessions of O'Neill's heroes. His "ha'nts" take us down through those layers of psychological protection O'Neill sought to penetrate many years before in The Emperor Jones. Beyond even More Stately Mansions, O'Neill here drives his hero's confession back to the earliest breakdowns of affiliation between mother and child, past experience which is unique to the "haunted Tyrones," back to the infant scream of separation. Jim's confession leads finally to one of the most terrifying metaphors in literature for birth itself, a metaphor that makes this play comparable to Sophocles' *Oedipus* in its probing of the sources of human pain and anxiety:

> It was like some plot I had to carry out. The blonde —
> she didn't matter. She was only something that belonged
> in the plot. It was as if I wanted revenge — because I'd
> been left alone — because I knew I was lost, without any
> hope left — that all I could do would be drink myself to
> death, because no one was left who could help me. (*His
> face hardens and a look of cruel vindictiveness comes into
> it — with a strange horrible satisfaction in his tone*) No,
> I didn't forget even in that pig's arms! I remember the
> last two lines of a lousy tear-jerker song I'd heard when
> I was a kid kept singing over and over in my brain.
>   "And baby's cries can't waken her
>   In the baggage coach ahead."
> Josie: (*distractedly*) Jim!
> Tyrone: I couldn't stop it singing. I didn't want to stop it!
> Josie: Jim! For the love of God. I don't want to hear!
>   (*The Later Plays*, pp. 392–93)

Josie does not "want to hear" because the story of the baby and the song of the baby and the mother who "will not hear" are not just figures in O'Neill's personal myth but resonate that wordless tale of violent emotional deprivation in the lives of so many human beings. Through the song and the sense of endless repetition created by the click-clacking rhythm of the train along the tracks, O'Neill catches the panic that many build a lifetime fortress around. Like all true tragedy, this play successfully fuses the details of a hero's personal suffering with that of a large portion of its audience — that large portion in this case for whom separation from maternal tenderness and sustenance was traumatic, be that separation in adulthood, adolescence, childhood, infancy, or at the instant of birth itself. The dark, helpless terror that is suggested by the image of the shrieking baby and the dead mother has had great impact in recent productions — in an age when, for many, science and reason have destroyed that confidence in myths of God and Heaven which for previous ages allayed the sense of isolation which is the legacy of man born of woman.

Josie, in response to Jim's tale and on behalf of the rest of us, does two things in rapid succession. First, she recoils from him, and second she embraces him: the two halves of a full and genuine kinship response. First, the resentment, the denial, the hatred of him not only for having desecrated the memory of his mother but for having revealed that deepest of all human terrors — second, the empathy and the compassion. The first without the second would be the height of coldness, but the second without the first would be the height of hypocrisy.

Then follows their Pieta-like union, which has been the center of a good deal of disagreement concerning this play. To some, it represents the moment at which Josie acquires the status in modern terms of the Virgin Mary herself.[15] To others, it is a tawdry representation of O'Neill's still-unresolved Oedipus complex, a "rather immature comment on the meaning of love."[16] I will not speak to the former, but to the latter I shall speak. I do not consider Jim's responses in this situation O'Neill's immature comment on the meaning of love. O'Neill asserts the child at the mother's breast as the sole still-unquestionable model of authentic human love, without which the universe seems endless and terrifying indeed. The mother-infant image is to O'Neill the greatest image of life-sustaining love because it combines the physical and the emotional. If we are cut off from either, we die: physically if we don't receive the nourishment, emotionally if we don't receive the tenderness. The Pieta-image which Josie provides is a scenic image of that nourishment and tenderness expressed in a fashion which also signals total and final forgiveness.

Unlike *The Great God Brown, A Moon for the Misbegotten* does not conclude with its Pieta image. The play goes beyond kinship into the facing of ultimate separation. It is finally a play which attempts to confront death. Many O'Neill plays make that attempt, but they usually end only in violence, dejection, or bitterness. In this play, O'Neill treats death precisely as he treats life. As with kinship, which is the center of life for O'Neill, so with death: there are both negative and positive charges. There is, as it were, a "dead part" of the idea of death as there is a live part. There is the death that Jim Tyrone associates with his guilt, his degeneracy, and his hostility — Jamie's "the dead part of me" in *Long Day's Journey*. This death is also identified in various ways throughout O'Neill with isolation and despair — the abandonment of, and the desire to destroy everyone and everything, culminating with one's own destruction. Obviously, this death is identified with suicide.

The idea of death in *A Moon for the Misbegotten* is finally just the opposite. Far from being associated with guilt, degeneracy, and hostility, this other death is associated with the transcendence of those qualities and the acceptance of both life and death. To achieve a sense of this other death, O'Neill once more resorts to the language of great poetry — this time Keats' "Ode to a Nightingale." Quite early in their conversation, Jim's mind turns to the lines which state what his mortally damaged being most longs for, and the mood of the lines clings to the remainder of the play — especially its last act:

> Now more than ever seems it rich to die,
> To cease upon the midnight with no pain,
> In such an ecstasy!

But it is pain Jim cannot escape, and it might well have provided him with the first kind of terrible death, like that experienced by Don Parritt in *The Iceman Cometh*, had he been unable genuinely to encounter Josie Hogan. Josie in her long night of nurture becomes Jim's nightingale. Following his great confession and the sustenance taken at her breast, Jim can die in peace — which is all, O'Neill is telling us, a man really needs, whether his death be near or far.

Following Josie's giving herself to Jim in a manner far more profound than she earlier thought was his goal, she must in love accept the immediate inevitability of his death. She must accept it in the same way she earlier yearned for a permanent affiliation with him in life. It is Josie rather than Jim this play's final act concentrates on. Josie knows early with her mind that Jim is in poor condition, but it is only in knowing with her body how ill he really is that her acceptance of his death can come. It is after the several hours of holding Jim's head against her breast and then his body between her legs, restoring in some small measure the love that he has been so long separated from, that Josie realizes she has borne "a dead child in the night." Jim Tyrone has been damaged emotionally by his deprivation of love as a man would be damaged physically whose brain slowly, over a long period of time, had been denied adequate supplies of oxygen. Josie's holding Jim in the two positions she does throughout the night represents birth — in this case, rebirth. But Jim's deprivation has been too long and too great. Though here reborn, he is in fact all but dead from his drinking. Thus, both the joy of birth and the desolation of death have been part of Josie's long night — life and death in seemingly unending juxtaposition, like the two opposing halves of feeling central to kinship itself.

Because Jim has brought her to accept herself — has in fact given her life — the Josie we see in the final scenes is able to accept others, to breathe into them the life that Jim has breathed into her. Her first task is to transform a leprechaun into a deeply feeling human being. Knowing Josie's joy and pain, Phil for the first time expresses his feeling without comic posturing. His games and deceptions, as far as Josie is concerned, are over. The unexpected high note on which the play ends is a burst of unalloyed love between father and daughter, a note which directly counters the cold, if comic, scheming which began the play. The kinship between father and daughter which ends this play is the kinship which O'Neill sought for but could not yet allow himself completely in *A Touch of the Poet*. Whether Josie will marry or not is really pretty insignificant in the light of her feelings toward her father, and his toward her, at the end of the play — feelings that are the essence of O'Neill's language of kinship:

> Josie: . . . Don't be sad, Father. I'm all right — and
> I'm well content here with you. (*Forcing her
> teasing manner again*) Sure, living with you has
> spoilt me for any other man, anyway. There'd
> never be the same fun or excitement.
> Hogan: (*plays up to this — in his fuming manner*) There'll
> be excitement if I don't get my breakfast soon,
> but it won't be fun, I'm warning you!
> Josie: . . . Och, don't be threatening me, you bad-tempered
> old tick. Let's go in the house and I'll get your
> damned breakfast.
> Hogan: Now you're talking.
>
> (*The Later Plays*, p. 409)

Jim Tyrone has done what he lived to do — to give life to others and to create the conditions in which he might die in peace. Like many tragic heroes before him, he arrives at the start of the play beyond hope of rehabilitation. His emotional tissues, like those in his throat, can no longer be restored, a fact which Josie comes to realize from the wordless contact of their bodies. To her own surprise she can finally wish him, without bitterness on her part or the evoking of bitterness on ours, the peaceful death in his sleep which is her benediction following her final exchange with Phil. Jim's death has brought life to others, as a hero's death should. He has grown in self-knowledge through the courageous gesture of his confession; and in gaining that knowledge, just before his unavoidable death, he becomes a light to those who follow.

Conclusion

THE PASSAGE from which the title of this book is taken sums up the direction of this book. Writing about Strindberg's triumph over the hypocrisy and superficiality of the past, O'Neill invokes a phrase from *Dance of Death* to denote a determination to get beyond the sordidness which is the surface of most human relationships:

> . . . we "wipe out and pass on" [Strindberg's phrase] to
> some as yet unrealized region where our souls, maddened
> by loneliness and the ignoble inarticulateness of flesh,
> are slowly evolving their new language of kinship.[1]

O'Neill in his last plays, after years of distorting and disguising the most deeply troublesome issues of his life, was able to "wipe out and pass on," to fight relentlessly through maddening loneliness and fear into the region of his new language. Along with those few playwrights who might genuinely be called great, O'Neill takes us beyond the fascination that accompanies the recognition that his problems — in one way or another and to greater or lesser degree — are our problems. O'Neill's personal suffering, reflected early in so many disguises and finally faced so directly and honestly, also fired in him a perception of close human relationships which others have had in our time but few have successfully made the center of an artistic vision.

In a sense, we are fortunate (if O'Neill was not) that he lacked the courage to confront his past directly and honestly in his earlier works. Other recent dramatists, having had such courage early in their careers, have turned out lesser works. As O'Neill learned about others through painfully learning about himself, he also learned about his art. When his confrontation finally came in psychological terms, he was ready for it in artistic terms. He had mastered his uniquely individual craft as a playwright. He could convey his tragedy deeply and sympathetically. He could give us, effortlessly and with dignity, his sense of the value of life that underlay that tragedy. There have been other autobiographical dramatists in our time; there have been other philosophical dramatists. But none has so turned autobiography and vision into the deeply resonant imitation of life that O'Neill did in his last works.

Appendix
Motifs in *Long Day's Journey Into Night*

THE MOST RECOGNIZABLE MOTIFS associated with the present life of James Tyrone, Sr., are the following:

His bitter disappointment over his wife's condition

His controlled alcoholism

His use of alcohol to help him communicate with his sons

His daily desertions of his wife to seek companionship

His aristocratic affectations

His Irish and Roman Catholic pride

His boisterous manner

His pride in his health and physique

His resentment at his sons' "ingratitude"

His fear of attack by his sons

His supposed miserliness

His fear of poverty

His distrust of new ideas and recent writing

His resentment of the role which made him rich and famous

His near-deification of Shakespeare

Those associated with James Tyrone, Sr.'s memories of the past are the following:

His early poverty and sense of social humiliation

His long-suffering mother

His hatred of manual labor

His family's desertion by his father and the rumors of that father's suicide in Ireland

His romantic courtship of Mary Cavan

His need for Mary's company after their marriage

His nightly desertions of Mary

His drink and social success

His philandering

His becoming a matinee idol

His promise as a Shakespearean actor

His "selling out" in search of financial security

The most recognizable motifs associated with the present life of Mary Tyrone are the following:

Her social pretensions

Her propriety and at times Puritanical attitudes

Her envy of neighbors

Her hysteria concerning her younger son's health

Her fear of her elder son

Her narcotic withdrawals

Her use of the upstairs spare room as location for taking drugs

Her dilated pupils when under the influence of morphine

Her fear concerning the appearance of her hair

Her use of the arthritis in her hands as front for her addiction

Her persistent denials of the reality of her condition

Her contempt for doctors

Her desire for and fear of Roman Catholic confession

Her fear of the fog

Those associated with Mary Tyrone's memories of the past are the following:

Her father's consumption and alcoholism

Her proper upbringing

Her love of her girls' boarding school

Her desire to be a nun

Her desire to be a concert pianist

Her infatuation with the matinee idol

Her wedding gown

Her enforced accompanying of her husband and desertion of her first child

Her loneliness in hotel rooms

Her jealousy of her husband's admirers

Her resentment of her husband's drinking and social life

Her loss of a second child

Her blaming first child for death of second
Her conceiving a third child as replacement for second
Her difficult childbirth
Her dependency on strange doctors
Her use of morphine to alleviate pain
Her addiction and its discovery by first child, then second
Her pride in her first child

The most recognizable motifs associated with the present life of Jamie Tyrone are the following:

His bitterness and cynicism
His brilliant wit
His contempt for and mockery of his father
His quick recognition of his mother's renewed addiction
His ability to articulate his feelings through poetic quotations
His "Broadway" diction
His dependency on brother and father
His jealousy of his brother
His support for his brother
His emotional honesty

Those associated with Jamie's memories of the past are the following:

His early disillusionment with his mother
His early successes at school
His dismissal from colleges
His drinking, whoring, and gambling
His ability to give others pleasure
His elegance in dress
His failure as an actor

The details of his mother's death and his responses to it as described in *A Moon for the Misbegotten*

The trip to California
His mother's sudden illness
The deathwatch
His false lamentation
His resentment of his mother's death
His drinking on the train
The blonde whore on the train
His being too drunk to go to his mother's funeral

The most recognizable motifs associated with the present life of Edmund Tyrone are the following:

> His persistent hope that his mother has reformed
> His repeated disillusionments
> His anger at his mother
> His guilt at his anger at his mother
> His dependency on his brother
> His imitation of his brother in drink and wit
> His shock at his brother's cynicism
> His radical opinions
> His developing admiration for his father
> His consumption
> His love and recitation of recent poetry
> His ambition to be a writer
> His high-strung, nervous personality
> His love of the fog
> His fear that he might be like his mother

Those associated with Edmund's memories of the past are the following:

> His shock at learning of his mother's addiction from his brother
> His early emulation of his brother
> His sense of an ideal past before his mother's "fall"
> His running away to sea
> His love of the sea
> His prodigal return

The following motifs are associated with the family group:

> Laughter over an anecdote involving the humiliation of the proud (Shaughnessy's pigs)
> Father indignant at sons
> Sons taunt father
> Mother defends father against son
> Mother joins sons against father
> Father and reluctant sons flatter mother
> Father and sons plead with mother
> Father and sons observe mother in withdrawal

The following are associated with exchanges between James and Mary:

> Father commends mother on her renewed health (by observing her increase in weight)

Mother resentful of father's land speculations
Mother resentful of father's drink
Mother pleads for understanding
Mother resentful of father's miserliness
Father accuses mother
Mother attacks doctors
Father late for meals

The following are associated with exchanges between James and Jamie:

Father castigates son for his failures
Father castigates son for his dissolute behavior
Father castigates son for his innuendos about mother
Mutual accusations about causes of mother's condition
Son castigates father for his miserliness
Son attacks brother to father
Son defends brother to father
Father fears son's cynicism
Son financially dependent on father
Inevitable directness between father and son

The following are associated with the rare exchanges between Mary and Jamie:

Son recognizes the "signs" of his mother's addiction (eyes)
Son savagely cynical toward mother
Son reveals slight hysteria at mother's condition
Communication between mother and son long gone
Mother fears son's reactions

The following are associated with interchanges between James and Edmund:

Son attacks father's miserliness
Father attacks son's opinions
Father proud of son's literary achievements
Father fears son's demise
Son hurt by father's fears
Father reveals past to son
Son begins to understand father
Mutual fears and hopes about mother
Mutual dependency upon alcohol

The following are associated with interchanges between Mary and Edmund:

> Mother hysterically anxious about son's health
>
> Mother critical of son's behavior
>
> Son states his belief in mother
>
> Son indirect in his suspicions
>
> Mother hurt by suspicions
>
> Son's disillusionment rooted in mother's condition
>
> Son hurt by mother's denials
>
> Son accuses mother of being a "dope addict"
>
> Mother accuses son for having been born
>
> Communication between mother and son breaks down

The following are associated with interchanges between Edmund and Jamie:

> Brothers jest about drink, whores, father's eccentricities
>
> Elder brother cynical about mother
>
> Younger brother defends mother, attacks elder brother
>
> Elder brother lords it over younger brother
>
> Elder brother confesses feelings toward younger brother
>
> Elder brother declares his love for younger brother

Notes

Introduction

1. "The God of Stumps" (Review of *Desire Under the Elms*), *The Nation* 119 (26 November 1924): 578.

2. The first full-length studies of the O'Neill canon were primarily concerned with ideas implicit in the works. The studies are all interested in O'Neill the man, but they contain little about his life. What each critic found, moreover, differed substantially from what the others found. Barrett H. Clark, *Eugene O'Neill: The Man and His Plays* (New York: Dover Publications, 1946), a book published in its original form in 1926, praises O'Neill for his great power and success in finding hope in man despite life's many and great discouragements. Sophus K. Winther, *Eugene O'Neill: A Critical Study* (New York: Russell and Russell, 1961), a revision of a book published in 1934, also is impressed by O'Neill's power in representing life's perils uncompromisingly and courageously, but finds far less hope in the plays than does Clark. Winther concentrates on the social and economic evils to be found in the plays and leads the long line of those critics since the 1930s who identify O'Neill's debt to nineteenth century revolutionary philosophy—notably that of Friedrich Nietzsche. On the opposite side is Richard Dana Skinner, *Eugene O'Neill: A Poet's Quest* (New York and Toronto: Longmans, Green and Co., 1935), a work which sees in O'Neill's work up to and including *Days Without End* an uncompromising, honest, and powerful struggle to re-assert the Roman Catholicism of his youth. The most comprehensive more recent full-length treatment of the historical and cultural influences on O'Neill is John Henry Raleigh, *The Plays of Eugene O'Neill* (Carbondale, Illinois: Southern Illinois University Press, 1965).

Cyrus Day, who published important articles on *Lazarus Laughed* and *The Iceman Cometh*, was at work on a full-length study of O'Neill at the time of his death in 1967. I am deeply grateful to his wife, Camilla Day, for allowing me to consult his notes in 1976. Day sharply differentiated O'Neill from the other writers of the 1920s who, like him, were facing the loss of faith. O'Neill, Day's notes suggest, kept seeing inner turmoil as the real concern of his earlier plays rather than social protest. Day also felt that as O'Neill brooded more and more deeply on the meaning of life, he began to rely more and more on books, rather than on the direct observation of life, to determine his themes. The more he read Nietzsche,

Schopenhauer, Jung, and (indirectly) Freud, the more strained and remote from reality his plays became.

See also note 13 below.

3. Tiusanen's study establishes the concept that a basic scenic image exists for each O'Neill play, an image which keeps audience attention focused on the play's central issues. It is a work indispensable to directors of the plays and extremely helpful to all students of O'Neill. Chabrowe's more recent study focuses on the two types of play central to the O'Neill canon — one ritualistic in nature, the other naturalistic. These two types culminate for Chabrowe in the differing brilliance of *The Iceman Cometh* and *Long Day's Journey into Night.* Another important study of form in O'Neill's plays is Egil Tornqvist, *A Drama of Souls: Studies in O'Neill's Supernaturalistic Technique* (New Haven: Yale University Press, 1969).

4. To these might be added Frederic I. Carpenter, *Eugene O'Neill* (Boston: Twayne Publishers, a division of G. K. Hall & Co., 1979).

5. Doris Alexander, *The Tempering of Eugene O'Neill* (New York: Harcourt, Brace and World, 1962); Arthur and Barbara Gelb, *O'Neill* (New York: Harper and Row, 1973); and Louis Sheaffer, *O'Neill: Son and Playwright* (Boston: Little, Brown and Company, 1968), followed by *O'Neill: Son and Artist* (Boston: Little, Brown and Company, 1973).

6. "Ideas in the Plays of Eugene O'Neill," in *Ideas in the Drama,* ed. John Gassner (New York: Columbia University Press, 1964), p. 104. (The entire paper appears on pp. 101–24.) See also Eric Bentley, *Theatre of War* (New York: The Viking Press, 1972), p. 68. Bentley's specific statement on the subject is the following: "He [O'Neill] lives, as it were, in a trance, writing and rewriting the story of the two Jameses, Ella, and Eugene. Or parts of the story. Or the story at a remove." Bentley goes on, however, to de-emphasize this aspect of O'Neill's creative processes.

7. *The New Yorker,* 7 November 1931, p. 28.

8. See John Henry Raleigh, "Eugene O'Neill and the Escape from the Chateau d'If," in *O'Neill: A Collection of Critical Essays,* edited by John Gassner (Englewood Cliffs, New Jersey: Prentice-Hall, Inc., 1964), pp. 7–22. Raleigh demonstrates the influence of James O'Neill's *The Count of Monte Cristo* on O'Neill as well as O'Neill's efforts to overcome that influence.

9. See Joseph Wood Krutch, introduction to Eugene O'Neill, *Nine Plays* (New York: The Modern Library, 1932).

10. See Arthur H. Nethercot, "Madness in the Plays of Eugene O'Neill," *Modern Drama* 18(1975): 259–79. Nethercot documents what Louis Sheaffer calls O'Neill's "preoccupation with insanity," but never links that preoccupation with O'Neill's mother's addiction, even though he identifies (p. 267) Mary Tyrone's addiction with madness in *Long Day's Journey.*

11. My outlook contrasts with that of Eugene Waith in "Eugene O'Neill: An Exercise in Unmasking," *Educational Theatre Journal* 13(1961): 182–91. Waith sees in many O'Neill plays a tearing away of the masks of altruism or affection most of his characters wear to reveal the hatred or hostility beneath. Without commenting on masks as such, I consider both the altruism and hostility as natural to O'Neill's characters, neither one, especially in the late plays, effectively disguising the other, but each one instead rhythmically alternating with the other.

12. See "Strindberg and Our Theatre," in *American Playwrights on Drama,* ed. Horst Frenz (New York: Hill and Wang Dramabooks, 1965), p. 2.

13. Two full-length studies have recently appeared which have direct bearing on the two phases of my work here. One is Jean Chothia, *Forging a Language: A Study of the Plays of Eugene O'Neill* (Cambridge University Press, 1979). The other is Virginia Floyd, *Eugene O'Neill at Work* (New York: Frederick Ungar, 1981).

Chothia's book anticipates in some degree what I have to say about O'Neill's "language of kinship." She finds, as I do, that O'Neill, having begun to show promise integrating language with feeling in the early plays, became overly dependent on melodramatic situation and exclamatory language in his middle years. In his late plays, however — especially *The Iceman Cometh* and *Long Day's Journey* — Chothia feels that he brought that early promise to fruition. Those plays successfully integrate feeling and language. Chothia is more interested than I in the relationship of language and stage image, but she is in no way concerned with significant autobiographical forces shaping those images. Her chapter on O'Neill's "literary biography," for example, is almost exclusively about the playwright's early reading.

Floyd's long-awaited study, on the other hand, confirms much that I say about autobiographical elements in all the plays — early, middle, and late — and adds to our knowledge of that subject in providing a great deal of material drawn from O'Neill's newly released notebooks, where early drafts of published plays, ideas for plays, scenarios, and even dialogue from uncompleted plays are to be found. It is interesting to note, in connection with my conclusions, that the uncompleted play which O'Neill intended to be his last and greatest, "The Last Conquest," Floyd presents as a massive exploration of the "duality of man" from which ultimately emerges a feeling of hope for the human condition (see pp. xxi–xxii and 317–45).

1 — The Rhythm

1. In *"Children of the Sea" and Three Other Unpublished Plays by Eugene O'Neill*, ed. Jennifer McCabe Atkinson (Washington, D.C.: The National Cash Register Company, 1972). In addition to its World War I theme, the play may suggest the *shock* associated throughout O'Neill's plays with the discovery of something terribly shameful — i.e., O'Neill's discovery of his mother's addiction during his adolescence.

2. An excellent discussion of this infrequently cited play appears in Tiusanen, *O'Neill's Scenic Images*, pp. 66–71.

3. See Sheaffer, *Son and Playwright*, p. 385.

4. (New York: Random House, 1955), 3 volumes. All quotations are taken from this edition except those from plays not included in it. References following each quotation are to volume and page number(s) only. In no case do they refer to act and scene.

5. O'Neill's mother's full name, of course, was Ella Quinlan O'Neill, which was in *Long Day's Journey* rendered into Mary Cavan Tyrone. Sheaffer also notes the similarity between Emma Crosby and Mary Tyrone in *Son and Artist*, p. 39.

6. See Sheaffer, *Son and Artist*, pp. 12–13. Sheaffer recognizes the similarity to O'Neill's father but not that to O'Neill's mother.

7. See Carpenter, *Eugene O'Neill*, p. 93.

8. This exceedingly melodramatic play (*The Straw*) has some genuinely powerful moments. Its plot concerns a youthful hero's relationship with a dying girl in a TB sanatorium. Obviously based on O'Neill's own experience in such a sanatorium in 1913, the play

may also suggest O'Neill's ambivalent feelings toward his mother. The hero at first hurts the girl badly by ignoring her when she needs him. Then, in sincere guilt and new-found love, he dedicates himself to her for the remainder of her days. This pattern reflects O'Neill's feeling that he rejected his mother when she needed him, followed later by his intense and unrelenting guilt. The pattern is picked up in numerous plays throughout the O'Neill canon.

9. See Engel, *Haunted Heroes*, pp. 10–15.

10. *Shell Shock*, according to Jennifer McCabe Atkinson, ed., *"Children of the Sea" and Three Other Plays*, p. xiv, was written in 1918. The *S. S. Glencairn* plays were written between 1916 and 1918.

11. For a discussion of the kind of popularized Eastern philosophy this mysticism was based on, see Doris M. Alexander, "Eugene O'Neill and *Light on the Path*," *Modern Drama* 3(December 1960): 260–67.

12. I take the phrase "scenic image," and its connotations, from Tiusanen, *O'Neill's Scenic Images*.

2 – Breaking the Rhythm

1. Jones's life on the chain gang is never dramatized, of course, so there is no sure evidence that *kinship* of the kind I have been discussing would have existed there. But I am persuaded that it would have for the following reason. That *The Emperor Jones* and *The Hairy Ape* directly reflect one another in theme and form has been suggested in Emil Roy, "Eugene O'Neill's *The Emperor Jones* and *The Hairy Ape* as Mirror Plays," *Comparative Drama* 2(Spring 1981): 21–31. (Note, among other things, that the last names of the heroes are "Smith" and "Jones.") Kinship is clearly evident among the stokers in *The Hairy Ape*, as I shall shortly be pointing out. Thus, if the form of *The Hairy Ape* does in fact mirror that of *The Emperor Jones*, then the chain gang would reasonably have been for Jones what the stoke hole is for Yank: that is, a "home" in which camaraderie alternated with violent hostility. In Jones's case the hostility led to a murder. It barely misses that in Yank's case.

2. See Skinner, *A Poet's Quest*, pp. 131–41. Skinner's is a perceptive discussion of this play which, like mine, sees the theme of inter-racial marriage as secondary.

3. See Bogard, *Contour in Time*, p. 193; and Carpenter, *Eugene O'Neill*, p. 103.

4. The existence of the prize fighter suggests the influence on this play of the black prize fighter Jack Johnson and his white wife. See Sheaffer, *Son and Artist*, p. 119.

5. Clark, *The Man and His Plays*, p. 99, first noted the similarity in the endings of *All God's Chillun* and *Desire Under the Elms*. See also Michael Hinden, "The Transitional Nature of *All God's Chillun Got Wings*," *Eugene O'Neill Newsletter* 4 (May–September 1980): 3–5.

6. As he would again, of course, in *Mourning Becomes Electra*, O'Neill here disguised his agonies concerning his family by using a plot from Greek mythology and drama – in this case the myth of Theseus, Hippolytus, and Phaedra as dramatized in the *Hippolytus* of Euripides. See Edgar F. Racey, "Myth as Tragic Structure in *Desire Under the Elms*," *Modern Drama* 1 (May 1962): 42–6; also Bogard, pp. 213–14.

7. Floyd recognizes the parallel between the older Cabot brothers and Jamie, in *Eugene O'Neill at Work*, p. 54. Sheaffer identifies Ephraim Cabot with O'Neill's father in *Son and Artist*, pp. 129–30.

8. See *"Desire Under the Elms:* A Phase of O'Neill's Philosophy," in *Eugene O'Neill: A Collection of Criticism,* Ernest G. Griffin, ed. (New York: McGraw-Hill, 1976), pp. 59–66.

9. See Murray Hartman, *"Desire Under the Elms* in the Light of Strindberg's Influence," *American Literature* 33 (1961): 360–69. Hartman analyzes the relationship of Eben and Abbie in terms of a "mother fixation" on O'Neill's part which was influenced by Strindberg's similar affliction.

10. Chester Clayton Long observes how central sexual passion is to this play in *The Role of Nemesis in the Structure of Selected Plays by Eugene O'Neill* (The Hague and Paris: Mouton & Co., 1968), pp. 106–7.

11. See Carpenter, *Eugene O'Neill,* p. 106.

II — The Valley of the Shadow

1. Sheaffer, *Son and Artist,* p. 86. (The italics are mine.)

2. See *Son and Artist,* pp. 94–115. Sheaffer sees O'Neill's reactions during the year and a half between his mother's and his brother's deaths, especially during the summer of 1922, as simply the somewhat more than usually riotous behavior of the volatile artist. He does not consider that behavior in relation to the recent death of Ella O'Neill or the circumstances surrounding it. But what Sheaffer describes, he himself says "tells of self-hatred, and impulse toward self-abasement"; and in the light of what had happened the previous March and the obvious intensity of O'Neill's guilt in response to those events, I feel impelled to connect them with O'Neill's bizarre behavior that summer. O'Neill, we are told, partied furiously. He insulted his wife publicly, struck a woman reporter, and one night "urinated into a half a bottle of whiskey and then drank from it." These actions represent something more than O'Neill's typical "August depression." They reveal a self-destructiveness and a violent desire to escape from overwhelmingly painful thoughts related to the recent past. Those thoughts would ultimately find worthier outlet in O'Neill's plays. It is noteworthy to add that Jamie was a guest, not altogether welcome, at O'Neill's Cape Cod cottage during a good part of that summer, serving as a constant reminder of Ella's death and the circumstances surrounding it.

3. Sheaffer describes this trip in *Son and Playwright,* pp. 215–21.

4. See John H. Stroupe, "O'Neill's *Marco Millions:* A Road to Xanadu," *Modern Drama* 12(February 1970): 377–82. Stroupe specifically links Marco's self-condemnation and inability to love with O'Neill's relationship with his family (p. 381).

3 — In Memory of Jamie

1. James R. Scrimgeour identifies Dion with Jamie in "From Loving to the Misbegotten: Despair in the Drama of Eugene O'Neill," *Modern Drama* 20 (March 1977): 37–53; and Sheaffer sees this parallel, as well as that between Cybel and Josie Hogan, in *Son and Artist,* pp. 169–70. Norman Chaitin meanwhile recognizes the clear similarity between William Brown the successful architect and Eugene O'Neill the successful playwright of the 1920s in "The Power of Daring," *Modern Drama* 3(May 1960–February 1961): 231–41. The most convincing case for linking O'Neill with Brown and Jamie with Dion is made by Floyd in *Eugene O'Neill at Work,* pp. 46–51. Floyd also sees qualities in some of the dialogue between Brown and Dion as anticipating dialogue between the brothers in *Long Day's Journey.*

2. That O'Neill may well have intended this speech to refer explicitly to the two years Jamie spent "on the wagon" before his mother's death is suggested by a correction he made in the first long-hand manuscript of the play on file in the Eugene O'Neill Collection at the Beinecke Library at Yale University. Following the words "until at last," O'Neill had first put the preposition "in," then crossed that word out and used the preposition "through" instead. The words "two tears," which follow, fit logically with "through" but would hardly have followed the preposition "in." "In," however, might very well precede the words "two years" — the two years Jamie spent as his mother's companion. "Through two tears" is in fact *gauche* in the speech as it stands; "in two years" would have been both more graceful and more reasonable in the light of Jamie's painful history. O'Neill, in other words, may have been intentionally obfuscating at this point, as he does elsewhere, to prevent the easy identification of characters with individuals in his immediate family.

3. Tiusanen makes a highly creditable attempt at interpreting them. See *O'Neill's Scenic Images*, pp. 182–206. See also Tornqvist, *Drama of Souls*, pp. 122–28.

4. Cyrus Day, "*Amor Fati*: O'Neill's Lazarus as Superman and Savior," *Modern Drama* 3(December 1960): 297–305. On the relation of the play to Nietzsche, see also Winther, *Eugene O'Neill*, pp. 95–108; Engel, *Haunted Heroes*, pp. 177–96; as well as numerous articles and doctoral dissertations of the past twenty years.

5. *The Great God Brown* (III. 269).

6. Nietzsche's treatment of the myth may be found in *Thus Spake Zarathustra*, (translated by Thomas Common). See *The Philosophy of Nietzsche* I, xxi (New York: Random House Modern Library, 1937), pp. 85–8.

7. Leonard Chabrowe, *Ritual and Pathos — The Theatre of O'Neill*, pp. 45–54. See also Winther, note 4 above; Doris Alexander, "Lazarus Laughed and Buddha," *Modern Language Quarterly* 17(1956): 357–65; Egil Tornqvist, "O'Neill's Lazarus: Dionysus and Christ," *American Literature* 41(March 1969–January 1970): 543–54.

8. Raleigh notes the similarity between the central characters of this play and of *Long Day's Journey*, in *The Plays of Eugene O'Neill*, p. 47.

9. Chabrowe shows convincingly how Lazarus anticipates Hickey in *Ritual and Pathos*, pp. 86–99. Chabrowe in these pages relates *Lazarus Laughed* to *The Iceman Cometh* as the two most important examples of O'Neill's "ritual" drama.

10. That Miriam's image is increasingly that of mother rather than wife is mentioned in Skinner, *A Poet's Quest*, pp. 188–89. Her lines while dying from eating a poisoned peach recall the dope-dreaming Mary Tyrone.

11. Skinner, *A Poet's Quest*, p. 188, notes the similarity between Caligula and Brown.

12. See Sheaffer, *Son and Artist*, photographs on pp. 18–19.

4 — Strange Interlude and Dynamo

1. Sheaffer, *Son and Artist*, p. 230.

2. Engel — *Haunted Heroes*, p. 202 — observes, referring to Professor Leeds, that "the father is to Nina what the mother is" to other O'Neill heroes. Engel, p. 211, further makes clear that he considers Nina the feminine counterpart of such obvious representatives of O'Neill himself as Dion Anthony, William Brown, Reuben Light, and John Loving.

3. The biographies and the plays of the twenties suggest that following the deaths of father, mother, and brother, O'Neill was very much in a mood to run away from his emotional problems. The William Brown of *The Great God Brown* ends in a state of constant fugue and certainly the underlying spirit of *Lazarus Laughed* is a frantic search for some means to get away from death and the past. But the figures in O'Neill's personal life in those years whose existence insisted that he could not escape, that he had to face himself and his responsibilities, were his wife and children. And so, like many men before him and since, he felt he had to escape his wife and children. The biographies leave little doubt about the authenticity and depth of his love for Agnes Boulton, but as it was the authenticity of the love itself that contributed to the pain of self-knowledge, he had to reject that love. Stated in other words, O'Neill was ripe for an affair, and an affair was what Carlotta provided. She provided it so well that he finally allowed himself to destroy an essentially stable marriage, and quite possibly the stability of his young son Shane in the bargain.

4. It is worth noting that O'Neill, throughout his career, kept probing the sources of his pain rather than dwelling, as so many artists do, solely on the pain itself and on the effects of it.

5. S. J. Perelman delightfully embellishes this point by providing the inimitable Groucho Marx a near-perfect parody of *Strange Interlude* in the film *Animal Crackers*, which was produced during the years of the O'Neill play's immense popularity on stage and screen. Perelman particularly satirizes O'Neill's use of the interior monologue.

6. O'Neill had not made his final break with Agnes at the time he wrote the play. He seemed determined to remain with her right up to the day he actually did leave her. See Sheaffer, *Son and Artist*, pp. 271–92.

7. Bogard, *Contour in Time*, p. 301, discusses this parallel in some detail.

8. See Sheaffer, *Son and Artist*, p. 242. Sheaffer identifies Charlie Marsden with two avowedly homosexual writers of the day who were friends of O'Neill's. O'Neill in his notes referred to Charlie as "bisexual." See Floyd, *Eugene O'Neill at Work*, p. 71.

9. Sheaffer, *Son and Artist*, p. 309, notes the play's greater than usual similarity to *Long Day's Journey*. It strikes me that this similarity is about par for the course. See also Floyd, *Eugene O'Neill at Work*, p. 146.

10. Fife's made-up crime, which concerns the murder of a husband by his wife and her lover, directly anticipates *Mourning Becomes Electra*.

11. On O'Neill's debt to *The Education of Henry Adams* for the idea of the dynamo, see Raleigh, *The Plays of Eugene O'Neill*, pp. 247–48; Sheaffer, *Son and Artist*, pp. 306–7; and Carpenter, *Eugene O'Neill*, pp. 138–39. Despite the recent suggestion of D. H. Lawrence as a source (see Susan Tuck, "'Electricity is God Now': D. H. Lawrence and O'Neill," *Eugene O'Neill Newsletter* 5 [Summer/Fall 1981]: 10–15), there is little question that the idea comes from Adams. In his chapter entitled *The Dynamo and the Virgin*, Adams says that he feels the forty-foot electric dynamo he saw at the St. Louis Exposition of 1893 "as a moral force, much as the early Christians felt the Cross." And he goes on, a few lines later, to observe that "before the end, one began to pray to it" (*The Education of Henry Adams* [New York: The Modern Library, 1931], p. 380). That O'Neill may have considered Adams's feeling over-stated, however, is suggested by the characterization of Reuben Light.

12. Sheaffer notes the similarity of this play and *The Hairy Ape*, and also quotes O'Neill recalling in a letter of this period that *The Hairy Ape* opened on the night his mother lay dead in a mortuary. Thus the connection between *Dynamo* and the death of Ella O'Neill is made explicit by O'Neill himself. See Sheaffer, *Son and Artist*, pp. 389–90, 308.

13. Engel, *Haunted Heroes*, p. 235, discussing Mrs. Fife, calls attention to the "decline" of the Earth Mother in O'Neill's plays, which he finds "indicative of O'Neill's increasing pessimism."

14. See Sheaffer, *Son and Artist*, pp. 313–35.

15. Skinner, *A Poet's Quest*, pp. 203–210, is most sensitive to the "frenzy" which underlies this play.

5 — *Mourning Becomes Electra*

1. *The New Yorker*, 7 November 1931, p. 28.

2. See Bogard, *Contour in Time*, pp. 345–50; Doris Alexander, "Psychological Fate in *Mourning Becomes Electra*," *PMLA* 68(December 1953): 923–34; Sheaffer, *Son and Artist*, p. 371. One ought not overlook, too, O'Neill's reactions to the Anglo-Puritan ethic underlying the play. See Raleigh, *The Plays of Eugene O'Neill*, pp. 55–61.

3. Sheaffer finds qualities of "James O'Neill old-time theatre" in the play (*Son and Artist*, p. 371).

4. O'Neill has done this before and will do so again, but I am reluctant to call this a pattern in his works because the process is essentially different in each case. Ned Darrell and Charlie Marsden do not represent the same division as do Orin and Lavinia. Dion and Brown represent a division in his own personality, but still more represent O'Neill in his relationship with his brother, as do Lazarus and Caligula. The Mannon and Brantome strains in the play under consideration represent still another division, and that between John and his alter ego Loving in the play to follow — *Days Without End* — another division still. And so on down to *The Iceman Cometh*, where all the personae of *Long Day's Journey* divide in a plethora of different ways.

5. Observe here the echo of the unproduced "Shell Shock," briefly discussed in Notes to Chapter 2, note 1.

6. Carpenter, *Eugene O'Neill*, p. 130.

7. See Raleigh, *The Plays of Eugene O'Neill*, p. 21, for a discussion of this song in relation to the rhythm of the sea. This is important to my discussion in that O'Neill implicitly links the song to Brant's "blessed isles." Tiusanen, *O'Neill's Scenic Images*, p. 232, notes the similar evocative effect of the song to that of the "melancholy singing" in *Moon of the Caribees*.

8. See Rolf Scheibler, *The Late Plays of Eugene O'Neill* (Berne, Switzerland: Francke Verlag, 1970), especially pp. 14–39. In these pages Scheibler does a good deal with the theme of man's lost harmony with nature as it applies to *A Touch of the Poet*. What he says applies to *Mourning Becomes Electra* equally well, if not better.

9. This view is in some measure anticipated by Engel in *Haunted Heroes* when he identifies the blessed isles with "the Mother, the counterpart of Cybel" (p. 242), and when he suggests that what O'Neill achieved in the play was "narcosis" rather than "catharsis" (p. 258).

6 — *Days Without End* and *Ah, Wilderness*

1. See Travis Bogard's excellent discussion of the great cycle in *Contour in Time*, pp. 371–407. See also Floyd, *Eugene O'Neill at Work*, pp. 215–22.

2. Sheaffer, *Son and Artist*, p. 413.

3. For Skinner, a critic who approaches O'Neill from a conservative Roman Catholic perspective, the ending of course *made* the play. See *A Poet's Quest*, pp. 234–42.

4. The most obviously autobiographical factor in *Days Without End* is not its most important. John's betrayal of his wife parallels O'Neill's betrayal of Agnes Boulton with another woman (Carlotta), and John's great guilt over Elsa is most obviously O'Neill's over Agnes and their children. But by the time O'Neill wrote this play, his wife-betrayal had fused in his mind with the earlier, greater mother-betrayal. The play makes no distinction between the two betrayals, really; but by using a modification of his mother's name for the wife, and by so greatly emphasizing the wife's near death, O'Neill makes abundantly clear which betrayed figure of the past he was chiefly agonizing over.

5. Loving's very name indicates that he is intended to stand for more than simply the hero's hateful, vindictive side. Loving is like Jamie in being cruel and cynical only to be kind. In finding all hope and belief illusory, he advocates death as the sole solace for man. Floyd also notes the similarity between Loving and Jamie in *Eugene O'Neill at Work*, p. xxvii. Her later discussion of *Days Without End* (pp. 149–67) sees the play primarily in autobiographical terms.

6. To "call" as in playing poker is also a possible meaning here, but the implications would be the same. John — i.e., O'Neill — would still have to *show* what he's got.

7. For a lucid description of O'Neill's various drafts of the play, see Doris V. Falk, "The Way Out: The Many Endings of *Days Without End*," in *Eugene O'Neill and the Tragic Tension* (New Brunswick, New Jersey: Rutgers University Press, 1958), pp. 144–55. See also Sheaffer, *Son and Artist*, p. 410; and Floyd, *Eugene O'Neill at Work*, pp. 149–67.

8. See John Shawcross, "The Road to Ruin: The Beginning of O'Neill's Long Day's Journey," *Modern Drama* 3 (December 1960): 289–96. Shawcross's is the first of several attempts since to discover the parallels between *Ah, Wilderness* and *Long Day's Journey*. The most recent even considers the earlier play foreshadowing the "pessimism" of the later play. See Thomas Van Laan, "Singing in the Wilderness: The Dark Vision of O'Neill's Only Mature Comedy," *Modern Drama* 22 (1974): 9–18. O'Neill did in fact project a despairing sequel to the play (see Floyd, *Eugene O'Neill at Work*, pp. 240–41), but that fact cannot obscure the sentimental optimism of *Ah, Wilderness* itself.

9. Carpenter, *Eugene O'Neill*, p. 143.

10. Sheaffer, *Son and Artist*, p. 404.

7 — Remnants of a Cycle

1. See Charles Fechter, *Monte Cristo* (James O'Neill's version), in *America's Lost Plays* (Bloomington, Indiana: Indiana University Press, 1965), 15:1–70. Joseph Wood Krutch was the first to identify Con Melody as James Tyrone, in "The O'Neills on Stage Once More," *Theatre Arts* 42 (October 1958):16–17, 71. For the most recent statement on similarities between the Tyrones and the Melodies, see Virginia Floyd, introduction to "An American Perspective," in *Eugene O'Neill: A World View* (New York: Frederick Ungar, 1979), p. 195.

2. Rolf Scheibler, *The Late Plays of Eugene O'Neill* (pp. 25–26), sees Melody Castle as a symbol of Con's lost harmony with nature. The whole point, however, about the "mel-

odies" of childhood is that they give rise to "castles" in the air. Melody Castle is not a symbol of Con's lost harmony with nature so much as it is a symbol of O'Neill's lost childhood.

3. Eugene O'Neill, *A Touch of the Poet* (New Haven, Connecticut: Yale University Press, 1957).

4. Nora may have a real-life antecedent, of course, in O'Neill's loving childhood nurse Sara Sandy (see Sheaffer, *Son and Playwright*, passim.) and the use of the name Sara in this play, although for another character, may indicate O'Neill was thinking about his distantly remembered nurse as he wrote the play. Sara Sandy may also underlie the Earth Mothers in other O'Neill plays — perhaps Mrs. Fife in *Dynamo*. But she does not figure in *Long Day's Journey*, and I am trying to keep my focus on the generation of the characters in that play. Had she been sufficiently important to O'Neill, she probably would have at least been referred to there, and she is not.

5. Refers to Ella *Quinlan* O'Neill and Mary *Cavan* Tyrone. Tiusanen, p. 261, and Bogard, p. 387, note parallels between Deborah Harford and Mary Tyrone. See also Floyd, *Eugene O'Neill at Work*, p. 297. Interestingly, Deborah is identified with Thoreau's mother in Mordecai Marcus, "Eugene O'Neill's Debt to Thoreau in "A Touch of the Poet," *JEGP* 62 (1963): 270–79. This, of course, is consistent with the idea that Simon Harford and his cabin are suggested by Thoreau's *Walden*.

6. A shebeen-keeper's daughter not unlike Sara Melody is central to Synge's *Playboy of the Western World*, while O'Casey's *Purple Dust* is full of humiliations of the rich and proud by the poor and humble.

7. These dates are Sheaffer's. See *Son and Artist*, pp. 448 and 481.

8. In June 1976, Mr. Donald Gallup, then Curator of the American Literature Collection at the Beinecke Library at Yale University, allowed me to look at a photocopy of O'Neill's typescript of *More Stately Mansions*. Mr. Gallup asked me to make no notes and to use no quotations which did not already appear in published form. In my discussion of the play, I have used only the two published versions of the play (see notes 9 and 10 below), though I have naturally been influenced in my interpretation by the typescript I read at the Beinecke Library. I feel deeply indebted to Mr. Gallup for allowing me to consult this material.

9. From the recording of *More Stately Mansions*, edited and abridged, as produced on Broadway, by Elliot Martin (New York: Caedmon Records, TRS 331). Quotation is taken from the opening scene.

10. Eugene O'Neill, *More Stately Mansions*, shortened from the author's partly revised copy by Karl Ragnar Gierow and edited by Donald Gallup (New Haven, Connecticut: Yale University Press, 1964).

11. The tumult and instability of O'Neill's marriage to Carlotta occupies a major portion of the later chapters of Sheaffer's *Son and Artist*.

12. This one quotation sums up the O'Neill enigma which almost every important O'Neill critic — Clark, Krutch, Winther, Skinner, Engel, Alexander, Bentley, Tom Driver, Mary McCarthy, Robert Brustein, Bogard, Sheaffer, Raleigh, Carpenter, Scheibler, and Floyd — have sought in one way or another to deal with. Even those critics chiefly concerned with aesthetics or theatrical image — Chabrowe, Tiusanen, and Tornqvist — must face it time and again. It underlies what has made readers and audiences return to O'Neill relentlessly even when there appears no way around the despair which seems so overwhelming in his plays. It surely was what Cyrus Day was trying to come to grips with where his unpublished notes indicate, as they do repeatedly in varying ways, that O'Neill was "too much a child of his age to accept the faith of his fathers, and too much a mystic not to want to believe."

8 — The Iceman Cometh

1. The strong affinity between Ibsen's play and O'Neill's was first discussed in Sverre Arestad, "*The Iceman Cometh* and the *Wild Duck*," *Scandinavian Studies* 20 (February 1948): 1–11, and has been observed by numerous others since. For other parallels between Ibsen and O'Neill's late plays, see Egil Tornqvist, "Ibsen and O'Neill," *Scandinavian Studies* 37 (1965): 211–35.

2. This response was typically expressed by the screenwriter Dudley Nichols, who discussed the play with O'Neill in the early 1940s. In spite of its focus on death, Nichols did not feel the play was pessimistic, or even gloomy. Like others, of course, Nichols accepted the inevitability of the life-lie. See the Gelbs, *O'Neill*, pp. 831–32. Floyd suggests that the explicit theme of an early version of the play is that close friendship and human warmth are the sole means of human survival. See *Eugene O'Neill at Work*, p. 268.

3. Eric Bentley attacks what he considers the intellectual limitations of *The Iceman Cometh* in "Trying to Like O'Neill," *Kenyon Review* 14 (July 1952): 476–92. He is effectively answered, I think, in Robert Brustein, *The Theatre of Revolt* (Boston: Little, Brown & Co., 1962), pp. 339–48.

4. Sheaffer (*Son and Artist*, p. 494) convincingly demonstrates that Charles E. Chapin — a "prominent newspaper executive" who in 1918 shot his wife (while she slept) out of love and concern for her welfare — is a model for Hickey. Similarly, Sheaffer and others have identified O'Neill's close friend of the teens Terry Carlin as a model for Larry Slade. (See Sheaffer, *Son and Artist*, pp. 62, 428; Alexander, *The Tempering of Eugene O'Neill*, p. 211; and Carpenter, *Eugene O'Neill*, p. 153.) Similarly, too, other real-life models for the figures who appear or are referred to in *Iceman* have been identified: Hippolyte Havel for Hugo Kalmar (Doris Alexander, "Hugo of the *Iceman Cometh*: Realism and O'Neill," *American Quarterly* 5 [Winter 1953]: 357–66; Emma Goldman for Rosa Parritt (Winifred L. Frazer, *E.G. and E.G.O.: Emma Goldman and The Iceman Cometh* [Gainesville: University Presses of Florida, 1974]); James Findlater Byth, O'Neill's alcoholic press agent, for Jimmy "Tomorrow" (Sheaffer, *Son and Artist*, pp. 490–91); and a composite of the big-time Tammany politicians of the early twentieth century for Willie Oban's father (Raleigh, *The Plays of Eugene O'Neill*, p. 67). Having no reason to quarrel with any of these identifications, I only observe that the persons of O'Neill's immediate family may be seen beneath the real-life models in almost every case. Alexander (*The Tempering*, p. 211) and Carpenter (*Eugene O'Neill*, pp. 157–58) acknowledge this as far as O'Neill himself and Larry Slade are concerned, while Sheaffer sees parallels between O'Neill and both Hickey and Parritt (*Son and Artist*, p. 499).

5. Robert J. Andreach identifies the real remembered women in the play as varying manifestations of the Virgin Mary, which considering O'Neill's ambivalence toward the church is a reasonable corollary to their identification with his mother. See "O'Neill's Women in *The Iceman Cometh*," in *Eugene O'Neill: A Collection of Criticism*, edited by Ernest G. Griffin (New York: McGraw-Hill, 1976), pp. 103–13. The Holy Mother could always be equated with the real mother whenever O'Neill was in the throes of his guilt. When Andreach goes on, through biblical parallels, also to equate the whores in the play with the Virgin Mary I suspect he goes too far. They are not, after all, virginal whores like Josie Hogan, who may well be associated with the Blessed Virgin. Nor do the whores resemble Josie, as do other possible Blessed Virgin counterparts — Cybel, for example.

6. For Rosa's probable historical model, see Frazer reference in note 4 above.

7. Engel, in *Haunted Heroes*, without the knowledge of O'Neill's life which was to

come later, seems to recognize a sense of unrevealed information about Larry throughout the play, and of exorcism, in his responses late in the play. Says Engel:

> Larry's bitterness is intensified as the play progresses,
> and the disparity between that emotion and the facts which
> O'Neill gave to account for it is widened. Larry continues
> to be a mysterious figure even after we supplement the in-
> adequate facts with inferences. Never completely divulged,
> the content of his pipe dreams is insufficient motive and
> cue to his acrimonious expressions of self-loathing, mis-
> anthropy, nihilism. Larry is increasingly distressed as certain
> other characters in the play try to disinter his "dead and
> buried" dreams. . . . In one instance were it not for the
> author's interpolation the significance of a remark would go
> unnoticed. For when, near the end of the play, Larry, moved
> by horrified pity mumbles, "God rest his soul in peace,"
> O'Neill informed the reader of the play that a *long-forgotten
> faith* [has returned to Larry] *for a moment* . . . [sic] Having
> called attention to the phenomenon, O'Neill never again referred
> to it. What spiritual trauma was responsible for the dis-
> affection remains hidden (p. 285).

8. Similarities between *Iceman* and *Waiting for Godot* were noted by several critics in reviews of the 1956 revival of *Iceman* by Jose Quintero. See reviews by Richard Watts, Jr. and Thos. R. Dash as summarized in Jordan Y. Miller, *Eugene O'Neill and the American Critic* (Hamden, Connecticut: The Shoe String Press, Anchor Books, 1973), p. 352.

9. William R. Brashear deals well with Larry's immense compassion, in "The Wisdom of Silenus in O'Neill's *Iceman*," *American Literature* 36 (1964): 180–88. See also Brashear's remarks on this play and *Long Day's Journey* in "O'Neill and Shaw: The Play as Will and Idea," *Criticism* 8 (1966): 155–69.

10. See Martin Buber, "What Is To Be Done," in *Men of Dialogue*, ed. E. E. William Rollins (New York: Funk & Wagnalls, 1969). Buber defines the rot in human relationships as that which makes "meaning degenerate into convention, respect into mistrust, modesty in communicating into stingy taciturnity" (p. 6).

11. Joe's last name obviously calls to mind Mott Street in New York's Chinatown. By using the name, O'Neill seems to be linking Joe not only to black America but to America's racial minorities generally.

12. Chabrowe, *Ritual and Pathos*, pp. 73–99, sees the entire play as a Dionysian celebration of life. He focuses on repeated rituals of singing and dancing in the play, including its cacophonous finale. The songs at the close of the play themselves do not "constitute a celebratory ritual," says Chabrowe, but "embedded as they are in a structure of dialogue with a pattern of repetition, they contribute to an overall rhythmic effect which does make for celebratory ritual" (p. 95).

13. Eric Bentley clearly recognizes the kind of opposition in emotional attitudes that I label the "language of kinship" in this play. See "Eugene O'Neill," in *Theatre of War* (New York: The Viking Press, 1972), pp. 64–92, especially pp. 87–92. But Bentley feels, as I do not, that the negation overwhelmingly outweighs the affirmation. Similarly, Winifred L.

Frazer sees the many expressions of love in the play as finally having to do not with life but with death. See *Love as Death in The Iceman Cometh* (Gainesville: University of Florida Press, 1967); and "King Lear and Hickey: Bridegroom and Iceman," *Modern Drama* 15 (December 1972): 267–78. As love and hate are one to Frazer, so love and death "result in the same thing" (*Love as Death*, p. 35).

Other critics, however, sense varying degrees and types of tragic affirmation inherent in the alternations of feeling in the play. Brashear finds in Larry's compassionate side an "affirmation of human value *in spite of* the apparent meaninglessness of life ('The Wisdom of Silenus," p. 186). Tom F. Driver — in "On the Late Plays of Eugene O'Neill," *Tulane Drama Review* 3 (December 1958): 8–20 — feels that O'Neill is strongest "wherever we care to look at man coming to terms with himself in a world of total darkness," but accepts Engel's idea that death is philosophically central to the play. Carpenter finds that "*Iceman* gives highest expression to O'Neill's lifelong belief that emotion is more important than action . . ." (p. 157). And Henry Alonzo Myers, in *Tragedy: A View of Life* (Ithaca, New York: Cornell University Press, 1956), says that O'Neill "seems to identify ambivalence with the tragic predicament of modern man, who is simultaneously attracted toward and repelled from objects, persons, and even life itself; [sic] Shakespeare identifies the tragic predicament of man in all times and places with equivalence, with the two-sided nature of human feeling whereby . . . man, in accordance with his capacity for feeling . . . is fated to enjoy and suffer in equal measures. O'Neill may be said to have shown, perhaps better than any other modern dramatist, the sickness of an age and an aspect of tragedy particularly noticeable in our time. . . . *The Iceman Cometh* contains O'Neill's most explicit identification of ambivalence with the tragic predicament of modern man" (pp. 99–100). See also Tiusanen, *O'Neill's Scenic Images*, pp. 264–84.

9 — Hughie

1. Virginia Floyd identifies the Night Clerk with O'Neill in *Eugene O'Neill: A World View*, p. 204. She also identifies Erie with Jamie in *Eugene O'Neill at Work*, p. 327.

2. *The Later Plays of Eugene O'Neill*, edited by Travis Bogard (New York: Random House, The Modern Library, 1967.) All quotations from *Hughie* and *A Moon for the Misbegotten* are from this edition.

3. This "human bond, founded on an illusion," is described in precise terms by Raleigh, *The Plays of Eugene O'Neill*, pp. 28–30 (quotation from p. 30). See also Tornqvist, *A Drama of Souls*, pp. 151–53; Tuisanen, *O'Neill's Scenic Images*, pp. 316–21; and Robert Butler, "Artifice and Art: Words in *The Iceman Cometh* and *Hughie*," *Eugene O'Neill Newsletter* 5 (Spring 1981): 3–6. Floyd even sees their bond in quasi-religious terms, in *Eugene O'Neill: A World View*, p. 205. On the other hand, Ruby Cohn finds the relationship an image of "absurdity" in that each character must bear witness "to the other's reality" — in "Absurdity in English: Joyce and O'Neill," *Comparative Drama* 3 (Fall 1969): 156–61 (quotation from p. 160) — while Falk, *Eugene O'Neill and the Tragic Tension*, p. 202, associates their union with death.

10 — Long Day's Journey Into Night

1. *Long Day's Journey Into Night* (New Haven, Ct.: Yale University Press, 1955). This is the sole edition of the play in print.

2. See Judith E. Barlow, *"Long Day's Journey Into Night:* From Early Notes to Finished Play," *Modern Drama* 22 (1979): 19–28. Barlow has discovered in the typescript of the play far more hostility and recrimination than appears in the published version. She suspects that O'Neill may have gained in compassion as he re-worked the play. Under any circumstances, however, and using a different metaphor from mine, she recognizes what I have been calling the language of kinship. Of both earlier and later versions of the play, she says: "The warp and woof of *Journey* are the inextricably woven threads of love and hatred in the family" (p. 28). See also Chothia, *Forging a Language*, pp. 168–81, a section she entitles "Empathy and Alienation: O'Neill's Structuring of the Play."

3. Bogard, *Contour in Time*, p. 438, notes the similarity between Fat Violet and Josie Hogan.

4. Carpenter, *Eugene O'Neill*, p. 161, finds in the confrontation of Jamie and Edmund in Act Four, and in Jamie's confession, the "true climax of the play." Jamie's description of the existence and nature of their conflict "provides the final moment of illumination, and of tragic catharsis." Waith, on the other hand, finds only that Jamie reveals all the hate which resides under his "guise of love," in "Eugene O'Neill: An Exercise in Unmasking," pp. 190–91. Similarly, Robert B. Heilman sees the "love-hate paradox" implicit in Jamie's confession as a "dividedness" which "deepens into a permanent malady," in *The Iceman, the Arsonist, and the Troubled Agent: Tragedy and Melodrama on the Modern Stage* (Seattle: University of Washington Press, 1973), p. 107.

5. Mary McCarthy, "Dry Ice" (review of the original production of *The Iceman Cometh*), *Partisan Review* 13 (November–December 1946): 577–79. The acerbic Mary McCarthy later tempered her opinion of O'Neill, thanks to *Long Day's Journey*, which in 1961 she described as "the great play of his old age," suggesting that it "achieves in fact a peculiar poetry." See *On the Contrary* (New York: Farrar, Straus, and Cudahy, 1961) pp. 306–7.

6. Joseph Golden praises the play in terms which may serve as a corollary to what I have said. The following comes from *The Death of Tinker Bell: The American Theatre in the Twentieth Century* (Syracuse, N.Y.: Syracuse University Press, 1967), pp. 44–45: "*Long Day's Journey* will remain perhaps the most singular triumph of his entire career and one of the legitimate glories of the American drama. Tempered by twenty years of bravado, of ghost-hunting, of personal anguish that bordered, at times, on suicidal impulses, he was ready to face himself, somewhat more wary of the extravagances of the past. And the result was remarkable. Here is a play that derives its ultimate power *not* from plot — which is at best a crude mechanical 'system' — but from a process of character revelation that is awesome in its grinding inevitability; not from the usual sordid probes into the subterranean streams of humans compulsively tearing away from one another, but from a compassionate insight into profoundly lost humans groping blindly, sometimes viciously, often pathetically, *toward* one another; not by melodramatic swirls and eruptions, but by a tightly compressed, well-controlled development of human interrelationships."

11 — A Moon for the Misbegotten

1. On the play's "elegiac" tone, see Bogard, *Contour in Time*, pp. 449–53.

2. See Bogard's quotation and discussion of O'Neill's deletion from the play of a fairly long speech made by Jim Tyrone about his "brother" (pp. 432–33). This deletion suggests now O'Neill's desire not to disguise autobiography but to transcend it.

3. Sheaffer in *Son and Artist*, p. 329, alludes to "John ('Dirty') Dolan — a onetime

tenant of James O'Neill — as a possible model for Phil Hogan and to his daughter Josie, who is almost 'freakish' in size." See also Sheaffer, *Son and Playwright*, pp. 259–62. But Sheaffer says nothing to suggest any real similarity of personality between these people and the characters in O'Neill's play, certainly nothing to parallel the similarities between the Tyrones and the O'Neills.

4. On Ibsen and O'Neill, see Tornqvist, "Ibsen and O'Neill." On Strindberg and O'Neill, see S. K. Winther, "Strindberg and O'Neill: A Study in Influence," *Scandinavian Studies* 31 (1959):103–20; Murray Hartman, "Strindberg and O'Neill," *Educational Theatre Journal* 18 (October 1966): 216–23; and Thomas C. Dawber, "Strindberg and O'Neill," *Players* 45 (1970): 183–85; as well as other studies going back to 1928. At the meetings of the Modern Language Association in New York in December 1981, I presented a paper on Chekhov and the late O'Neill. This paper was not so much of influence as of similarity in dialogue, especially that between mothers and sons.

5. See Carpenter, *Eugene O'Neill*, p. 162; Falk, *Eugene O'Neill and the Tragic Tension*, p. 177; and others.

6. See Edmund's quotation of Baudelaire's "Epilogue," *Long Day's Journey*, Act Four, Yale edition, pp. 133–4. In this poem, Baudelaire directly links his love for his "enormous trull" to his love for the city of Paris. O'Neill, of course, used the highly influential translations (adaptations really) by Arthur Symons. For "Epilogue," see Baudelaire, *Prose and Poetry*, translated by Arthur Symons (New York: Albert and Charles Boni, 1926), pp. 86–7.

7. See Baudelaire, *Prose and Poetry*, p. 117.

8. Josie is included by Rudolph Stamm among several women characters who "prove that O'Neill has a knowledge of a kind of love that cannot be explained as a life-giving illusion . . . ," in *The Shaping Powers at Work* (Heidelberg: Carl Winter, 1967), p. 270.

9. For complete reference to *The Late Plays of Eugene O'Neill*, see Chapter 9, note 2.

10. *The Late Plays of Eugene O'Neill*, pp. 71–2.

11. This viewpoint was clearly articulated by Dan Isaac in a paper he delivered at a section on O'Neill's later plays held at the Modern Language Association convention in Chicago, December 1977.

12. See Sheaffer, *Son and Artist*, pp. 595–6.

13. John J. Fitzgerald, "Guilt and Redemption in O'Neill's Last Play," *Texas Quarterly* 9 (Spring 1966): 146–58, is a systematic, if not altogether clear, analysis of the play's construction in terms that Fitzgerald's title implies. James R. Scrimgeour, "From Loving to the Misbegotten: Despair in the Drama of Eugene O'Neill," *Modern Drama* 20 (March 1977): 37–53, on the other hand, sees Jim Tyrone's great confession as an exorcism which "invites us to share in the experience of despair" (p. 49).

14. Ingmar Bergman's 1978 film *Autumn Sonata* is the most compelling example — a film which may well have been influenced by O'Neill's later plays, given their well-known popularity and availability in contemporary Sweden.

15. See Scheibler, *The Late Plays*, pp. 98–9. Carpenter, *Eugene O'Neill*, p. 162, and Tiusanen, *O'Neill's Scenic Images*, pp. 311–13, praise the scenic image of the pieta in the play but are more cautious about assigning religious implications to it.

16. Falk, *Eugene O'Neill and the Tragic Tension*, pp. 177–8. For another negative response to the pieta image so important to this play, see Eric Bentley, "Eugene O'Neill's Pieta," in *The Dramatic Event* (New York: Horizon Press, 1954), pp. 30–3.

Conclusion

1. Strindberg and Our Theatre," in *American Playwrights on Drama*, ed. Horst Frenz (New York: Hill and Wang Dramabooks, 1965), p. 2.

Index

Adams, Henry, 223n11
Aeschylus (*Oresteia*): 76–7, 79, 81, 82
Ah, Wilderness: 101–5; Aunt Lily anticipates Evelyn Hickman (*The Iceman
Cometh*), 102; Aunt Lily anticipates
Mary Tyrone, 102; Aunt Lily as
Earth Mother, 102; compared with
Lazarus Laughed, 104; Essie Miller
unlike Mary Tyrone, 101; kinship in,
105; Nat Miller unlike James Tyrone
Sr., 101; Richard as a sentimentalized
adolescent Eugene O'Neill, 104; Rich-
ard compared to Juan in *The Foun-
tain*, 19; Sid Davis anticipates Hickey
(*The Iceman Cometh*), 103; Sid Davis
based on James O'Neill Jr. (Jamie),
102–3; similar to *Long Day's Journey*,
101, 225n8; similarity to *Long Day's
Journey* questioned, 101–2
Albee, Edward (*Zoo Story*): 163
Alexander, Doris: 2, 218n5, 220n11,
222n7, 224n2, 226n12, 227n4
All God's Chillun Got Wings: 30–35;
compared with *Desire Under the
Elms*, 30, 35, 220n5; compared with
More Stately Mansions, 32; Ella anticipates Mary Tyrone, 7, 30–2; Ella
contrasted with Mary Tyrone, 182;
Ella Downey Harris and Ella Quinlan
O'Neill, 30–2; Jim anticipates Edmund Tyrone, 31–2; kinship in, 9,
25, 32–4; loss of kinship in, 9, 30,
34–5; racial theme in, 30–1
Andreach, Robert J.: 227n5

Animal Crackers (screenplay by S.J.
Perelman), 223n5
Anna Christie: 23–6; Anna represents
Eugene O'Neill, 18–9; Chris anticipates James Tyrone Sr. and Mary Tyrone, 18–9; compared with *The Iceman Cometh, Long Day's Journey*,
and *A Moon for the Misbegotten*,
26; kinship in, 9, 23–5; romantic conclusion of, 27
Arestad, Sverre: 227n1
Aristotle: 4, 11
Asselineau, Roger: 36, 221n8
Atkinson, Jennifer McCabe: 219n1,
220n10
Autumn Sonata (film by Ingmar Bergman): 231n14

Ballad of Reading Gaol (Oscar Wilde):
189
Baudelaire, Charles: 183, 197, 231n6,
231n7
Beckett, Samuel: 121; *Waiting for
Godot*, 142, 145–7, 162–3, 228n8
Benchley, Robert: quoted, 3, 76, 218n7,
224n1 (ch 5)
Bentley, Eric: 218n6, 226n12, 227n3,
227n13, 231n16
Bergman, Ingmar: 231n14
Beyond the Horizon: Mayo brothers an-
ticipate Tyrone brothers, 19; roman-
tic nature of Robert Mayo's death,

233

Beyond the Horizon (*cont.*)
27; Ruth Mayo anticipates Mary Ty-
rone, 17
Barlow, Judith E.: 230n2 (ch 10)
Bogard, Travis: 2, 3, 220n3, 223n7,
224n2, 224n1 (ch 6), 226n5, 226n12,
229n2, 230n3 (ch 10), 230n1 (ch 11),
230n2 (ch 11)
Bound East for Cardiff: see SS Glencairn
plays
Boulton, Agnes: *see* O'Neill, Agnes
Boulton
Brashear, William R.: 228n9, 229n13
Brustein, Robert: 226n12, 227n3
Buber, Martin: 145, 228n10
Butler, Robert: 229n3
Byron, George Gordon, Lord: 110
Byth, James Findlater: 227n4

Carlin, Terry: 227n4
Carpenter, Frederic: 218n4, 219n7, 220n3,
220n11, 223n11, 225n9, 226n12,
227n4, 230n4, 231n5, 231n15; quoted,
84, 224n6, 229n13
Chabrowe, Leonard: 2, 7, 54, 218n3,
227n7, 222n9, 226n12; quoted, 228n12
Chaitin, Norman: 222n1 (ch 3)
Chapin, Charles E.: 227n4
Chekhov, Anton: 193–4, 231n4
Chothia, Jean: 230n2 (ch 10); *Forging a
Language* discussed, 219n13
Clark, Barrett H.: 217n2, 220n5, 226n12
Cohn, Ruby: 229n3
Commins, Saxe: O'Neill's conversation
with Commins, February 1922 (quo-
tation from Louis Sheaffer, *Eugene
O'Neill: Son and Artist*), 42–3, 221n1
(intro. to Pt II)
Count of Monte Cristo, The (American
drama by Charles Fechter and James
O'Neill, based on the Dumas novel),
218n8, 225n1 (ch 7)

Dance of Death, The (August Strind-
berg): 8, 209, 232n1
Dash, Thomas R.: 228n8
Dawber, Thos. C.: 231n4
Day, Cyrus: 53, 217n2, 222n4, 226n12
Days Without End: 92–100; autobio-
graphical, 92–3, 225n4; compared

Days Without End (*cont.*)
with *The Iceman Cometh*, 99; compared with *Lazarus Laughed*, 99;
compared with *A Moon for the Mis-
begotten*, 96, 97; conclusion, 92, 100,
142, 225n3; Elsa and Ella Quinlan
O'Neill, 94, 96, 98; Elsa anticipated
Mary Tyrone, 2, 98; Father Baird and
John Loving anticipate James Tyrone
Sr. with both Edmund and Jamie Ty-
rone, 7; Father Baird anticipates Nat
Miller (*Ah, Wilderness*), 94–5; Father
Baird unlike James Tyrone Sr., 94;
John and Loving represent two sides
of O'Neill's nature, 93; John and Lov-
ing compared to the two sides of
Larry Slade's nature (*The Iceman
Cometh*), 137; kinship in, 96, 105;
Marx in, 95; Nietzsche in, 95; Zen
Buddhism in, 95
Desire Under the Elms: 35–9; Abbie
Cabot anticipates Mary Tyrone, 38;
Abbie as Earth Mother, 38; based on
Euripides (*Hippolytus*), 77, 220n6;
compared with *All God's Chillun*, 35,
39, 220n5; despair in, 27, 28; Eben
anticipates Edmund Tyrone, 35;
Eben's dead mother and Ella Quinlan
O'Neill, 37–8; Eben's half-brothers
anticipate Jamie Tyrone, 35; Ephraim
compared with Deborah Harford
(*More Stately Mansions*) and Mary
Tyrone, 39; Ephraim anticipates
James Tyrone Sr., 35–6; Ephraim and
Eben anticipate James and Edmund
Tyrone, 7; kinship in, 25, 36; loss of
kinship in, 9, 28, 30, 35, 36–7; mur-
der of baby compared to Parritt's sui-
cide (*The Iceman Cometh*), 140
Diff'rent: Emma Crosby anticipates
Mary Tyrone, 7, 17–8, 219n5
Dowson, Ernest: 183, 186
Driver, Tom: 226n12, 228–9n13
Dynamo: 71–5; anticipates *Mourning Be-
comes Electra*, 223n10; electric dy-
namo compared to gorilla in *The
Hairy Ape*, 74; electricity as god in,
74; Ella Quinlan O'Neill and, 223n12;
Hutchins and Reuben Light anticipate
James and Edmund Tyrone, 7;
Hutchins Light anticipates James Ty-
rone Sr., 72; Mrs. Fife as Earth
Mother, 73–4; Mrs. Fife as mockery
of Earth Mother figure, 74, 75, 196;

Lang, Fritz: *Metropolis* (film): 71
"Last Conquest, The" (title of an uncompleted play by O'Neill, discussed in detail by Virginia Floyd in *Eugene O'Neill at Work*): 219n13
Lawrence, D. H.: 223n11
Lazarus Laughed: 53–9; anticipates *The Iceman Cometh*, 55, *Moon for the Misbegotten*, 56; Caligula represents Eugene O'Neill, 56–7; compared *Ah, Wilderness*, 104, *Days Without End*, 99; Lazarus and Uncle Sid (*Ah, Wilderness*), 54; Lazarus anticipates Hickey (*Iceman Cometh*), 55, 134, a variety of characters in other O'Neill plays, 55; Lazarus compared with Jamie Tyrone, 187, represents James O'Neill Jr., 54–6; loss of kinship in, 58; Miriam anticipates Mary Tyrone, 222n10; Nietzschean ideas in, 58; Tiberius represents Eugene O'Neill in, 57–8; Tiberius represents James O'Neill Sr. in, 57
"Leave-Taking, A" (Algernon Swinburne): 142, 164–5
Long, Chester Clayton: 221n10
Long Day's Journey Into Night: 164–90 and *passim*; anticipated in *Ah, Wilderness*, 101–2, 225n8; autobiographical motifs in, 4–6, 181, 211–16; compared with *Anna Christie*, 26; compared and contrasted with *Strange Interlude*, 71, 181; conflicting interpretations of, 230n4 and 230n5; Edmund's speech on the sea compared with Paddy's (*The Hairy Ape*), 184; Ella Quinlan O'Neill viewed with new detachment in, 164–5, 181–2; Fat Violet compared with Josie Hogan (*Moon for the Misbegotten*), 230n3; Jim Tyrone as development of Jamie Tyrone, 187; kinship in, 10–11, 165–78, 182–90; kinship obstacles in, 178–82; kinship related to illusion in, 180; last act anticipated in *Hughie*, 182; Mary Tyrone contrasted with Ella Downey (*All God's Chillun*), 182; Mary Tyrone contrasted with Mrs. Keeney (*Ile*), 182; Roman Catholic Mass paraphrased, 190; significance of Swinburne quotation in, 165
Long Voyage Home, The: *see* the SS Glencairn plays

McCarthy, Mary: 189, 226n12, 230n5
Manheim, Michael: 231n4
Marco Millions: 44–6, 221n4; Ella Quinlan O'Neill's death in, 44–5; loss of kinship in, 45–6; Princess Kukachin anticipates Mary Tyrone, 44–5
Marcus, Mordecai: 226n5
Martin, Elliot: 226n9
Marx, Groucho: 223n5
Marx, Karl: 95
Metropolis (Fritz Lang film): 71
Milton, John: *Paradise Lost*, 128
Miller, Jordan Y.: 228n8
Monterey, Carlotta: *see* O'Neill, Carlotta Monterey
Moon of the Caribees: *see* the SS Glencairn plays
Moon for the Misbegotten, A: 191–208; autobiographical motifs in, 5, 213; compared with *Anna Christie*, 26, *Days Without End*, 97, *The Emperor Jones*, 204, *Strange Interlude*, 7, *Touch of the Poet*, 112, 193; Detroit police chief closing play in 1947, 202; "elegiac" tone of, 191, 230n1; Josie Hogan in, 195–8; Josie anticipated by Sara Harford (*More Stately Mansions*), 196; Josie and kinship, 231n8 and *passim*; Josie as Earth Mother in, 195–7; Josie compared to Fat Violet (*Long Day's Journey*), 230n3; Josie contrasted with Cybel (*Great God Brown*), 195–6; Keats quotations in, 191, 207; kinship in, 11, 128, 198–208; Phil Hogan anticipated by Con Melody (*Touch of the Poet*), 193; Pieta-like image in, 206, 231n15 and 231n16; possible real-life models for Phil and Josie Hogan, 230–31n3; significance of change from "Jamie" to "Jim" Tyrone, 200
More Stately Mansions: 116–25; compared with *All God's Chillun*, 32, *Mourning Becomes Electra*, 125, *Strange Interlude*, 67 and *passim*; compared and contrasted with *The Iceman Cometh*, 151–2; Deborah Harford anticipates Mary Tyrone, 7, 17, 118–9; Deborah and Sara Harford (combined) as Earth Mother, 122; Ella Quinlan O'Neill in, 120; kinship in, 120–4; marriage to Carlotta Monterey reflected in, 120; negates seeming optimism of *Touch of the Poet*,

Eugene O'Neill's New Language of Kinship

was composed in 10-point Compugraphic Palatino and leaded two points
by Metricomp Studios,
with display type in Monotype and Foundry Goudy Old Style by
J. M. Bundscho, Inc.;
printed by sheet-fed offset on 55-pound, acid-free Glatfelter Antique Cream,
Smythe-sewn and bound over boards in Joanna Arrestox B,
also adhesive bound with paper covers drawn on
by Maple-Vail Book Manufacturing Group, Inc.;
and published by

SYRACUSE UNIVERSITY PRESS
Syracuse, New York 13210